DUNDEE

The Discovery

DUNDEE

A VOYAGE OF DISCOVERY

EDITED BY
GRAHAM OGILVY

MAINSTREAM
PUBLISHING
EDINBURGH AND LONDON

First published in 1999 by
MAINSTREAM PUBLISHING COMPANY (EDINBURGH) LTD
7 Albany Street
Edinburgh   EH1 3UG

ISBN 1 84018 218 0

A catalogue record for this book is available from the British Library

Typeset in Sabon
Reprographics by Inside Image Limited, Edinburgh
Printed and bound in Great Britain by The Bath Press Ltd, Glasgow

Contents

Acknowledgements

Staff of the local studies department at the central public library, Wellgate, especially David Kett, Senior Resource Officer, Neighbourhood Resource Development; Ian Flett, Dundee City Archivist; Eileen Moran, Dundee Central Library; Clara Young, Heritage Programme Officer, McManus Galleries; Laura Adam, Ninewells Medical Museum; Vera Morrocco; Gordan Douglas; Alan Richardson; Joyce Lorimer, D.C. Thomson and Co. Ltd; Angus and Dundee Tourist Board; Steve Scott; David Martin at Fotopress; Alan Woodcock; Ed Gorrie; Alan Grant; Petra McMillan; Sandra Burke; Macdonald Black; Bill Dow; Barker and Dobson; Sandy Forbes's Dundee Philatelic Society; Christine McGregor; Peter Rundo; John Clancy; Allan Neave, Dundee Guitar Festival; Gordon McPherson; Simon Crookall and Nik McHugh, RSNO; Donald Gordon, DSO; Rachel Gardiner, Music Development Officer; Rod Gordon, Arts and Heritage; Kevin Murray, MIDI; Susan Allen; Pat Carson, Dundee Operatic; Dorothy Hunter, Tomson-Leng; Helen Wylie, Downfield Musical Society; Sandra Fraser, Tayport Amateur Musical Society; Garry Fraser, Broughty Operatic; Sheena Wellington; Kay Simson, Dundee Choral Union; Anna Newell and Nicola Young, Dundee Rep; Graeme Stevenson and Dr John Brush, University of Dundee; and the history department, particularly Professors Chris Whatley and Murdo Macdonald, and Bob Harris, Billy Kenefick and Louise Miskell.

Notes on contributors

GRAHAM OGILVY is a writer and journalist who lives in Dundee.

NIALL SCOTT was educated at Dundee High School and the University of Aberdeen. He was medical correspondent with *The Courier* for ten years from 1985. He is currently director of the City of Discovery campaign and an executive with Beattie Media.

CRAIG MILLAR is a senior reporter with Grampian Television. He served ten years with *The Courier*, *The Evening Telegraph* and *The Scotsman*, before switching into broadcasting with BBC Radio Scotland and then Grampian Television. In 1989 he was appointed Scotland correspondent for the former breakfast television station TV-am. He rejoined Grampian in Dundee in 1991.

FRANK O'DONNELL is a reporter with The Scottish News Agency. After psychology and business from Edinburgh University, he travelled the seven seas, working in the USA, Canada and Australia. He was previously a reporter with *The Carrick Gazette* in Girvan, Ayrshire.

ALISON BALHARRY was born and brought up in Dundee. She currently lives in Glasgow and works as a producer with BBC Scotland. She is a co-founder of *artifax*, an arts, music and listings magazine for Dundee, and was co-editor between December 1997 and December 1998.

BRIAN LINDSAY was born and brought up in Dundee. He was educated at Lawside Academy and the University of Dundee. He is a broadcaster and co-editor of *artifax,* Dundee's arts, music and listings magazine.

CAROL POPE gained a 'first' in psychology at the University of Stirling, then followed her own idiosyncratic career path including four years as a syndicated columnist. She has written for many newspapers and magazines and her book *Baby Monthly* accompanied the BBC2 series of the same name. She was launch news editor of the magazine *Writers News* and is currently press officer at the University of Dundee.

ROB ADAMS founded Dundee Jazz Festival in 1983. Now an established freelance writer based in Edinburgh, he covers jazz, folk and roots music for *The Herald*.

SANDY McGREGOR left Morgan Academy on a Friday and started in newspapers the following Monday. He is chief reporter of *The Courier* and *The Evening Telegraph*. He has written about most sports and participated – with breathtaking mediocrity – in a number of them.

WILLIAM BOYLE is a prominent solicitor in Dundee, where he has practised for 25 years. He was educated at Lawside Academy and the University of Dundee.

TOM PETERKIN is a reporter for *Scotland on Sunday*. Prior to that he worked for the Scottish News Agency and *The Courier* for four years. He is a graduate of Edinburgh University, where he was the 'yard of ale' champion.

NORMAN WATSON is a journalist for *The Courier* and the author of several books, including *Dundee's Suffragettes* (1990) and *Daughters of Dundee* (1997). He lectures part-time on historical and medical issues and was elected to the senate of the Open University in 1997.

HELEN BROWN is a feature writer with *The Courier* with a special interest in the arts. She is also a member of the Scottish Food Writers' Circle. A history graduate of Edinburgh University, she studied the piano from the age of seven and also sings professionally in concert and oratorio throughout Scotland.

CHARLES McKEAN is a Professor of Scottish Architecture at the University of Dundee. He was previously secretary of the Royal Incorporation of Architects in Scotland. He is author of 18 books including *Dundee: an Illustrated Architectural Guide*.

TOM SHIELDS is the long-serving diarist of *The Herald* newspaper.

Dundee, now a city of leisure and tourism as well as education and commerce

Introduction

This book is a celebration of Dundee and, above all, the spirit of its people who are carving out a new identity for their city as it enters the third millennium. Drawing on its rich history, Dundee has set about discovering itself, some might say rediscovering itself, in order to meet the challenges of a rapidly changing world. It is a voyage of discovery that has seen Dundee emerge as a university and pioneering city, developing new technologies and new medical treatments. The same determined spirit has spilled over into a vibrant artistic community and a robust sports scene. It is that pioneering spirit that the contributors to this book have sought to capture.

Dundee: A Voyage of Discovery was conceived as part of the city of Dundee's millennium celebrations and its publication has been generously supported by Dundee City Council and Scottish Enterprise Tayside. The writers and journalists who have contributed did so at very short notice and deserve thanks for their commitment to the project. They have produced a book of which Dundee can be proud, a volume packed with fascinating detail that catalogues the city's impressive achievements. The views expressed in this book are those personally held by the authors.

In addition to those people listed in the acknowledgements, I would also like to thank Dundee's former Lord Provost Merv Rolfe, Les Roy and Anne Rendall of Dundee City Council, Sandra Burke of SET and Niall Scott of Beattie Media for their support in having this book published. Bill Campbell and the Mainstream team also deserve recognition for their efforts in turning the book around quickly.

Thanks are extended to James Rougvie, Donald Stewart and John Clarke for proof-reading.

Photographs were generously contributed by D.C. Thomson and Co. Ltd and also by David Martin of Fotopress, Alan Richardson, Gordon Douglas, Charles McKean along with Ian Jacobs and Michael Boyd of the Scottish News Agency.

One of Dundee's sixty-seven stunning parks and woodland spaces

Dundee Delineated

Inspiration, Imagination and Innovation

Graham Ogilvy

Dundee is, and always has been, a city of ideas. 'Inspiration, Imagination and Innovation' are the three 'I's that have characterised both the city's past and its present. In the last 400 years, Dundee has pioneered a breathtaking number of social, religious and political reforms, technological advances and medical breakthroughs.

If innovation is the common thread that runs through this book, determination, dissension and defiance are the human qualities that shine through the achievements of a truly ingenious people. Despite, or perhaps because of, its historical isolation, Dundee has played a considerable part in shaping modern Britain's political, financial, scientific, commercial and medical life.

Curiously, Dundee, and Dundonians, have always been rather reluctant to seek the limelight and boast of the city's accomplishments. But, as it enters the twenty-first century, the air of self-apology that once dogged the city has been dispelled. At the same time, the feeble schoolboy ditty of 'jute, jam and journalism', the woefully inadequate mnemonic device that so cruelly caricatured the city, has been well and truly buried.

Even during the five decades or so of the ascendancy of the textile industry – and note there is no place for the linen industry within the curse of the three 'J's – such a description was simply inaccurate. This book testifies to that. What was the relevance of the three 'J's when Dundee aviator Preston Watson dreamed of defying the laws of gravity; when Dundee doctor Thomas Maclagan discovered the basis for aspirin; when Robert Fleming founded the great financial trust movement that played such an important role in the opening up of the American West; and when the men of Dundee's shipyards built the RRS *Discovery*, one of the marvels of its day? Observers might rightly ask what this mediocre mantra has got to do with today's city of education, electronics and engineering and medicine, media and music? The three 'J's were simply three of Dundee's ideas – not bad ones at that, but only three from a cauldron of creativity that boiled with ingredients from every field of human endeavour and produced sensational results.

Today, the jute industry has been consigned to history. To the credit of the Dundee Industrial Heritage Trust, an organisation of concerned business people and individuals anxious to capture the experience of Dundee's days as Britain's 'Juteopolis', the award-winning Verdant Works is now the only place in Dundee where the raw jute that once blew across the streets can be seen. Appropriately, for what is a museum to a brilliant commercial idea and its equally brilliant technical exploitation, the Verdant Works was awarded the title of European Museum of the Year in 1999 for the best industrial museum, a reflection of the ingenuity and imagination of its interactive displays.

Yet the Verdant Works is more than just a museum devoted to the jute industry. It is a monument to the blood, sweat and tears shed by generations of mill workers. The industry thrived on low wages and large-scale poverty, earning Dundonians a reputation for being diminutive. In 1904 an army recruitment drive in the city had to reject half of all volunteers because they were too small or too light. The scourge of rickets, bad housing and poor nutrition meant that the average Dundonian was several inches shorter and several pounds lighter than the national average. To see just how small they were, examine the accompanying photograph of German pilots under arrest alongside Dundee's defiant defenders during World War II; both pilots seem bemused at the Lilliputian stature of their captors.

The imagery of King Jute, effectively deposed more than 50 years ago, is rightly blamed for the erroneous but lingering perception of Dundee as a mill town in a state of perpetual decline. Not all of the legacy of the textile industry is so negative, however, and the cornerstone of the new Dundee as a campus city was laid in the last century by the textile heiress Mary Baxter, who donated a considerable part of her fortune for the endowment of the college that is now the University of Dundee, on the strict condition that women were allowed to study as well as men.

The industry also bred an extraordinary self-reliant, hardy and industrious people, the foundation of the Dundee of tomorrow. The truth is that Dundee defies easy definition and glib categorisation, not because of its geographical location, diverse economic base or imagined remoteness, but because of the incredible individualism of its people, who are capable of strong-minded and forcefully expressed opinion on the one hand and an almost crippling reserve, especially when it comes to revealing successes, on the other. One takes Dundee for granted at one's peril.

Typically, it is the most creative of the three 'J's, journalism, that continues to flourish in Dundee. The publishing empire of D.C. Thomson and Co. Ltd not only produces its well-known stable of newspapers, magazines and comics but

Nazi airmen captured at Tentsmuir are marched along Bell Street to the Drill Hall, 12 March 1941 (courtesy of Dundee City Archives)

also produces journalists and media folk by the score. During the '80s, in an era when British industry did not distinguish itself by its track record of reinvestment, D.C. Thomson spent £40 million building one of the most sophisticated printing plants in Europe at its Kingsway Works and spent millions more on high-tech editing systems. Fleet Street executives and managers still make the pilgrimage to Dundee to see the latest technology in action. The company is a partner in Scotland on Line, the leading Internet provider, and has been no slouch in diversifying into other media and television investments. It has developed an important contract print business and now prints millions of brochures and even the daily newspapers of other proprietors.

Success, of course, encourages detractors. But even in a city that prides itself on its record of recycling, the hoary old stories of paternalistic attitudes, general strikes and kailyards are wearing a bit thin. How do these square with the high-tech realities? How do they explain the continued success of titles like *The Courier* and *The Sunday Post*? And critics should think twice before scorning the likes of *The Scots Magazine*, Britain's oldest magazine, first published in 1739 and still entertaining more than 300,000 readers monthly, or *The Dandy*,

Britain's longest-running comic whose early editions from 1938 onwards are now collectors' items, or the evergreen *People's Friend*. (While reporting on the 125th anniversary of the *People's Friend* a few years ago, the author conducted a telephone survey of Scottish news editors to obtain their guesses as to the circulation of the women's weekly. Back came the replies: '40,000?', '85,000?' and 'Is it still printed? I remember my granny used to get it.' All were stunned to learn that it sold a massive 435,000, with sales rising.)

There are plenty of newspaper barons who would like to get a slice of a 'kailyard' like that, and there are plenty of media professionals who owe their start in the business to D.C. Thomson. In addition, Radio Tay, the University of Dundee and other local news organisations have also played a role in producing journalists, and there is scarcely a newspaper, magazine, radio station or television channel that does not have staff connected in some way to Dundee.

Dundee and D.C. Thomson have been synonymous for a century. The company remains a valued employer and loyally retains its headquarters in the city. Yet while its newspapers are influential in setting the parameters for political debate, they have rarely been able to impose their conservative views on a city that prizes political radicalism and ideological non-conformity.

For centuries, Dundee has been a hotbed of new ideas. Ground-breaking concepts were eagerly seized upon by Dundonians long before they became fashionable and safe. During the Reformation, Dundee was known as Scotland's Geneva because of its prominent role in pursuing religious reform and supporting the Protestant cause. George Wishart, one of the Reformation's greatest martyrs, was a hero in Dundee, where he had returned to comfort plague victims. He survived attempts on his life in Dundee and Angus but was finally burned at the stake on 1 March 1546.

Two hundred and fifty years later, the port of Dundee, which had smuggled banned Protestant tracts from Europe, clandestinely imported illegal copies of Tom Paine's *Rights of Man* from revolutionary France. It was also at this time that one of Dundee's most remarkable sons and political visionaries came to prominence. George Mealmaker, a humble but well-educated weaver, led a society demanding democratic rights and helped to found Scotland's first modern democratic party to admit working people as members. After the suppression of the 'Friends of the People' and the transportation to Australia of their leaders, including a Dundee Unitarian minister, Thomas Fysche Palmer, Mealmaker established the United Scotsmen and wrote its constitution and principles.

Tragically for him, Mealmaker was, of course, 200 years ahead of his time. Among his shocking demands was the creation of a Scottish Parliament and the vote for working people. In 1798 Mealmaker was tried for sedition and sent to Botany Bay for 14 years. Support and admiration for him was such that a 17-

year-old cooper from Fife was sentenced to seven years' transportation rather than give evidence against him. A third of the convicts on their ship died during the terrible journey to the other side of the world. Mealmaker survived but died in Australia in 1807, just a year after his old comrades collected a 6,000-strong petition in Dundee appealing for clemency. The Scottish Parliament had its first martyr from Dundee. Remarkably, two centuries later it was another Dundonian working-class leader, Harry McLevy, who, as Scottish TUC President, was instrumental not only in winning a Scottish Parliament but also in virtually single-handedly gaining acceptance of the need for proportional representation within Labour's ranks.

When it comes to politics, however, the only predictable thing about Dundee is its unpredictability. William Pitt, while Prime Minister, remarked that he 'knew the price of every MP except one – George Dempster', the MP for Dundee from 1761 to 1790. Dempster supported the American colonists in their fight against British rule. He might even have known the family of Samuel Johnston, who, born in Dundee in 1733, went on to lead the rebel colonists, become the first senator for North Carolina and serve as state governor for three terms.

From the very earliest development of modern, non-dynastic politics, therefore, Dundee produced fiercely independent characters and defiant, dissenting voices, a trend that was to become the hallmark of Dundee politics. Consider Dundee's MPs since Dempster. They include George Kinloch, who was outlawed for his support of popular rights; Alex Wilkie, elected in 1906 as Scotland's first ever Labour MP; and Winston Churchill, then a leading Liberal and the scourge of the Tory party, elected in 1908 only to be defeated in 1922 by Neddy Scrymgeour, the one and only MP for the Prohibition Party of Great Britain that was founded in Dundee. E.D. Morel, a pacifist and remarkable campaigner who exposed the horrors of his native Belgium's rule in the Congo, was returned in the same election as Scrymgeour; Florence Horsbrugh, the first ever woman MP for the Conservative Party, was returned in 1931 as a National Government candidate by the fickle mill lasses whom Churchill had observed turning out in great numbers to seal his fate; and John Strachey, the controversial left-wing intellectual of the '30s, represented Dundee while serving as Defence Minister in Attlee's famous Labour government. Despite Dundee's reputation as a Labour stronghold, it kept alive the flickering flame of nationalism by returning SNP leader Gordon Wilson for much of the '70s and '80s. Today the two strands of socialism and nationalism are represented in John McAllion, the MP for Dundee East and a rare dissenting voice among the serried ranks of New Labour.

But one of the most outstanding of Dundee's political figures in the twentieth century is also the least well known, yet his amazing life story embraces so much of Dundee's recent history. Bob Stewart started work in the jute mills in 1887 as

The high-tech newsroom at D.C. Thomson's (courtesy of D.C. Thomson and Co. Ltd)

a ten-year-old 'half-timer', a child labourer who divided his time between school and work in the mills. At 16, after three years' full-time work in the mills, he became an apprentice joiner and was eventually to work on the building of the RRS *Discovery* in Gourlay's yard, where he was a shop steward. Sickened at the impact of drink on the working classes, like many trade unionists, he became a strict teetotaller. In 1908 he was the full-time organiser of the Scottish Prohibition Party and was elected to Dundee Town Council as a Prohibition councillor. During that year of terrible unemployment, when soup kitchens had to be organised to feed thousands of starving families, Stewart persuaded the council to create work for the unemployed – and the trees in Blackness Road are the living memorial to a man who is largely forgotten in his native city. Stewart's strongly held convictions saw him oppose the fearful slaughter of the Great War, in which thousands of Dundonians were killed. As a conscientious objector, he was court-martialled four times and spent two and a half years as a prisoner in Dudhope Castle, Wormwood Scrubs, Calton Jail, Edinburgh Castle and, finally, the old Dundee Prison.

During his time in prison he heard about the Russian Revolution, an event that inspired him just as the French Revolution had inspired young Mealmaker more than a century earlier. Stewart was attracted to the new ideas of 'scientific socialism' and joined the Communist Party. Like Mealmaker, he was tried for sedition but served only three months in a Welsh prison for a speech he had made to a crowd of miners. He graduated to become one of the leaders of the British communist movement and served as the party's acting general secretary when its leaders were arrested during the general strike of 1926. In 1931 he stood as a Communist in his native Dundee, winning over 10,000 votes, and it is in that year that his memoirs, *Breaking the Fetters*, end.

Now, for the first time, it can be revealed why Stewart's memoirs, published in 1967, end more than 30 years earlier. With the rise of fascism in Europe, Stewart went to Moscow, where he worked with the Communist International. He became one of a group of Comintern secret agents who risked their lives to act as couriers smuggling money, false documents and spying equipment into Nazi Germany, Fascist Italy and war-torn China – which explains why a Dundee mill laddie who helped to build the *Discovery* later came to be pictured with Chairman Mao Tse-tung. The full story of Bob Stewart's anti-fascist work, and the tragic consequences it had for his family, lies buried in the Moscow vaults of the KGB; perhaps one day it will be told.

Keeping pace with democratic developments in Dundee have been the extraordinary strides made by Dundee's women. Since the dark misogynist days of the witch hunts when Grizzel Jaffray was burned at the stake for witchcraft, the women of Dundee have tenaciously fought for, and won, their rights. In the process they have acquired a reputation for independence and resourcefulness,

George Wishart . . . Administering the Sacrament *by James Drummond (courtesy of Dundee Art Galleries and Museums)*

qualities tested to the utmost during the days of jute when they were frequently the breadwinners of the family and brought up children as well as working full time. The grim '30s imagery of tenements and 'kettleboilers', the name given to Dundee's unemployed men who stayed at home while their wives went to work, is only part of the story of Dundee women, however, and it obscures so much more.

The city gave birth to one of the world's first feminists. Fanny Wright is remembered by a small plaque at her former home in the Nethergate, but in the United States she is revered as North America's founding feminist. Wright, the daughter of a Dundee linen merchant who was a supporter of George Mealmaker, fled to America with her father during the government crackdown on the radicals. In the United States of the 1820s she was demonised as a 'Red Harlot' for her championship of women's rights and her efforts in setting up a new model community in 1825 that aimed to give black slaves their freedom. Just across the road from her birthplace in Dundee, the university has carried on a noble tradition with the appointment of Scotland's first Professor of Gender Studies, Gerda Fiann.

The strength of Dundee's women, whose legendary feistiness is tempered with a warm compassion, is probably best exemplified in the exploits of the Victorian mill girl turned missionary Mary Slessor. Her portrait now graces bank notes and her life story is to be the subject of a feature film. In Calabar, now a part of Nigeria, the memory of the tiny Dundonian mill lassie who saved the lives of hundreds of native girls who would otherwise have been killed at birth by adopting the babies is still revered. In time, 'Ma', as she was known across the 2,000 square miles where she practised her own special blend of practical missionary work, that must have shocked the tight-laced missionaries of the time.

Slessor's example inspired others to follow, and Dundee women became pioneers in a whole range of professions from medicine to the law. The city produced Scotland's first woman university professor in Margaret Fairlie, a gynaecologist who used up her own savings to buy radium for Dundee Royal Infirmary in the early days of radiation treatment. In the legal profession, Dundee can claim Scotland's first woman sheriff in Margaret Kidd and, most recently, Scotland's first woman advocate general, Lynda Clark. It was also a daughter of Dundee, Williamina Fleming, who pioneered women's entry into the world of astronomy by becoming Harvard University's curator of astronomical photographs, discovering hundreds of stars and charting the first map of the skies, and Dundee's formidable army of women mill workers elected Britain's first female trade-union leader when, in 1971, Margaret Fenwick was appointed general secretary of the Jute, Flax and Kindred Textile Operative's Union.

Bob Stewart, the legendary Dundee councillor who worked on the Discovery, *entertains Chairman Mao Tse-Tung in 1955. Stewart was an underground agent smuggling funds to the anti-Nazi resistance in Germany and the Chinese Red Army during its struggle against Chiang Kai-shek (courtesy of Dundee City Archives)*

Dundee's doughty women were fighting for their rights long before the Edwardian suffragettes, who had a strong presence in the city, or the 'women's libbers' of the '60s and '70s. The country's first known example of a marriage contract was drawn up in the 1830s at the behest of a local woman, one Mary Ritchie, who wanted to protect her £10,000 fortune, and in the 1820s a crowd of Dundee women angered at flourishing prostitution in the city resorted to the expedient of burning both of the town's brothels to the ground.

Those early pioneers of women's rights could scarcely have imagined the advances that have been made and Mary Baxter would marvel at how her vision of a university which allowed entry to girls has become a reality. Dundee is now a campus city with one of the highest ratios of students per head of the population in the country, with more than 22,000 students now educated at the city's educational establishments. Miss Baxter's University College has grown to become the University of Dundee, and the Dundee Technical Institute, created in 1888 with funds from a trust established by Mary's brother, Sir David Baxter, is now the University of Abertay.

The latter has gone from strength to strength in the '90s. Abertay's new library is a welcome and tasteful addition to Dundee's architecture, but the university is as at home with the old as it is with the new and Dudhope Castle

Mary Baxter would be gratified at the number of women among Dundee's 22,000 students

Dundee: a city transformed and renewed

is now home to Abertay's successful Dundee Business School. The university works closely with industry, providing a range of services to companies. It recently set up Britain's first degree course in computer games to reinforce and capitalise upon Dundee's reputation as Europe's computer-games capital, partly a reflection of the high esteem in which former Abertay student David Jones, founder of DMA and creator of 'Lemmings', is held.

Traditionally, the strength of the University of Dundee has lain in its vocational departments. Its engineering, law, dentistry and medicine faculties have trained thousands of graduates since the university was granted its charter in 1967. Now it is famed for its research into the life sciences which has put Dundee on the map as one of the great cancer-research centres of the world, and a unique interdisciplinary approach bringing surgeons and biochemists together is developing new methods of cancer treatment.

The monumental achievements in the life sciences can sometimes overshadow other areas of excellence within the university. The arts and social science faculty, for example, has a long and distinguished track record. How many politics departments can claim the general secretary of NATO and a government minister, George Robertson and Brian Wilson, among their former students? The department of English has encouraged something of a literary revival in the city through the success of its writer-in-residence scheme. The long-term benefits of this scheme are now being witnessed and, as we shall see later in this book, Dundee has become a city of poets. The university's merger with the Duncan of Jordanstone College of Art has underwritten the continued success of what is Scotland's largest art college with one of Britain's most highly regarded schools of television and electronic imaging.

In keeping with an established 'town and gown' tradition, the university has collaborated in the development of Dundee Contemporary Arts, where it has located the university's Visual Research Centre. The university, working in partnership with the city council, has contributed greatly towards the generation of a 'cultural quarter' in which DCA, the Dundee Rep theatre, private galleries, antique shops, coffee bars and wine bars will shortly acquire a new neighbour in the shape of a £9 million science centre.

In true democratic Dundee fashion, however, this quarter is in no sense exclusive. In its first few months of opening, DCA, housed in an attractive building and complete with two cinemas, café bar, shop, print studio and exhibition area, established itself as a popular venue for local people with an imaginative programme of exhibitions and community-education events. In doing so, it is following in the footsteps of the innovative Dundee Rep that pioneered community drama with its city-wide production of *Witch's Blood* and community dance programmes. The Rep has also inspired a number of popular plays on Dundee themes, often by writers with little theatrical experience. *They Fairly Mak Ye Work*, *A Man at Yir Back*, *Toshie*, *The Mill Lavvies* and *On the Line* are a few examples of how a theatre can interact with the community.

Physically, the Dundee of today is incomparably more attractive than the city of 30 years ago. In spring and summer it is a city in bloom thanks to the award-winning efforts of the council's parks department. Public art has been a feature of Dundee's renaissance since the early '80s, when Bob McGilvray and his Dundee Public Arts team were initially regarded with some scepticism. Now, public art is an integral part of the new Dundee. In the newly refurbished city centre and tucked away in nooks and crannies all over the city, murals, sculptures and imaginative furniture delight and entertain, while often reflecting Dundee's history. Architecturally, too, there has been an effort to improve the quality and aesthetic appeal of new buildings in the city centre, with the Bank of Scotland headquarters and the new Overgate shopping centre two prime examples.

Fifty years ago, a famous postcard satirised the city. 'Bonnie Dundee' was pictured huddled under a blanket of smog from the dozens of mill smokestacks. Today it is a garden city that takes pride in its open spaces and magnificent vistas over the Tay. And, with new hotels appearing all the time, Dundee has now managed to create what was once unimaginable, namely a tourism industry.

When, in 1980, the author was asked by *The Scotsman* to write an article on tourism in Dundee, it seemed an impossible task. Of the thousand words written, only half were devoted to the city, the rest focusing on the undoubted charms of Dundee's fantastic hinterland of Angus, Fife and Perthshire and the hunting, shooting, fishing and golfing that they had to offer. At that time Dundee possessed a museum and art gallery in the McManus Galleries that had changed little since the war and Camperdown Park had yet to develop its imaginative wildlife centre. The *Discovery*, the vessel that was to become a symbol of Dundee's recovery, had yet to arrive. Discovery Point had not even been considered. There was no award-winning museum at the Verdant Works. The old mill that now tells the tale of Dundee's textile past was still a scrapyard. There was no science centre in the pipeline. There were no bowling alleys or multi-screen cinemas. There were no flights to London even on a weekly, let alone a daily basis. The Dundee Contemporary Arts centre had not even been conceived. The old mills in the centre of town that have been transformed into flats, nightclubs and artists' studios lay abandoned and derelict. No investors had come forward with a £250 million plan to demolish the mouldering '60s-style Overgate monstrosity and replace it with the type of exciting new shopping centre recently opened. The High Street and the city centre had yet to receive their £50 million facelift and the city did not possess a decent bookshop. Many of the pubs were dour places compared with today's hostelries, and pub food had still to develop beyond pie and beans. The conference business that today accounts for a large slice of Dundee's £70 million annual tourism income was virtually non-existent.

The credit for much of this transformation belongs to the Dundee Project, a partnership between what is now Scottish Enterprise and the city council. It was established in 1982, partly as a response to the series of hammer blows that Dundee has received during the Thatcher era when numerous engineering factories, mills and the local shipyard were the subjects of closure. With morale in the city desperately low, the Dundee Project's billboards announcing forthcoming developments were greeted with some cynicism, and some Dundee folk are still annoyed at what they see as the piecemeal development of the Waterfront, where the architectural standards expected in the city today are not evident.

Yet the Project team persevered in its efforts not just to plan strategically for the long term but also to boost the morale of the city. Its first masterstroke was the return of the *Discovery* in 1986. There followed Dundee 800, the celebration in 1988 of Dundee's Octocentenary that saw the inimitable Henny King lead a year-long programme of events. The feel-good factor returned to the

Her Majesty the Queen at the opening of the new library at the University of Abertay, Dundee (courtesy of Prospect PR Ltd)

city after the depression of the early '80s. As sponsored sporting events came to the city and the Tay estuary, the results of the early planning and negotiations started to filter through. The Technology Park, recently joined by a Medical Park, and other modern industrial and commercial premises were developed. Dundee Airport was developed and extended, and Scotland's largest pedestrianised shopping precinct was created in a revamped city centre.

And if, during this period, Dundee lost a number of familiar names, it also retained many. With the headquarters of C.J. Lang in the city, Dundee remains an important centre for food and grocery distribution. NCR is a world player in the development of automatic telling machines and draws heavily on graduates from the local universities. Michelin in Dundee are the UK's most important manufacturers of tyres. Bonar Carelle prints most of the crisp packets and confectionery wrappers for the UK's leading brands. The Wright Dental Group supplies perhaps Dundee's most unlikely exports in the millions of sets of dentures it sells around the world. The Scottish Crop Research Institute is at the forefront of biotechnology innovation. Curiously, Dundee is also host to Scotland's two leading firms of chartered surveyors, with both Graham and Sibbald and J. and E. Shepherd retaining their head offices in the city. The

The University of Abertay library, symbolic of the high standards in the city's modern architecture (courtesy of Prospect PR Ltd)

Alliance Trust remains in the city that give birth to the financial trust movement and continues to outperform its rivals on a regular basis.

New names, too, have appeared on the scene. TRAK microwave is at the forefront of its field and – fittingly, for the City of Discovery – a Dundee-made component was on the first space vehicle to land on Mars. Shield Diagnostics are part of a burgeoning medical sector that has grown up in the city alongside the growth of life sciences at the University of Dundee. Tayside Optical Technology develops complex gratings for some of the world's most advanced satellite systems. Another company, Cyclacel, in which the university has a share, is developing the commercial applications of the cancer-research breakthroughs made in the city. DMA Design is creating computer games eagerly sought after by children across the globe. The high-tech sectors that these companies represent are the seed beds for the successful businesses, and jobs, of the future. It may not happen tomorrow but, make no mistake, it will happen.

Dundee's future is, as it always has been, in the ideas of its people, and in sector after sector Dundee is at the cutting edge of developing new technologies. It is somehow fitting, and not at all surprising, that the twentieth century

The men who went to Mars – a TRAK microwave team with their component sent to outer space

opened with Dundee expertise involved in the exploration of what was then man's last frontier, Antarctica, and that it ends with that same expertise playing a role in the exploration of man's final frontier, outer space. As for the millennium ahead, the City of Discovery is again on a voyage into the future, seeking new cures, new treatments, new crops and new technologies that will benefit mankind. And of one thing you can be sure: somewhere in the city by the Tay, as you read this, a man or a woman in an office, a laboratory, a library or a factory has just had an idea . . .

2

The Fame of Their Deeds Is Immortal

Dundee's Astonishing Medical Pioneers

Niall Scott

Even in a city that keeps secrets like a mother guards her children, the house at 136 Nethergate is a wonderfully understated memorial to a great wee slice of history. Jammed in a busy student thoroughfare, the elegant but anonymous tenement offers little to command the notice of passers-by. Beyond its douce exterior, however, the Nethergate house has as captivating a heritage as the RRS *Discovery* herself.

A small plaque on the wall commemorates the life of 'The Great Red Harlot' Fanny Wright (1795–1852), one of the earliest proponents of free love, birth control and equal rights for women – but few can be aware that the building was also home to a man whose legacy lives on in bathroom cabinets from Rangoon to Rio.

It was in 1874 from surgical rooms in these well-appointed premises that Dr Thomas Maclagan, a 'lad o pairts' from Scone, wrote the seminal chapter in the story of aspirin, one of the most important drugs in history. Given aspirin's influence on society, Maclagan's house in Nethergate – presently a busy solicitors' practice – ought to be a shrine for the sore, shivery and hung-over millions who rejoice in the drug's healing and preventative

Thomas Maclagan, the pioneering Dundee doctor who discovered aspirin (courtesy of The Scotsman*)*

powers. The ubiquitous tonic of the twentieth century has become one of the most widely used pharmaceutical products in the world, but without Thomas Maclagan's home-grown enterprise and inquiring mind, aspirin as we know it today might not have existed.

Dundee's part in the story of instant pain relief remains one of medicine's best-kept secrets – but then the City of Discovery can also lay claim to the pioneers of X-rays, antihistamines, acupuncture, big-game post-mortems and pay-per-view surgery, yet has largely eschewed celebration of its diverse achievements, even at a time when it is pushing the envelope and commanding international notice in so many areas of science and medicine.

For students of history, of Dundee and of medicine, the stories of the city's medical innovators still offer the rarity of unexplored and unexploited territory. The son of a physician, Maclagan was schooled in Perth before entering Glasgow University at the age of 15 to study the humanities. He entered the Edinburgh Medical School in 1855, qualified in 1860 and travelled for postgraduate study in Paris, Munich and Vienna. Fate played a large part in bringing him to Dundee as Resident Medical Superintendent of the Royal Infirmary during the fever-ravaged winter of 1864. Maclagan promptly fell seriously ill with typhoid fever and was granted a leave of absence to recover his health.

Musing upon his illness and believing that his predecessors' poor diet and heavy workload had contributed to their deaths, he introduced an improved dietary regime at DRI and prescribed the use of medicinal wine – an enlightened strategy of health promotion that was subsequently to reduce hospital mortality in Dundee to one of the lowest levels in the country. Between 1865 and 1866, Maclagan became the first in Scotland to make practical and investigative use of the clinical thermometer in the fever wards of a hospital, a device which had hitherto been regarded in medical circles as little more than a toy.

Once the fever epidemic had abated in 1866, Maclagan left his post at DRI to go into general practice and eventually settled in the surgical rooms at 136 Nethergate, where he and his wife Isabella Scudamore raised a family of three. Perplexed by the suffering of a steady stream of patients admitted to hospital each year with acute or chronic rheumatism, Maclagan applied himself wholeheartedly to the pursuit of a remedy.

The age-old theory that nature plants the remedy close to the cause and the common association between rheumatism and low-lying, damp localities led Maclagan, on a good scientific hunch, to the willow tree. Using salicin, the bitter principle that can be simply extracted from the bark of the white willow tree in early spring, Maclagan began an uncontrolled trial among eight Dundee patients suffering from rheumatism in November 1874. The results were spectacular. The patients' pain and fever decreased markedly within 48 hours of oral administration of Maclagan's preparation. Further trials followed and in 1876 Maclagan published his results outlining the value of salicin in the treatment of acute rheumatism. He considered his use of salicin to be 'no haphazard experiment' but a method that boasted a fair foundation 'in reason and analogy'.

From the results of Maclagan's studies and parallel investigations in Germany, acetyl-salicylic acid (aspirin) was born. It was fully two decades after Maclagan's experiments with salicin in the Nethergate house, however, that a young German scientist named Felix Hoffman arrived at a process that allowed the synthetic manufacture of acetyl-salicylic acid and gave the new drug its brand name. Although Hoffman himself was to rely on Maclagan's work to further the development of aspirin, the passage of time has now largely erased the Dundee chapter from the official version of the genesis of the wonder drug.

John Crichton, one of the most skilled surgeons of his day, in a painting by John Zephaniah Bell (courtesy of Dundee Central Library Photographic Collection)

Maclagan's discovery, his influence on the treatment of rheumatism and the effect of his therapy upon grateful patients were eventually to prompt his departure from Dundee. In 1879 he moved to a medical practice in London at the insistence of the Earl and Countess of Southesk after salving the Earl's acute rheumatism with salicin. After his death, Maclagan's contemporaries rated him as influential as Lister and Simpson as the innovator of a specific therapy for rheumatism, a view which is still propounded by medical historians today.

Were it not for Laura Adam, the Curator of the Medical History Museum at Ninewells Hospital and Medical School, Maclagan's story, and those of his fellow innovators like Blair, Pirie, Riley and Crichton, would most likely remain consigned to the bottom drawer of history. Adam has painstakingly researched their work and mounted a series of inspired exhibitions in the University Medical School at Ninewells which underline Dundee's long traditions of medical innovation and discovery. Recognition for Thomas Maclagan is, she argues, long overdue. 'From the results of Maclagan's studies and

Dr George Alexander Pirie, whose pioneering work with X-rays cost him his sight (courtesy of Medical History Museum, Ninewells Hospital)

contemporaneous investigations in Germany using salicylic acid, aspirin was developed, one of the most widely used drugs of this century as an analgesic as well as an anti-rheumatic drug,' she says. 'Maclagan's claim of specificity for salicylates in treating rheumatic disorders is as substantial and credible now as when first made.

'Dundee gave Maclagan his seminal experience with fever and Maclagan responded energetically to the particular medical needs of the local community. He applied himself to the major problems of his general practice – fever and rheumatism. He came up with a remedy, a non-steroidal anti-inflammatory drug which, after chemical development, remains a specific treatment for rheumatism. It would not be correct to say that he invented aspirin, but there is no doubt he played a very significant part in its

Dr George Alexander Pirie with colleagues in the 1920s. Radiation damage to Dr Pirie's hands led to their ultimate amputation. Rather gruesomely, they are preserved in formaldehyde by the Medical History Museum at Ninewells Hospital, Dundee (courtesy of Medical History Museum, Ninewells Hospital)

development. It seems appropriate to link Dundee with Maclagan and his discovery of the values of salicin.'

Patrick Blair's place in Dundee's medical history is assured by dint of the fact he was the first doctor in Britain to dissect an elephant – although history does not seem to record who was second. A surgeon-apothecary, Blair practised medicine in Dundee from 1700 to 1715, was awarded an MD by the University of Aberdeen in 1712 and was elected a Fellow of the Royal Society the same year. He created a physic garden in the city between 1700 and 1708, one of the earliest in Britain to be established as a specialist resource for dispensatory medicinal plants, although its location is sadly now unknown. The unfortunate elephant who shares Dr Blair's place in folklore had toured Europe as part of a travelling exhibition and was *en route* to Dundee with its keepers on Saturday, 27 April 1706, when it collapsed on the Broughty Ferry Road. Hearing of its demise, Patrick

Dr James Riley, one of Dundee's earliest cancer specialists, who discovered the origin of histamine, the substance which brings misery to allergy sufferers. Dr Riley's discovery led to the development of the now commonly used antihistamines (courtesy of Medical History Museum, Ninewells Hospital)

Blair saw the opportunity to make a unique anatomical study and hurried to the scene with Provost Yeaman. As the elephant could not be moved, the dissection had to take place in the open air 'amongst a throng and rabble' and in 'mighty hot weather'.

In 1710, Blair published a very detailed and accurate account of the dissection in the Transactions of the Royal Society and won great admiration as a result. The fame of the event also helped save his life after the 1715 Jacobite rebellion. Dundee was a Jacobite stronghold at that time and Blair was captured and imprisoned in Newgate after the Battle of Preston. Sentenced to death, he was reprieved after his friend Sir Hans Sloane approached his gaolers with an account of Dr Blair's eminence. Blair died in London in 1728 having reached the letter 'h' in his alphabetical *Treatise of Dispensatory Plants*.

John Crichton, after whom Dundee's Crichton Street is named, was one of the first surgeons employed to work at Dundee Royal Infirmary after it opened in March 1798. He served as attending surgeon until 1855 and earned a reputation as one of the most skilled surgeons of his day. With no football to watch on a Saturday, the townspeople would cram into Crichton's operating theatre to see him at work.

These events proved so popular that it became necessary to add a protective rail around the operating table to prevent the 'spectators' from jostling the surgeons as they worked. Crichton's special area of expertise was lithotomy, the removal of stones from the urinary tract. He was extremely skilled in this procedure, and his records show that among 200 operations on patients ranging in age from two to 85, only 14 patients had died, an outstanding success rate given this was before the days of effective anaesthesia or antisepsis. He attributed his success to 'serenity of mind and a hand that never trembled'. In 1839, he became the first doctor in Dundee to practise the ancient Chinese art of acupuncture.

George Alexander Pirie was one of the early pioneers in the use of X-rays in clinical medicine, a speciality for which he paid a high price. He experimented with X-rays at Dundee Royal Infirmary from 1896 until 1925, when he was

Medical research – a tower of strength in the new Dundee. Professor Sir Philip Cohen (centre left) at the official opening of the Wellcome Trust Building in May 1998 (courtesy of David Martin/Fotopress)

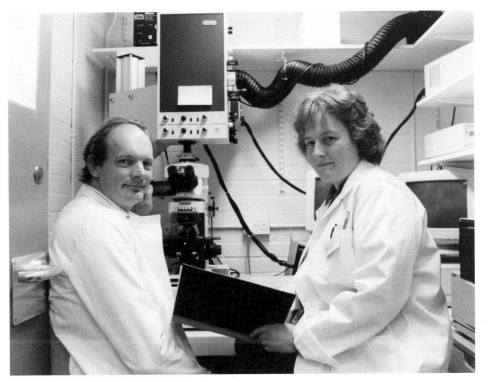

Professor David Lane, discoverer of p53, and his wife, Professor Birgitte Lane, working side by side (courtesy of David Martin/Fotopress)

forced to retire due to ill health brought on by his long-term exposure to radiation. After little more than a decade of experimentation, Dr Pirie began to suffer from tumours on his hands and his eyesight started to fail. Eventually he lost both hands, and when he was no longer able to continue working, he was awarded a Civil List pension and a Carnegie Hero Trust medal and pension. A macabre memorial, Pirie's hands are preserved in formalin and retained by the Medical History Museum at Ninewells Hospital.

An interview with Dr Pirie published in *The Courier* of 1929 gives an insight into his courage and doggedness in the painful pursuit of scientific breakthrough: 'My hands began to give me trouble. The skin cracked open, and it amused my comrades to see me going about with sticking plaster all over them. Sometimes I would waken at night and find them tingling like fire. I was urged to give up the X-ray work and merely superintend, but I could never bring myself to cause others to take a risk that I would not take myself. I was told nothing could be done. I like to draw a veil over those days.'

Pirie's name is inscribed on the Memorial Stone erected in Hamburg in 1936 to honour the pioneers of X-rays who suffered radiation injury or lost their lives pursuing clinical applications of Röntgen's discovery. The citation reads, 'They were heroic pioneers for a safe and successful application of X-rays to medicine. The fame of their deeds is immortal.'

Dr James Riley was one of Dundee's earliest cancer specialists, but his investigations were to lead to a major breakthrough in a completely different area of medicine. During the Second World War he served as a surgical specialist commanding a mobile surgical unit in the Far East. His surgical career was cut short after he contracted skin lesions on his hands while serving in Malaya and he switched his interests and energies towards radiotherapy. Appointed consultant radiotherapist at Dundee Royal Infirmary in 1948, he continued to research malignant diseases and noticed that skin tumours in mice were associated with the development of mast cells, first described by Paul Ehrlich in 1877. So called because they were usually found in tissues with enhanced nutrition ('mast' means 'food'), the function of mast cells remained a mystery at the time of Dr Riley's earliest observations. He devoted his life's work to their study and discovered that mast cells were storage sites for histamine, the substance which causes the symptoms of allergic reactions like rashes and hay fever. Before Dr Riley's discovery, the origin of histamine was unknown.

This breakthrough stimulated research around the globe and prompted the search for new drugs capable of inhibiting the release of histamine from mast cells. Subsequent investigations resulted in the discovery that sodium cromoglycate could prevent this release, and this compound is now widely used to prevent asthma.

Thanks to Laura Adam's research into Riley and his fellow innovators, several of the new roads on the Ninewells Hospital campus in Dundee now bear the names of many of the city's forgotten medical pioneers, among them George Pirie Way and Thomas Maclagan Way.

There are now tentative plans for a further memorial to Thomas Maclagan in the city that nurtured his formative and most creative years as a physician. Even 120 years after the first experiments with salicin, it would not be an inappropriate gesture given the way Maclagan's discovery has touched the practice of so many aspects of medicine, even more so because there is now good evidence that the true age of aspirin is just beginning. Over three thousand studies are published every year highlighting potential new uses for the drug. Some 12 billion aspirin tablets worth £1.3 billion are consumed worldwide. It is already recognised as an invaluable protector against heart attacks and, as an adjunct to some forms of infertility treatment, a daily dose can double the chances of a successful pregnancy. It is undergoing tests as a preventative agent against Alzheimer's Disease and may have applications in early screening for asthma. Particular excitement, however, has been prompted by the discovery that aspirin can halve mortality in cancer, the very disease that claimed the life of Thomas Maclagan, its Scottish pioneer, in 1903.

To the west of Maclagan's old house, a new building rises above the rooftops of the sprawling west-end campus of the University of Dundee. Here, the lights never go out. This is the Wellcome Trust Building, £22 million worth of state-of-the-art laboratory space and home to one of the principal architects of Dundee's renaissance. In the context of a global war against diseases such as cancer and diabetes in which armies of researchers in every continent are closing in on the enemy, the Dundee institute is increasingly viewed as command HQ.

Its director, Professor Sir Philip Cohen, came to Dundee 28 years ago by way of the University of Washington in Seattle. The young biochemist was attracted to Dundee by the reputation of Peter Garland, then the dynamic head of the city's new medical sciences institute. Garland had fought a personal battle to re-establish biochemistry as a force in Dundee and made a point of headhunting about a dozen bright young scientists, Cohen among them, in the '60s and early '70s.

Cohen was one of the few to see the enormous potential in a city whose image and self-esteem had been mired by the ravages of recession and a brief but infamous flirtation with corruption. He was sold on its beauty, its proximity to sea and mountains and its promise. A quarter of a century later, Cohen is credited with being the father of medical science in Dundee and a catalyst in the city's reinvention. The same qualities that persuaded him to put down roots in the City of Discovery he now uses to entice fellow scientists to the city. Not that there is much enticing left to be done. Cohen's reputation and that of Dundee are such that the city has become a natural first choice for many of the emerging stars of science. Outside the traditional scientific strongholds of Oxford and Cambridge, Dundee is now home to the UK's largest population of life scientists. Given their pick of Oxbridge or Dundee, most will now plump for the latter.

Cohen's research interests – the role of protein phosphorylation and dephosphorylation in cell regulation and human disease – are relevant to the broad tapestry of human frailty. Abnormal protein phosphorylation and its effect on cell behaviour is a cause or consequence of many major diseases, including cancer, diabetes and a number of hereditary disorders, such as muscular dystrophy. Cohen has forecast that many of the major drugs that will be developed in the next millennium will work at this level by inhibiting the enzymes which regulate cell behaviour. He speaks as much from experience as anticipation. Cyclosporin, the widely used immuno-suppressant that prevents tissue rejection after organ transplantation, acts by inhibiting a protein phosphatase identified by his lab in Dundee in 1981. More recently, he led the team which discovered an enzyme which plays a vital role in the cellular process which allows insulin to store glucose. The discovery opened new doors in research into diabetes and spawned the search for a new drug capable of switching the enzyme on and off, thereby obviating the need for patients to inject insulin daily.

Professor Sir Alfred Cushieri, the pioneer of 'key-hole' minimal-access surgery (courtesy of the University of Dundee)

These discoveries are a taste of what is to come. Drug companies and investors are attracted to Cohen's intellect like bees to honey. He has established a new division of Signal Transduction Therapy in which his lab is working with five leading pharmaceutical companies to develop specific inhibitors of the enzymes which influence a number of disease processes.

Ian Stewart was editor of Dundee's morning newspaper *The Courier* during the '80s and early '90s when a headstrong biochemist from the University of Dundee began to attract headlines for his efforts to establish a scientific citadel in Dundee. In 1992 he led with a story announcing a new science research centre for Dundee and predicting the city's growth at the cutting edge of life-sciences research. It was the biggest story in town, and remains so.

Shaped by the ambitions of Cohen and the university mandarins who shared his belief in the city's potential, the phrase 'City of Discovery', until then only associated with Scott's historic ship and Dundee's embryonic ambitions as a tourist centre, suddenly found a whole new resonance, and one that promised new directions, new wealth and new jobs for Dundee. The media leapt upon it and the city moved up several gears virtually overnight. 'Philip Cohen has probably been the single most influential character in the development of science and medicine in Dundee in the twentieth century and one of the biggest influences in science in this country,' says Stewart. 'Years ago he forecast that the scientific community would become one of the single most important economic forces in Dundee. It seemed far-fetched at the time, but he has an annoying habit of being proved right.

'He has been vital to Dundee's reinvention. Recruitment is the key to success. He recognised that for science to flourish in Dundee we must be able to attract the top people – and that effort has resulted in the growth of a family of scientific stars. Quality attracts quality, and in Dundee Philip has ensured we have the best of the best.'

Courted by Cohen, the Wellcome Trust saw the opportunities in Dundee and plans for a new research centre were launched. The Wellcome Trust Building in the Hawkhill was completed in 1997 with major backing from Wellcome, the university and Scottish Enterprise Tayside. Even Sean Connery was attracted by its possibilities and made a personal donation of £40,000.

Few doubted that there would be any difficulties attracting scientists to Dundee to work under Cohen. Few foresaw, however, just how successful he might be. His allegiance to science and to the community he and colleagues have built in Dundee is absolute. 'Philip is utterly and personally committed to the process of discovery,' says Allen Mackenzie, director of development at the University of Dundee. 'That's what drives him. Philip's wife Tricia was bequeathed a very large legacy by a former neighbour some years ago and she and Philip made up their minds right away to use the money to fund new lab premises in Dundee. They didn't give it a second thought. He puts his heart and soul into the job and expects only that those who work with him will do the same. It can be difficult to keep pace with him.'

It was not a huge surprise when Cohen was given a knighthood in 1997 for his services to science and research. The same year he won the Louis-Jeantet Prize for Medicine, second only to the Nobel Prize in prestige. The greatest prize, however, is perhaps more elusive. 'The attraction is to find out, to discover, something totally novel that no one has found out before,' is Cohen's response to those who struggle to pin down what fuels his seemingly endless energy and enthusiasm. 'It is an ethos. We have recruited well and it is not a case of us being able to offer large salaries, far from it. It is not what we have to offer an individual, it is what they can offer us. People want to be part of what is

Professor Wolf (courtesy of Alan Richardson)

going on here, and we want people who will fit in well. In many ways, we are just one big, happy family.'

David Lane joined Philip Cohen's happy family in Dundee in 1990. 'A quiet, unassuming biochemist who will one day be a household name' is how *The Times* described him in a shortlist of pioneers tipped for the top in the new millennium. Had it not been for Cohen's peculiar persuasiveness and dogged pursuit of his quarry, however, Lane would be a quiet, unassuming biochemist working in London. Badgered by Cohen to relocate to Scotland over dinner, wine and a stroll by the banks of the Tay, Lane resisted and kept asking, 'Why Dundee?' Then he looked out over the river and suddenly realised the question should be, 'Why not Dundee?' The penny dropped. He now tells the story in public as much against himself as the preconceived and faintly ridiculous notion that for UK scientists with ambitions to reach the top, all roads must lead to Oxbridge or London.

Lane's decision to come to Dundee was another milestone in the city's evolution as a scientific hothouse. Lane, then Principal Scientist at the Imperial Cancer Research Fund in London, had discovered the p53 suppressor gene that controls the growth of tumours in many common cancers. Like Fleming's discovery of penicillin from mould, Lane stumbled on p53 almost by accident. When a rogue protein repeatedly turned up during lab experiments looking at the role of tumour-causing viruses in 1978, it was simply dismissed by researchers as an 'irritating contaminant'. Lane, then a 26-year-old undertaking a post-doctoral fellowship in cancer research, wasn't so sure and felt compelled to look closer.

His investigations led to the identification of the gene p53 and transformed the cancer-research agenda. Variously described as the cell's 'most elegant defender' and, by Lane himself, as 'the guardian of the genome', p53 is the policeman which stops cells heading down the path to cancer. Healthy cells contain a small number of p53 proteins. If a cell's DNA is damaged in a way that threatens the development of a cancer, p53 triggers a response which directly inhibits cancerous growth. But if p53 is absent, damaged or unable to respond to the cell's cry for help, cancer has a clear run.

Lane believed that p53 played a pivotal role in the suppression of human cancers and postulated it should be possible to demonstrate the gene's protective qualities in a living organism. Talking through the theory with fellow biochemist Professor Peter Hall over a few pints in a Dundee pub in 1992, the two men decided on an unorthodox course of action. Knowing it could take months to obtain the necessary licences for animal experiments, Hall volunteered himself as a human guinea pig. He exposed a small patch of skin on his arm to radiation damage from a sunlamp. Over the ensuing fortnight, Lane took regular skin biopsies from his friend's forearm. If Lane's theory was correct, the skin samples should show increased levels of a protein manufactured by p53 in response to the damage caused by exposure to the sunlamp. The results of the experiment were of groundbreaking importance. Levels of the p53 protein in Peter Hall's skin rose quickly within hours of the sunlamp experiment, then tailed off gradually over the next few days – hard proof of p53's role as a regulator of cell damage.

The gene p53 has now become the most researched gene in the world and recently won the 'Molecule of the Year' award from the respected journal *Science* – the genetic equivalent of an Oscar. There are now over 6,000 published studies on the gene, and the number is rising.

Lane's discovery brought medicine to a crossroads. We now know that p53 is mutated, damaged or absent in over 60 per cent of human cancers. In these cancers, p53 has lost its ability to police the process of abnormal cell growth. Turn that on its head, and if science can find a way of re-establishing healthy p53 in the disease process, we may be looking at a new therapy for cancer. It is this next stage in cancer research – the prospect of being able to take scientific discovery from the bench to the bedside – that is now exercising David Lane and his team in Dundee.

His personal emotional investment in the search for new cancer therapies has been well documented. At 19, he lost his father to bowel cancer and he has been committed to the fight ever since. 'It had a profound effect on me,' he says. 'My mother, sister, three brothers and I looked after him until the very end. I was just appalled that we could do nothing for him and I decided then that, if I could, I wanted to do something to stop this terrible illness.

'While heart disease still kills more people, there is something uniquely insidious about cancer. There can scarcely be a family in the land which hasn't been touched in some way by the disease. I required no motivation to follow this line of research.'

The burden of expectation lies heavy on his shoulders. Few scientists command such notice. Professor Gordon McVie, head of the Cancer Research Campaign, has publicly tipped Lane as a future Nobel Laureate, claiming, 'I don't think I have ever known anyone who is quite so talented and quite so generous at sharing his work with others. He has a burning desire to get the work he is doing in the laboratory into a practical treatment that will benefit patients.'

That day has finally arrived. Lane has recently joined forces with Professor Sir Alfred Cushieri, pioneer of 'keyhole' or minimal-access surgery at Ninewells Hospital, interventional radiologist Dr Graham Houston and Professor Roland Wolf, head of the Imperial Cancer Research Fund labs at Ninewells. Lane is to move his labs to Ninewells, where he will collaborate with teams led by Wolf and Cushieri with the principal aim of developing new techniques for attacking tumours.

Cushieri has been a dominant influence in the revolution that has transformed surgery in the last decade. The use of minimally invasive techniques for a range of operations reduces patients' pain, trauma and recovery time after surgery. It is the future of surgery and it is likely that over 70 per cent of all surgical procedures will one day be carried out this way. Cushieri's expertise led to the establishment of a dedicated Surgical Skills Unit at Ninewells – the first of its kind – to train surgeons from throughout the world in keyhole techniques.

Roland Wolf was initially another Dundee-sceptic who was converted to the cause by Philip Cohen – and a field full of mushrooms. Legend has it that Wolf, who in 1989 was head of the Imperial Cancer Research Fund Molecular Pharmacology Group at the University of Edinburgh, turned down the first invitation to work in Dundee. When Cohen promised to introduce him to a secret field stuffed full of wild mushrooms where he could indulge his hobby of mycology, Wolf warmed to Dundee and agreed to relocate his labs. He has since become a passionate and powerful advocate for the City of Discovery, its quality of life, its setting and the unique opportunities the University of Dundee offers for collaboration across the disciplines of life-sciences and medical research. His work is at the coalface of cancer, examining the environmental factors that cause the disease and the mechanisms by which drugs and chemicals exert their effects on cells.

In 1998, Wolf and his team identified a single gene that seems to determine an individual's susceptibility to developing cancer. It was a discovery that reverberated around the scientific world. The gene plays a crucial role in warding off carcinogens, like cigarette smoke. If it malfunctions, the body's natural defence systems are less effective at resisting. Like p53, the gene discovered by Roland Wolf and his colleagues in Dundee has fuelled the search for new therapies which will fight cancer at a genetic level. If anything, the implications of its discovery may be even more profound that those of p53. Because the gene appears to act as a first line of defence against cancer-causing agents, it holds out the promise of a therapy which prevents the disease from developing in the first place.

The prospect of Wolf joining David Lane and Alfred Cushieri in a collaborative push to pioneer new cancer therapies in Dundee has caused an air of expectancy and excitement which is almost palpable. 'I like to think it's serendipity,' says Allen Mackenzie. 'When these guys come together in a room you can feel the adrenaline pumping and the rush of intellectual energy. Most scientists and medics are by their nature extremely cautious, but these guys are as excited and animated as I have ever seen them. They're so damn close – and they know it. I'll stick my neck out and say it for them: something wonderful is about to happen.'

Professor Alfred Cushieri and Professor David Lane with the chairman of the Ninewells cancer campaign, Jacqui Wood (courtesy of D.C. Thomson and Co. Ltd)

Two high-profile biotechnology companies – Shield Diagnostics and Cyclacel – have already resulted from research projects at the University of Dundee, creating wealth and providing jobs. Over two-thirds of the hundreds of inward investment inquiries now come from UK and overseas biotech companies attracted by the strength of science in the city. 'Interest in the city from the science community globally is increasing all the time,' says Jack Martin of Scottish Enterprise Tayside. 'Not long ago it would be unusual to hear Dundee mentioned in the same breath as Oxford and Cambridge, but that has become the norm. In biotechnology terms, we are fast becoming a major international player. Industry wants to be close to scientific advance, and in Dundee we have a community of innovators who are pushing back the frontiers all the time. We expect to see the establishment of several more scientific-research spin-off companies over the next five to ten years.'

Jam tomorrow? Dundonians would be forgiven a good measure of home-baked scepticism in the face of such optimistic forecasts. Without the hard, visible evidence of new factories and new jobs, they might be entitled to question the relevance of biotechnology to a community which has become used to rebuilding from the slow and frequently painful death of its traditional industries.

Yet the people have kept faith with this element of the town's reinvention. In fact, without the people, it could not have happened. Since 1991, when the city began to assert itself as a focus for cancer and life-sciences research, over

£7 million has been gifted by the local community to provide new facilities for cancer research and treatment. That's about £50 from the pocket of every man, woman and child in the city. Dundonians have flung themselves from planes, shaved their own and each other's heads, swum the Tay, saved pocket money, run countless marathons, fasted, raffled, sponsored, begged and borrowed to reach fundraising targets which would have tested a community ten times Dundee's size.

The giving goes beyond simple charity for a worthy cause. Jacqui Wood moved to Dundee from the north of England in the early '90s and was quickly signed up to lead the Cancer Research Campaign fundraising cause in the city. 'There is something very special about the place and the people which is hard to pin down. The response to the cancer-research fundraising efforts was overwhelming, stunning – there aren't the superlatives to describe it,' she says. 'I don't think we could have done this anywhere else in Britain. The support from the people in Dundee was magnificent from the start and it is obvious that there is a quiet but very strong pride in the research and in the way Dundee has carved out this important niche for itself.

'So many people wanted to give and get involved – like the guy who just walked into Ninewells with a plastic carrier bag stuffed full of £1,000 worth of banknotes. He wouldn't say much, just that he wanted us to have the money. He handed us the bag, turned round and walked out without another word. The notes smelt really musty, like they'd been kept under a bed for a long time.

'A gentleman who had just lost his wife to cancer in one of the wards at Ninewells came into the office and wrote a cheque for £300, but he also insisted that we take his wife's purse. It had £5.37 in it. We all had lumps in our throats. The generosity and effort of the community inspired us all. It was unique.'

But the £7 million from the community has done more than simply provide the infrastructure and the impetus for life-sciences and cancer research in Dundee. It has given Dundonians ownership of the biotech revolution on their doorstep, real pride in the achievements of the scientists who are making it happen and genuine hope that disease and human pain, no matter how sinister, can be overcome.

The notion that this self-effacing city of Dennis the Menace, Dens Park and doggerel might one day find a cure for cancer is no longer fanciful or incongruous. After all, Thomas Maclagan's efforts in Dundee over a hundred years ago gave the twentieth century its most widely used drug. Don't tell anyone, but Dundee's gift to the new millennium will be just as special . . .

3

Dundee's Other Discoveries

A Fascinating Tale of Invention and Innovation

Craig Millar

Dundee has come a long way since a certain Mrs Keiller boiled a consignment of Spanish oranges and invented one of the world's best-known breakfast delicacies. The origins of marmalade are steeped in folklore, but the association between this tangy concoction and the beginnings of the Keiller dynasty in Dundee are undeniable and accepted all over the world.

In terms of pioneering invention and innovation, the apocryphal marmalade tale is not Dundee's only claim to fame. Far from it. In the City of Discovery there are instances of human foresight and ingenuity which have lain undiscovered by much of Scotland's population. In fact, Dundee can lay claim to a number of notable firsts that will come as a surprise to many.

Could it be, for instance, the place where electric light was first demonstrated, long before Thomas Edison patented the incandescent lightbulb? Is the longevity of our postal system a tribute to the acumen of a Dundee bookseller? Is it even possible that the historic claims of the Wright brothers to the first powered flight are undermined by two brothers from a prosperous Dundee family?

All these stories are shrouded by the mists of time and, in some cases, dogged by the fiercest controversy. But, at the beginning of the new millennium, it would be a mistake to believe that Dundee's innovative credentials are consigned to the past. On the contrary, they have never been more credible. Dundee is the world leader in bank automation. It is the home of the company which 'decked' IBM. Some of its technology is out of this world – literally. The creator of Super Mario is an admirer of computer games made here. While the origins of the potato chip lay in Dundee in the last century, work on a different kind of chip may revolutionise a multi-billion-dollar industry of today. And from the banks of the Tay, scientists have been developing technology which can feed the world's starving population.

No doubt Mrs Keiller's eighteenth-century ambitions were less dramatic. Her discovery of marmalade has not been substantiated in scholarly terms, but it has led to an automatic connection with Dundee in many minds. The story goes that her husband had a small grocer's business in the city. His entrepreneurial instincts led him to buy a consignment of oranges from a Spanish vessel seeking refuge from a storm. Apparently he purchased them cheaply and found that their bitter taste was such that he was unable to sell them at any price. As the oranges started to rot, his wife Janet came up with a brainwave. She had been taught by her mother to make a preserve called marmalet, something that might otherwise be known as quince jam. Instead of quinces she boiled the Seville oranges with sugar, and accordingly the first marmalade came into being. All this led to the formation of a company that was to be long associated with the city, James Keiller and Son Ltd. Indeed, the Keiller trademark was one of the first to be recorded in the British register.

If marmalade brought the Keillers international recognition, the pioneering efforts of a man born shortly afterwards have received comparatively scant acknowledgement. And yet the name of James Bowman Lindsay is one which is now increasingly associated with foresight, wisdom and even genius. Born in Carmyllie in Angus in 1799, Lindsay is judged to have been a man before his time, an innovator unknown to most of the world, and even most Dundonians, who may just have upstaged the likes of Edison and laid some of the groundwork for another inventor of global repute, Marconi.

Lindsay's constitution was far from being robust. In his early surroundings, he was ill suited to the physical rigours of country labour and so was apprenticed to the linen-weaving trade. However, this young man was studious and clearly intelligent. It is said he could often be seen tramping from Carmyllie to Arbroath between his handloom and the merchant's warehouse, reading to himself while carrying his finished cloth strapped to his back.

Aware of his thirst for knowledge, his parents saved to allow him to have a proper education and at the age of 22 he went to St Andrews

Bright spark: The remarkable James Bowman Lindsay, pioneer of electricity and telegraphy (courtesy of Dundee Central Library Photographic Collection)

University. He read theology, possibly with the intention of entering the Church. But he also studied maths, physics and chemistry, and it was these leanings which swayed him towards his appointment as Science and Mathematics Lecturer at Dundee's Watt Institute.

Lindsay's academic talents were double edged. He was absorbed by the wonders of science but also transfixed by the intricacies of languages. This inner conflict marked his adult life in Dundee. It was here that he embarked upon a number of scientific experiments which were to exhibit his gifted nature. Lindsay displayed the potential uses of electrical technology, including telegraphy and power from batteries, despite the fact that this was a form of energy in its infancy. 'At that particular time, nobody had the remotest idea what electricity consisted of,' says Bill Dow, a Lindsay admirer and a former head of science at Dundee College of Education. 'Lindsay was dealing with things that nobody really understood.'

But in a notice in *The Dundee Advertiser* of 11 April 1834, his visionary nature enabled him to proclaim, 'Houses and towns will in a short time be lit by electricity instead of gas, and heated by it instead of coal; and machinery will be worked by it instead of steam.' Just over a year later, *The Advertiser* reported his first major discovery.

> Mr Lindsay, a teacher in the town, formerly lecturer to the Watt Institute, succeeded, on the evening of Sunday, 25 July, in obtaining a constant electric light. The light in beauty surpassed all others, has no smell, emits no smoke and can be kept in sealed jars.

Lindsay foretold, 'The present generation may yet have it burning in their houses and enlightening their streets.'

He was among a number of people at the time who were seeking the secret of electric light, and it is not possible to claim categorically that he was the first. But according to Bill Dow, 'There is no doubt whatever that Lindsay managed to make some type of silent continuous light. There's no record of whether he did this by means of a hot wire or an arc. An awful lot of people say it must have been a carbon arc. I suspect he was probably using a platinum wire, but that's a supposition by me.'

It was a light strong enough to be able to read a book at a distance of ten inches and was comparable to the gas light of the time. However, Lindsay did not stop there. He had already paid heed to the work of the Danish physicist and chemist Hans Christian Oersted, who had discovered the deflection of the magnetic needle by an electric current in 1820. To Lindsay, this was a 'clear view of the application of electricity to telegraphic communication'. In 1845 he sent a proposal to *The Dundee Advertiser* for an 'autograph' telegraph. When suggestions were sought for a submarine Atlantic telegraph cable, Lindsay proposed the construction of a cable using uninsulated copper wire with joints welded by electricity. This is reckoned to be the first suggestion of the use of electricity for welding.

Lindsay then experimented with one of the earliest systems of wireless telegraphy by sending messages through water without the use of cable. It was, in effect, a direct current method of transmitting the equivalent of Morse signals. At a lecture on telegraphy in 1853, he claimed that by establishing a battery on one side of the Atlantic and a receiver on the other, a current could be passed through the ocean to America without wires. He patented his method of wireless telegraphy on 5 June 1854. It involved instruments and batteries connected to submerged metal plates. He gave demonstrations by sending messages through water at Carolina Port and Earl Grey Dock and then across the Tay at Glencarse. After witnessing one of them, *The Advertiser* enthusiastically reported the following:

> The experiment removes all doubt of the practicability of Mr Lindsay's invention and there is every reason to think that it will soon connect continent with continent in one unbroken line of communication.

The truth was, though, that over long distances Lindsay's telegraph was unworkable. But over shorter spans it did have practical applications, and it was deployed as a temporary measure by the postmaster general Sir William Preece when telegraphic wires to the Isle of Wight, Rathlin Island and Mull went down.

'Lindsay was invited to read a paper on his marine telegraphy to a meeting of the British Association in Aberdeen in 1859, attended by Professor Michael Faraday and Professor J.J. Thomson, who later became Lord Kelvin,' says another Lindsay devotee, Macdonald Black. 'I don't think they were terribly impressed, but when they found out that Lindsay had actually got it to work, they recognised he had the germ of an idea. In fact, Lindsay's experimentation preceded Hertz and Marconi, who both later became involved in the development of wireless telegraphy and the radio.'

But Lindsay's theological work was as important to him as electricity. What the *Dictionary of National Biography* described as 'a philological craze' diverted him from his experiments. Although Lindsay was sometimes the subject of ridicule, the so-called craze may also have been a sign of his genius; he used philology and astronomy to investigate the historical accuracy of the Bible.

For years Lindsay lived in modest circumstances. He devoted himself to his scientific pursuits, spending much more money on equipment and books than he did on himself. He neglected his physical well-being to the extent that when disease struck, his emaciated frame could not stand the strain. But to put Lindsay's position in history in some sort of perspective, it was around 20 years after his death that the American Thomas Edison displayed his incandescent electric lightbulb. He became a multi-millionaire. By the turn of the century, Marconi was showing how to convey wireless messages through the air.

Lindsay was modest and retiring, lonely and shy. On the recommendation of the Prime Minister Lord Derby, Queen Victoria granted him an annual pension of one hundred pounds in 1858 in recognition of his learning and extraordinary attainments. But few, even within the scientific community, took note. Marconi, however, subsequently paid glowing tribute. In a letter to Sir John Leng MP he said, 'I have always been a sincere admirer of Lindsay. Had he been more appreciated in his time and more fortunate, it is probable that wireless telegraphy would have been far in advance of what it is.' Marconi further wrote, 'The name of James Bowman Lindsay must go down to posterity as the first man who thoroughly believed in the possibility and utility of long-distance wireless telegraphy – and first found a solution which came nearer practical realisation than many were inclined to admit.'

Today, a growing number who believe history has neglected him pay homage. 'Though he was probably an eccentric in the extreme, I think he was also a genius,' says his great-great-great-niece, Marion Hume. 'He was certainly a man before his time and I think Dundee should be proud of him.'

Among Lindsay's contemporaries was another Dundee man who may also have been deprived of the credit properly due him for an invention which has since been routinely used across the world. The fiercest of debates has surrounded the question of who should be regarded as the creator of the postage stamps we take for granted every day. History has accorded the Englishman Sir Rowland Hill the title of originator of the Penny Post. But in the view of many, it was the ingenuity of Dundee bookseller James Chalmers that made it work. 'There is no doubt in my mind that Chalmers was the inventor of the pre-paid adhesive postage stamp,' says the Dundee Philatelic Society's Sandy Forbes. 'I feel his contribution to philately has not been fully recognised.'

Such opinion has been at the root of a bitter conflict down the generations between the descendants of Chalmers and Hill. It all began with the best of intentions. From the early 1820s onwards, James Chalmers was an enthusiastic advocate of Post Office improvement. Like other businessmen, he objected to the unreliability of the postal system and its cost. After three years of campaigning, he succeeded in reducing the time taken between London and Edinburgh by one day each way. But mail was still slow and the recipient had to pay. There was, however, a groundswell of opinion across Britain that something had to be done.

In 1837, Rowland Hill, once a schoolmaster in Kidderminster, published a

Stamp of approval: James Chalmers, inventor of the adhesive postage stamp, painted by an unknown artist (courtesy of Dundee Art Galleries and Museums)

pamphlet entitled *Post-office reform, its importance and practicability.* His aims were greater speed in deliveries and simplification of Post Office operations. Modern-day encyclopaedia entries tell us it was Hill who suggested that there should be a flat rate for sending letters, starting at one penny, for any distance inside Britain. He further submitted that the charge should be collected in the form of a payment for a stamp. The famous Penny Black, we are told, was the result of his efforts. The Penny Postage Bill was passed in August 1839. Rowland Hill was appointed to superintend the new system, became secretary to the Post Office and was eventually knighted.

However, in August 1879, an anonymous letter appeared in *The Dundee Advertiser* which led to a heated revision of Hill's role. The letter was signed 'A Dundonian of 50 years ago'. It turned out to be from David Prain, a former employee of James Chalmers.

> I have read with much interest your article in this morning's *Advertiser* on the late Sir Rowland Hill, and while, with others, willing gratefully to accord to him the honour of having introduced and perfected that postal reform, the benefits of which we are now enjoying, yet I cannot ascribe to him the merit of being the first to suggest the plan of uniform rates and adhesive stamps, as to my certain knowledge, the late Mr James Chalmers, bookseller, Castle Street, before the year 1837, propounded a plan almost identical with that which Mr Hill in that year had the honour of getting introduced with so much advantage to the correspondence and the finances of the country.

Further letters and an editorial in *The Advertiser* supporting this viewpoint were sent to Chalmers's son Patrick, who lived in Wimbledon in London. It prompted Patrick Chalmers to spend the rest of his life campaigning to have his father receive the recognition he ardently believed he deserved. It was Patrick's

Today's postage stamps, like the Scottish Definitives Collection, owe their origins to James Chalmers (courtesy of the Post Office)

contention that James Chalmers had actually invented the adhesive stamp in August 1834. He had shown his bookbinder, William Whitelaw, a sheet of paper gummed on one side and with the other side covered with a series of identical designs in white and yellow. In the book *James Chalmers: Inventor of the Adhesive Postage Stamp*, authors William J. Smith and J.E. Metcalfe claim that David Maxwell, a nephew of James, was given the job of cutting the sheets into small equal and identical rectangles, 'and thus, without knowing it, he was making history'.

In 1837 James told Robert Wallace, the MP for Greenock, about his stamps, and when the Penny Postage Bill was passed into law two years later, Wallace urged the Commons to adopt the adhesive stamp. According to Patrick, while Rowland Hill had introduced the new system, he had failed to make any practicable plan to make it work. James Chalmers entered a public competition with the intention of doing exactly that. His plan went to London, and he added a special note for Hill: 'If slips or stamps are to be used, I flatter myself that I have a claim to priority – it being now nearly two years since I first made it public in a communication to Mr Wallace, MP.' His stamps were to be printed in sheets of uniform size and shape and coloured according to the price. He suggested black for the penny stamps.

Patrick Chalmers and subsequently the authors, Smith and Metcalfe, claimed that while Rowland Hill's idea was for a cheap, flat-rate post, he decided on a stamped-folder system or stamped covers. The House of Commons Select Committee, however, felt that these were in danger of being forged. To prevent this, it was recommended they be made of special 'pelure paper' with interwoven threads. Chalmers's supporters maintain that it was his scheme that the government adopted, though recognition of that was not forthcoming. Patrick claimed that the adhesive stamp saved the Penny Postage Bill from failure, and he insisted that correspondence between his father and Hill which showed this to be the case was removed by Hill from the Treasury and was much later found to be in the possession of his son Pearson.

The war of words between Patrick Chalmers and Pearson Hill was, at times, venomous. Patrick summoned evidence from a number of different quarters in support of his father, including testimony from one of the earliest proponents of postal reform, the Reverend Samuel Roberts, who wrote that, rather than Sir Rowland Hill, 'It is now known that it was a thoughtful, calculating, unassuming, patriotic reformer of Dundee, of the name of James Chalmers, that invented the Adhesive Stamp, and it was very unjust in the authorities of the Post Office to withhold from the real inventor and to grasp to themselves the reward and honour due to another for an invention that proved so essential.'

Patrick also cited a good deal more supporting evidence, including the 1884 edition of the *Encyclopaedia Britannica*, although the reference reporting in his father's favour was later removed. The *Dictionary of National Biography* further credited James with the invention of postage stamps.

The dispute between the families eventually gravitated downwards to the grandchildren of James Chalmers and Rowland Hill. The whole truth may never be known. But according to Sandy Forbes, James Chalmers's claims are merited. 'It's like saying who invented the sewing machine or the light bulb,' he says. 'These things go down in history and can't be changed. But we would just like to see a little more recognition given to the work of James Chalmers.'

It would be unwise to treat the controversies surrounding Lindsay and Chalmers with a pinch of salt. But it would be entirely appropriate to do so with another Dundee invention of the nineteenth century – and perhaps with a little vinegar as well! Belgian emigrant Edward de Gernier probably had little idea that he was starting a national institution when he moved to Greenmarket in the late 1870s, for one has to ask where modern Britain would be if it were not for the humble chip.

A shoemaker by trade, Mr de Gernier's proud claim to fame was that he was the man who introduced chips to this country. The stallholders in the Greenmarket had made a man who was unsure of the 'Scotch' language feel at home. Taking to the market life, he opened his own pitch selling, as he said himself, 'the first chip potatoes, peas and vinegar stall in Great Britain'. Born out of this, of course, was the gastronomic delight which became known as the Dundee Buster and which remained popular for a century thereafter.

His venture was started on a Saturday night. At his stance, Mr de Gernier erected a small tent, with a few boards placed on boxes for seats, a brazier, a cooking pot and some cinders. Threepence was all that remained of his capital. But by the end of the night, such was the novelty of what we today would call fast food that he had made 19/6d. At a halfpenny a time, that means he sold 468 portions of chips.

His fame, or rather that of his chips, soon spread. *The People's Journal* commented that Mr de Gernier was interviewed by visitors from all parts

Top flight: Preston Watson, Dundee's aviation pioneer (courtesy of Dundee City Archives)

'regarding his remarkable discovery'. He was asked to go to Newcastle to start a business but was content in the Dundee Greenmarket. There was even a tale about two lads who walked all the way from Perth to sample one of Mr de Gernier's chip suppers. For these two youths the journey was apparently worth it. Connoisseurs of the fish supper have every reason, therefore, to lionise Mr de Gernier.

But just a few years afterwards, the endeavours of others in the locale may have played an important part in creating a much more significant legacy for mankind – air travel. However, the pioneering flights of one Preston Watson draw us once more into the realms of controversy. While parallels have been drawn between James Bowman Lindsay, Marconi and Edison, and between Chalmers and Hill, so too was Watson's name spoken of in the same breath as the intrepid American aviators the Wright brothers.

The Wrights are internationally renowned for making the first ever powered aeroplane flights. But for years there was speculation that Preston Watson and his brother James had beaten them to it. James, or JY, as he was known, spent much of the latter part of his life trying to prove it. As he did so, claim and counter claim emerged.

The Watson brothers were products of the prominent Dundee family that made up one half of the Watson and Philip wholesale food business. Preston had embarked upon a business career with these produce merchants but he had leanings towards mechanics and applied that to his true passion, flying. The

James Thomson, Dundee's visionary city architect (courtesy of Dundee City Archives)

burning question is: when did he get an aircraft off the ground and by what means?

In the early 1950s, a 77-year-old former farm manager, Harry Band, recalled emphatically that he had seen a flying machine near Errol in July 1903, five months before the Wrights' historic flight at Kitty Hawk, North Carolina. He told *The Courier*, 'I heard noises – something similar to a machine gun at a distance – but I couldna see actually what it was. It was away down over a field.' Harry's cousin told him, 'It was twa young daft devils tryin' tae kill thersel's fleein.'

He took a closer look and described the incredible contraption thus. 'It was like a lot o' bloomin auld window blinds and sticks tied thegither. There wis a thing whirlin' on the front of it as far as I could make out, when all at once the thing was up in the air. It would have flown ower the top o' an ordinary cottage.

It came down and made another hop. It reminded me of locusts I'd seen in South Africa.' Mr Band had returned from the Boer War in 1902. He was certain that the flight he witnessed happened in the summer of the following year.

In 1955, the claim to the first flight was shot down by a contemporary of Preston Watson, Mr John Milne of Dundee, along with Preston's one-time mechanic David Urquhart. Mr Milne was a fellow student of Preston in 1903 at University College, Dundee. Preston was being coached in higher physics by a Professor Kuenen. In a *Courier* interview, Mr Milne recalled, 'It was then that I was informed of the reason. There was a good deal of secrecy about the building of this first aeroplane. I was among the first to see the machine in its early stages of construction at the works of his cousin, Mr Yeaman, at Carolina Port.' He maintained, 'The framework was that of a glider. There were no wheels and no engine.'

Mr Milne claimed that it was in 1906 that Preston learned it was possible to purchase a Duthiel Chalmers engine from Santos Dumont in Paris. With the

James Thomson's controversial view of Dundee's city centre (courtesy of Dundee City Archives)

help of a tree, Preston had developed the forerunner of the modern catapult used on aircraft carriers. A blacksmith's anvil and two 56lb weights were hoisted to a 30-foot branch with a block and tackle and attached to a pulley. The falling weights jerked the plane forward and into the air. This system was used at Errol in tests to prove Preston's theories of flight and to assess the suitability of the machine for an engine. The plane was removed to Forgandenny, where the engine was fitted. David Urquhart, who said he flew the glider at Errol, insisted that powered flights at Forgandenny did not take place until 1906.

Then, in 1966, came another twist. A 74-year-old ex-detective constable, Alexander Paterson, who was apparently blessed with a photographic memory, produced his own version of events. According to his account, he had seen the Watson brothers achieve a sustained flight of about 200 yards at a field near Errol in the summer of 1903. Untying anchor ropes and pushing the plane into position, young 'Eck' Paterson and his school pal Ernie Bruce helped the brothers in their efforts to get the plane off the ground – but not without difficulty. There was more than one failed attempt. Perhaps significantly, Mr Paterson recalled that the brothers were 'forever adjusting the engine and arguing over details'.

On the third day of trying, according to Mr Paterson, it was actually James who made the first real flight, at his first attempt. He recalled, 'Preston spun the

Sir Robert Watson Watt, who invented radar, returns to Dundee to address a meeting, c. 1950. On his left is Lord Provost Richard Fenton (courtesy of D.C. Thomson and Co. Ltd)

propeller and we cut the tethering rope. Away she bounded, with us running barefoot in its wake. After a hundred yards or so the machine suddenly lifted and rose to about the height of the farm buildings.' The plane flew on for about 200 yards without touching the ground, then dipped and came down nose first. James was thrown out over the broken propeller. Mr Paterson was adamant that the flight took place in July.

His story, though, is at odds with that of James Watson himself, who gave his brother Preston credit for the first flight. Interviewed in 1953, he said, 'I made the second flight myself. The great thing was that I was lighter than he. To my amazement, the plane went up. I put the stick full forward and it continued to go up. Amazing sensation? Amazing be damned! I tried to go down as fast as I could. I crashed but got away with no broken bones.' James Watson admitted he could not be sure whether Preston's plane flew six months before or six months after the Wrights'.

Preston Watson built three planes between 1903 and 1913 at a cost to his father of £1,000 each. He invented a rocking-wing system for control purposes, which he patented in 1909. However, the propellers for Preston's aircraft were made by Kerr B. Sturrock, a Dundee shopfitter and joiner. His memories add further to the speculation. Mr Sturrock was sure that he made propellers for Preston's first engine before he was married in 1905.

NCR was a huge employer in its mechanical days in the 1940s and 1950s (courtesy of NCR)

Preston Watson's contribution to the debate would clearly have been invaluable, but he died doing what he loved best. While training with the Royal Naval Air Service in 1915, Sub-Lieutenant Watson's plane exploded above Eastbourne. It reportedly dropped like a stone and was 'smashed to atoms'. What remains intact, though, is the pioneering reputation of this flying Scotsman. Even if he never replaces the Wright brothers in the annals of history, Preston Watson can, with some justification, be regarded as an early hero of aviation.

One can only assume that the extent of today's air travel would astound the Watsons. But not so long afterwards, just a few miles up the Carse of Gowrie in Dundee, another local man's prescience in transport matters of a different kind became evident.

James Thomson, Dundee's city engineer and architect, devised a number of grand schemes for the betterment of a place he served for well over half a century, long before governments took town planning seriously. Among them was a plan for an outer ring road thought to be the first of its kind in Britain, the Kingsway. Thomson unveiled his proposals in 1918. The ring road would be seven miles long, connecting at both ends with the riverfront and forming junctions with Broughty Ferry Road, Arbroath Road, Pitkerro Road, Forfar Road, old Glamis Road, Strathmartine Road, Clepington Road, Coupar Angus

Road, Liff Road and Perth Road. Thomson envisaged the road as being 160 feet wide, 'unprecedented in Dundee'. It would comprise a central tramway track and two ample footways with six rows of trees. There would be two carriageways for traffic travelling in opposite directions.

With its separate track for swift tramway service, its easy gradients, its junctions with all main arterial roads and its rows of trees and strips of grass, he believed the ring road would become 'one of the most useful and attractive of traffic and pleasure thoroughfares'. Yet when construction began in the 1920s, there were complaints and misgivings on the grounds of expense and the fear that valuable customers would be diverted past the town. But the Kingsway was such a successful concept, and was built so well, that it was not until the 1960s that any major changes or improvements had to be made. That in itself is a great reflection on Thomson's vision.

When he retired in 1924, Thomson visualised Dundee 50 years on. The Kingsway, he predicted, would be one of the greatest thoroughfares and the finest boulevard in the country. The Tay Road Bridge would be a reality. The Caird Hall Square would be opened up and the Overgate improvement scheme completed. Thomson, presumably, would have been proud to have seen such things come to pass.

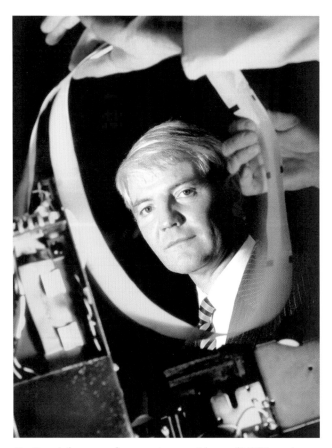

Dr Jim Adamson, former vice-president of NCR and managing director of its Dundee operations (courtesy of NCR)

They might never have done so if the ingenuity of a Dundee-educated scientist had not thwarted the plans of Hitler and Nazi Germany to invade Britain at the start of the Second World War. Born in Brechin, Sir Robert Watson Watt considered himself to be 'a man of Angus'. But as he was educated at University College, Dundee, where he gained his BSc, the city can take some credit for producing the man who became known as 'the father of radar'.

He was a pioneer of radio location and became superintendent of Britain's new Radio Division of the National Physics Laboratory at Teddington during the '30s. With the Nazis preparing for war, he set up five radio stations from headquarters established in Suffolk. Results proved his theories to be spectacularly accurate. By March 1936, his reporters were spotting approaching aircraft and other vehicles up to 70 miles away.

Radar became a weapon of inestimable value in defeating the Luftwaffe during the Battle of Britain. The 'First of the Few' making up the British fighter squadrons were forewarned about incoming German aircraft, who were mystified at the RAF's ability to intercept them. Watt's invention saved Britain, and arguably the world, from catastrophe. As well as being knighted, he was later awarded the US Medal of Merit.

The post-war era of reconstruction that victory ensured saw the arrival in Dundee of an American

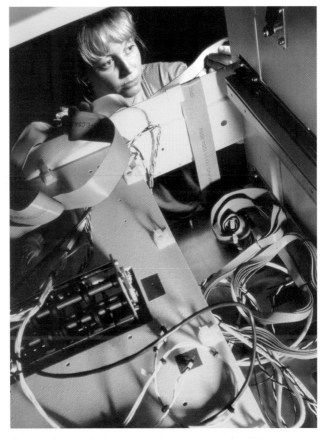

Research and design at NCR (courtesy of NCR)

multinational which became a cornerstone of the city's industrial fortunes. From among several other contenders, Dundee was selected as the British manufacturing site for the Ohio-based National Cash Register company NCR. When the company's Camperdown plant was officially opened in 1947, the President of the Board of Trade, Sir Stafford Cripps, referred to 'a happy marriage between the enterprise of America and the sterling skill and qualities of Scotland'.

In the 1950s, NCR became Dundee's largest employer as its cash-register business burgeoned. Job numbers reached a peak in 1969 with 6,000 staff working at seven factories. The approach of decimalisation brought demands for new and upgraded products, but the phasing out of £SD was a watershed. The electronic age had arrived and mechanical products were being made redundant.

When Dr Jim Adamson was appointed head of NCR's operations in the city, the picture appeared to be one of terminal decline. He recalls, 'When I went in 1980 they were due to shut the door. They had their fingers in every pie, they weren't making money and management and workforce were at loggerheads. The main reason for their demise was that they had nothing themselves. They really didn't have any heritage. They were just making products for anybody and they were a screwdriver shop for the whole of NCR. I saw a place with inherent talent but no real direction.' Adamson was told he had six months to turn the place around or it would close. He decided to have a go.

NCR had already been working on what was to become their saviour – the automated teller machine. Over the next few years, it was in Dundee that the ATM was developed into a world beater for the banking industry. 'In the most conservative industry in the world, we changed the habits of the world,' says Jim Adamson. 'If you think back to 1980, nobody used a cash machine. We went to bankers and convinced them to put this picture frame up on their wall and people would put plastic cards into it and get money out. They thought I was crazy when I was talking about this in the first instance. But now there's not a country in the world that doesn't have cash dispensers.'

NCR's third generation of ATMs based on reliability, flexibility and customer requirements brought global success. The 5070 ATM was capable of 5,000 transactions between each replenishment. It was based on a totally new software and electronics platform enabling connection to worldwide networks. The 5070 became the single most successful product in NCR's history. 'We were fighting the biggest and best in the industry,' says Jim Adamson. 'We took on IBM and beat the hell out of them. That isn't an easy task. We killed a few very big household names. Innovation was absolutely crucial.

'We had the smallest product, the lightest product, the fastest product and were bringing innovation to the product far quicker than anyone else. We were the first ones with colour on our ATMs, the first to handle multi-currencies, the first to put the machine on to the Internet. With all these things it was speed of innovation, and without that innovation we would have been knocked out of the business.'

Figures in 1998 showed that NCR had a 27 per cent share of the world ATM market. It was the 12th year in a row that the company had emerged as the world's top supplier. Nearly 220,000 machines had been dispatched from Dundee in the previous seven years to over 100 countries, and for the first time NCR had taken over the top spot in the United States.

But the technological creativity that has put Dundee on top of the world is continuing. For instance, bank customers can now withdraw money from a bank machine 'in the blink of an eye' thanks to iris identification technology. An NCR ATM fitted with the system supplied by American company Sensar means that the customer simply puts in his or her bank card and a camera mounted on the machine photographs the coloured portion of the eye, the iris. If the iris staring back matches the record on the databank, the ATM will allow instant access to the customer's bank account without need for a PIN. The entire process takes as little as two seconds and presents no danger to the customer's eye.

'When we started in this business in the 1980s, we focused on the quality and reliability of what we designed and produced, and that's still necessary in 1999,' says NCR's vice-president of financial solutions and general manager in Dundee, Danny O'Brien. 'The industry has changed, the market has changed and our customers have changed, and they have higher expectations of us as a supplier. Continuing innovation is essential. Because we're at the leading edge, it's important we show leading-edge technology and innovation.'

That sort of innovation could eventually mean the end of the bank card and customers having an actual conversation with a voice-activated automatic teller when they want to withdraw cash. But in the age of cyberspace, NCR now has company close to home when it comes to world-class cerebral agility. At Dundee University, scientists are working on methods which could revolutionise the production of silicon chips, an industry worth $150 billion worldwide.

Without silicon chips, modern-day life would probably come to a standstill. They make most electronic devices work, from computers to teamakers. Their manufacture relies on the ability to transfer, with perfect accuracy, the complex and tiny image of an integrated circuit on to the surface of the silicon. This has been achieved by the use of a device known as a photomask, a quartz plate coated with a layer of material on which the circuitry is chemically reproduced. The process involves a series of steps, each of which must be accurately controlled.

With the demand for evermore powerful and more complex silicon chips, the search for a simple method of producing high-resolution electronic structures becomes more urgent. Professor Jim Cairns and his colleagues have come up with a novel approach to their production which promises a single processing step, or a 'one-step chip'. The idea is to produce the complex metal circuitry patterns by using a range of newly synthesised chemicals known as organo-metallic compounds which, when bombarded with electrons, deposit high-resolution metallic tracks. 'The whole drive of the industry is to make smaller and smaller patterns because the more you can pack into the silicon, the more powerful, more versatile and more useful it becomes,' says Professor Cairns. 'In order to do that, the dimensions of the features of the chip have to continue to shrink, and we're developing the technology to allow that to happen.'

It is certainly true that Professor Cairns's work has global implications. But one Dundee company can claim to go a step further and boast that their technology is on a different planet. That is exactly where a component designed and manufactured by American-owned Trak Microwave ended up. A piece of kit called an iso-adapter, little bigger than a cigarette packet, ensured that NASA's Mars Pathfinder mission was a success. In 1997 this device allowed the space probe to beam back TV pictures from the surface of the Red Planet. If this

61

complex piece of equipment had failed, the 119-million-mile mission would have been a flop.

Trak Microwave is another Dundee success story, although, once again, it could all have been very different. From being a small company established in 1987 which 'haemorrhaged money', Trak has grown to become an international business with a staff of around 200. At one end of the spectrum, they make instruments which go into satellite- or space-based systems. At the other are the very commercial products which are primarily used in mobile-telephone infrastructure. Somewhere in between are military applications for missile and radar.

Being in Dundee has made an important contribution to Trak's success. 'There is a tremendous number of factors and the biggest factor is the skill level of the workforce that we have here,' says Trak's commercial business director Jacqui McLaughlin. 'It starts from the lowest level and goes to the highest level in the company.'

It is an extraordinary tribute to Trak's progress that an organisation such as NASA should look to Dundee inventiveness to assist missions in deep space. As Jacqui McLaughlin points out, Trak's reputation is strong. 'We're unique in all of Europe as a supplier of our type of products,' she claims. 'What we're finding now is that they're offering us more and more opportunities and broadening the scope of what we can do for them as well.' Similar Dundee-made components were also placed aboard another NASA mission to Saturn's moon, Titan.

Professor Jim Cairns (courtesy of Michael Boyd/Scottish News Agency)

While Trak staff are being credited with star status by NASA, another young Dundee firm is already in the megastar league. DMA Design are the creators of some of the world's most popular computer games. They are amongst the world's top ten in their field, with giants like Nintendo making plain their appreciation of what has come out of the city.

DMA's rise to global prominence was as rapid as it was astonishing. In a small way, its founder was influenced by the efforts of another computer genius. When David Jones was leaving school, Sir Clive Sinclair's ZX81 home computer had just come on the scene. Jones remembers it as 'an amazing little machine for the price'. Next came Sinclair's Spectrum, and by that time David, as an electrical engineer, was helping to make them at the Timex plant. 'I

David Jones, director of DMA Design, with his best-selling games (courtesy of David Martin/Fotopress)

knew them inside out. I was fascinated by them, and the whole UK had ZX Spectrum fever,' says David. 'The home-computer scene was just taking off in the UK. I worked with Clive Sinclair and met him on a couple of occasions. It was just terrific.'

David decided to leave Timex and go back to college to do a degree in software at what is now Abertay University. It was then that his first game was released. 'Menace' was so successful that David and some friends immediately followed it up with another smash hit called 'Blood Money'. It was even more popular and persuaded him to leave college to set up his own computer-games company, DMA Design. There was an element of risk. But staff at Dundee College of Technology, as it was at the time, were helpful. They suggested David could take a sabbatical and return to finish off his BSc in microsystems.

As it happened, he never did, largely due to DMA's creation of one of the most popular computer games of the '90s – 'Lemmings'. It featured dozens of tiny animated creatures who, without the player's help, would march into the jaws of doom in hundreds of highly imaginative ways. 'I knew it was a good game and it had the potential to be really big,' says David. 'But you can never tell in this industry.'

'Lemmings' was a huge worldwide smash, selling millions of copies, and created a whole new genre of computer games. Since then DMA have never looked back. They produced two hugely popular sequels and a number of acclaimed new titles. The company then became one of the first companies to be chosen for Nintendo's 'Dream Team', the hand-picked group of developers who would work on the first ground-breaking games for the new Nintendo 64.

David Jones and his colleagues met the president of Nintendo, and Miyamoto, the designer of the Mario series and one of the most respected figures in the video-games industry, came to Dundee to visit DMA. Nintendo's US chairman Howard Lincoln paid Jones this compliment: 'David Jones is one of the few people in the world who are really in that Spielberg category. He's capable of creating incredible software.'

DMA started with one employee. It now has around 90 staff. In 1997, the company was acquired by the leading UK developer and publisher Gremlin Interactive, and David is now the creative director of the combined group. He hopes that DMA's phenomenal success will produce benefits for Dundee and give it an identity in a new field. 'There are other companies in Dundee who are doing video games which are spin-offs from DMA,' explains David. 'I hope Dundee can become recognised for having great games companies and hopefully go some way to replacing some of the older industries that have fallen away.'

At one point, one of those companies, Visual Sciences, was top of the games charts with DMA. 'We were at number two and number three,' says David. 'To be honest, that's pretty amazing. If you had two artists who were number two and number three in the pop charts and came from the same city, people would probably sit up and take notice.'

Looking for anything profound in the initials DMA would be a waste of time – they actually stand for 'doesn't mean anything'. In terms of prestige for Dundee, it's a misnomer if ever there was one.

And now, bolstering David's wish that Dundee establish a reputation in video games, his alma mater has introduced what he describes as 'the best games-oriented degree in the world'. Abertay University has thrown its weight behind Dundee's standing as leading centre for computer games and virtual-reality development with its own state-of-the-art courses for future games boffins. When the university launched the MSc in Software Engineering (Games and Virtual Environments), it was thought to be a world first. Students from around the world have since enrolled on what is believed to be one of the first university-level degree courses in computer-games writing, the BSc (Hons) in Computer Games Technology.

While David Jones and Abertay have made an exhilarating world of virtual reality, there could be nothing more real than the basic human need for food. The work being done by scientists at the Scottish Crop Research Institute on the outskirts of the city can offer hope to those in disadvantaged parts of the world where proper nourishment is not automatically available.

SCRI has been thrusting forward in the field of food genetics. Professor Michael Wilson, who was until recently the institute's deputy director, would very much like to disabuse those who believe this is a concept which should be treated only with contempt. Looking out from the comfortable perspective of living in wealthy western Europe, it is for him a means of helping those who simply do not get enough to eat.

In tropical countries, viruses in particular cause real problems. Large percentages of the crops are lost to pests and pathogens, viruses and fungi. There is no natural resistance to some of these viruses. 'The basic premise of the genetic modification of crop plants is that it's technically possible to introduce a single gene or a few genes which through expressing particular proteins within the crop at very low levels give that crop new characteristics which in many cases you can't achieve by classical breeding,' says Professor Wilson.

SCRI is, for instance, involved in ways of shielding the peanut crops of Africa and India from viruses which can have a devastating effect. For subsistence farmers and their families, the peanut is a major source of protein. There is no resistance to the Indian virus. SCRI has been examining the biology of these viruses and how they are spread with the aim of designing genes based on viral sequences which can be introduced into the peanuts to protect them.

Six hundred million Chinese people rely on wheat as their main source of carbohydrate. Again the wheat is threatened by a virus transmitted by a fungus with the potential to wipe the crop out, and there is no effective resistance to this virus in Chinese wheat-breeding programmes. SCRI scientists are involved in attempting to introduce some specific single genes into the breeding lines of Chinese wheat which have been grown in Dundee. The lines of Chinese wheat contain genes derived from the virus. In 1999 these were due to be tested for protection against the virus.

To Michael Wilson, this is a far healthier way of treating the problem than using environmentally unfriendly chemical compounds. He claims, 'GM technology is not the universal panacea but it's a very powerful new technique which can be added to all existing breeding programmes.'

It is his firm belief that the genetic techniques being exploited at SCRI will help to feed parts of the world that would otherwise be in trouble. In other words, work being done in Dundee has the potential to reduce the world's starving population.

One can only wonder what Mrs Keiller would have made of that.

Dundee's nautical history re-enacted at Broughty Ferry Castle

4

Triumphs and Tragedies
Dundee and the Sea

Frank O'Donnell

At the turn of the nineteenth century it was the Antarctic and not outer space that captured the imagination as man's last frontier, and in the race to reach the South Pole and unravel the mysteries of those frozen wastes, Dundee was at the forefront of developing the new technology of the day. For, make no mistake, Captain Scott's Royal Research Ship *Discovery* was as much a pioneering vessel then as NASA's space shuttle *Discovery* is today. And it was no accident that the *Discovery*, now a metaphor for Dundee's emergence as a city of science and innovation, was built on the banks of the Tay. The building of the *Discovery*, one of the most remarkable vessels of its time, was the logical outcome of a maritime tradition that stretches back centuries and survives today in oil-rig-fabrication yards and marine-engineering design.

Dundee has always looked to the sea, its hinterland of hills and mountains making land travel difficult before the development of roads and the coming of the railways. As it emerged from its medieval chrysalis of Dondei, Dundee grew to become Scotland's second richest city, a powerful burgh with a thriving port.

There is clear evidence that Dundee harbour was being used for trade in the eleventh century with goods arriving for the Abbey at Coupar Angus. One of the earliest written references comes from Robert the Bruce's Charter of 1329, which mentioned a 'free harbour' existing at the time of Alexander III. In the Middle Ages the Tay emerged as an important trade passage to the Baltic and the rest of Europe. Wine was imported from the thirteenth century and, by 1620, 50,000 gallons were

Dundee's nautical tradition in stone – a detail from the Sailors' Home

imported from Spain and France, making Dundee Scotland's second largest importer of wine. 'Murmblade', Canary sugar, aniseed oil, 'toffie' from Flanders and olive oil from Spain were also landed in the port, the list of imports testimony to the wealth of Dundee at that time. In turn, the port exported wool, sheepskins and hides. From the fifteenth century, the rise of spinning, weaving and cloth manufacture was reflected in the trade of the harbour, presaging the emergence of the linen trade and, of course, ultimately jute.

The creation of modern Dundee began with the growth of the linen industry and the return of economic prosperity in the mid-eighteenth century. Dundee Town Council had control of the port but was initially slow to respond to the opportunities. At the turn of the nineteenth century, the harbour was rudimentary and the council seemed more interested in profiteering than in investing in the future of their most important asset. Between 1764 and 1815, £38,000 was collected in shore dues but only £9,000 was spent on the harbour.

Dundee's maritime history is splashed with tales of adventure and intrigue. One of the most celebrated is the Battle of Camperdown, where the British fleet scored an unexpectedly decisive victory over the Dutch in 1797. The British naval fleet was led by Scotland's most celebrated sailor, Dundonian Admiral Adam Duncan, and the victory has been hailed as one of the greatest ever, comparable in significance with the Battle of Britain. After three hours of intense battle, the leader of the Dutch fleet, Admiral de Winter, came on board the *Venerable* to hand over his sword as a symbol of surrender. Nine Dutch ships were captured and the remainder fled back to port. Had the Dutch won, their navy would have joined with the French to launch an army on Britain.

The significance of the victory cannot be overestimated. At the time it was a huge boost to a British navy riven with low morale, and the government seized upon the news to help lift the spirit of the nation: church bells were rung, guns were fired from the Tower and the city of London was illuminated. Duncan himself was swiftly made a viscount by the King on 17 October. Fourteen civic authorities, including Dundee, Edinburgh and Glasgow, presented him the freedom of their cities. Numerous societies, from the Royal College of Surgeons to the Marine Society of Merchants, elected him to honorary membership. And in March of the following year, Parliament voted to pay him and his two succeeding heirs an annuity of £2,000, tax free, backdated to the day of the battle.

When Duncan arrived in Dundee in January 1798 he was met with a military parade, while magistrates formed a procession and accompanied him along the High Street to the Town House, where a dinner was held in his honour. Similar welcomes followed in Edinburgh, London and elsewhere as civic leaders queued up to confer honours on a national hero. Viscount Duncan died in 1804 and was succeeded by his third and eldest surviving son, Robert Dundas Duncan

Haldane. He became the first Earl of Camperdown and set about planning what became Camperdown House, which was completed in 1828. The achievements of Duncan have been overshadowed until recently by those of Horatio Nelson and it was not until 1997, the bicentenary of the battle, that interest was renewed.

With Dundee fast becoming the linen metropolis of Scotland, pressure mounted from manufacturers and ship owners for investment in the harbour, but it was not until the arrival of jute 40 years later that it began to develop its potential. In 1815 the management of the port passed to a Harbour Commission made up of council representatives, businessmen, landowners and harbour users. The main imports then were hemp, flax, tow, cotton and timber, while linen, sail cloth, cotton bagging and thread were the principal exports. The Harbour Commission brought in Thomas Telford to design an extension to the port and the result was the West Graving Dock, opened in 1823. The King William IV, Earl Grey, Camperdown, East Graving and Victoria Docks followed.

From 1826 the Dundee, Perth and London (DP and L) Shipping Company, which still thrives, ran a twice-weekly service to London and Glasgow, expanding further when the company introduced steamships to outpace its rivals in Aberdeen and Leith.

The investment in the port was to have a positive effect on the shipbuilding industry and shipbuilding on the Tay would grow to become second only to that on the Clyde in importance in Scotland. Records show that ships were built in Dundee from 1782, but it was not until 1814 that the first engine-powered vessel, *The Tay*, was built by James Smart Shipbuilders. At that time there was no road between Perth and Dundee and over the next two decades numerous local steamers were built to transport people between the two cities.

One of those steamers was the SS *Forfarshire*, which catapulted Grace Darling, an unknown 23-year-old, to instant stardom thanks to a single act of courage on 7 September 1838. The previous night, in awful conditions, the SS *Forfarshire*, on a journey from Hull to Dundee with 60 people on board, had run aground on the Farne Islands, where Grace's father was the lighthouse keeper. Most of the passengers, who had been in their cabins below deck, were drowned. Incredibly, nine survivors clung to the rocks and Grace and her father bravely rowed out in the stormy seas to save them. The story hit the national newspapers and, to her great distress, Grace became one of the first ever media celebrities of Victorian Britain.

The episode came at the beginning of Victoria's reign and Grace Darling became a symbol of the heroic Victorian era. She became a symbol of British maidenhood and was celebrated as 'pious and pure, modest and yet so brave'. Countless books and magazine articles were written about her, not to mention

Dundee harbour in the late-eighteenth century (courtesy of Dundee Art Galleries and Museums)

Admiral Adam Duncan (courtesy of Dundee Arts and Heritage)

A bustling harbour scene as Dundee grows and develops shipbuilding on the Tay, by D.A. Andrews (courtesy of Dundee Art Galleries and Museums)

The age of steam has well and truly arrived in this river scene (courtesy of Dundee Art Galleries and Museums)

numerous poems and paintings which were created in her honour. Boat trips were organised to the Longstone lighthouse for people just to get a glimpse of her. Sadly, Grace died of tuberculosis only three years after the rescue, her early demise sealing her reputation as a heroine. She was buried at her native Bamburgh, where a monument in the churchyard was specially designed to be seen by passing ships. A Royal National Lifeboat Institution museum in the village still displays the original coble in which she rowed out with her father to rescue the survivors.

Shipbuilding expanded steadily in Dundee in the mid-nineteenth century in tandem with the whaling and jute industries. In 1850 more than 100 vessels of between 100 and 200 tons sailed from the port. Unlike Dundee, other neighbouring harbours important in the eighteenth century like Perth, Arbroath and Montrose failed to develop docks for deep-water ships, fast unloading facilities or adequate warehouse capacity for raw materials and were left behind by Dundee's rapid expansion.

The next step in the evolution of Dundee shipbuilding came in 1854 with the construction of the first iron ship. Apart from wooden-hulled whalers, iron-hulled screw-propelled steamships came to be the main product of all Dundee yards after this time.

At its zenith, the harbour sprawled over 119 acres and three and a half miles of quayside, and more than 200 ships and 18 whalers registered in Dundee traded around the globe. The jute industry's requirement for whale oil resulted in Dundee becoming Scotland's last great whaling port, and whaling also produced one of Dundee's great maritime heroes, the whaler James McIntosh, known as 'Toshie'. Toshie was the sole survivor of one of the boats of the schooner *The Chieftain*, which sailed from Dundee in the spring of 1884 under Captain T.F. Gellatly to search for seals and whales around Greenland. After a thick fog descended for several days, Toshie and two others became cast away in a boat. Both the other men died, but Toshie, barely alive, was rescued after 17 days by a passing ship. His ordeal resulted in both his legs being amputated, leaving him disabled but defiant.

Toshie's story became the subject of a play in 1984, the year of the centenary of the disaster, scripted by Dundee writer Stewart Brown. He explained, 'Toshie was iced to the boat when he was found. They had to hack him free before his legs were amputated below the knee by a surgeon on the Danish warship *Diana*. Toshie came home a hero and lived in Broughty Ferry. When he left on that tragic journey he had only one son, but by the time he died he had eight kids. It seems he lost his legs but nothing else!'

Upon his return to Dundee, Toshie was unhappy with his pair of heavy, solid teak artificial legs and set out to find a pair made from cork. Stewart continues the story. 'A Dundee minister, Reverend David Macrae, gave him a hand tricycle. Toshie then cycled to London and right up Fleet Street, where he was interviewed by the *Pall Mall Gazette*. Toshie's story of suffering was related in the London paper and after an appeal he was eventually given the cork legs.'

The story of Toshie helped locals to understand the dangers of whaling, but in 1883 Dundonians had a chance to view at first hand the prized creature which lured their menfolk to the icy waters of the Arctic for months at a time when a whale appeared off the coast. The arrival of the 'Tay Whale', as it became known, caused much excitement in the city. Few, however, predicted that after a month Dundee's whaling captain would have failed to capture a male humpback lying in their own backyard.

On Hogmanay 1883 the whalers sensed they were close to a capture after the whale was finally struck by harpoons from several boats. The massive creature, however, battled with the whalers and on New Year's morning it broke the harpoon lines and swam free, leaving the men to return empty-handed with the greatest 'one that got away' story of all time. The Tay Whale, however, was fatally wounded and was eventually spotted floating off the coast at Inverbervie, having succumbed to its injuries.

It was towed ashore by a tugboat and on arrival was greeted by a crowd of several thousand fascinated onlookers. It was later auctioned and bought for £226 by Dundee oil merchant John Woods, who quickly recouped his outlay by charging the public 6d. (two and a half pence) to view the creature from the deep. It is estimated that during the fortnight the Tay Whale remained on exhibition, 50,000 people came to see it, 12,000 on the first Saturday. Bus and rail companies put on special services to cope with the demand and local photographers took shots of visitors sitting in the mouth of the whale. The skeleton of the humpback was donated to Dundee museum by Woods, where it has remained as one of the most popular attractions for more than 100 years.

Dundee's shipyards continued to thrive, churning out ships for the First World War. But the slump that followed the war saw the closure of the Dundee Shipbuilding Company in 1920, and the Caledon became the city's sole representative in the shipbuilding industry. The Caledon continued to fly the flag during the Second World War, when it built cargo vessels as well as corvettes, frigates and even an aircraft carrier in Dundee.

While women dominated the textile industry in the city, shipbuilding and engineering were male preserves. The exception to this came during the war years, when woman were welcomed while labour was in short supply, but they were supplanted when the men returned from combat. It was not until equal-opportunities legislation in the 1970s that women became permanent full-time employees in the shipyards, ironically during their decline.

Dundee's great shipbuilding tradition finally ended in 1980 with the closure of the Robb Caledon yard. The steady decline did not ease the pain for the many

Victorian heroine: Grace Darling's daring exploits commemorated in The Wreck of the Forfarshire *by T.M. Joy, 1840 (courtesy of Dundee Art Galleries and Museums)*

thousands of men who had served apprenticeships within the yard. One of those was Eddie Bree, who worked in the Caledon Yard for 22 years, beginning in 1950.

> I joined as a catch boy. I caught the hot rivets from the heater boys and passed them on to the riveter. Back then I earned just one pound three shillings for a 44-hour week. I then became an apprentice welder and my wages went up to 25 shillings a week.
>
> I was paid off in 1960 when shipbuilding went into a slump but many men were taken on again in 1963 when Caledon got the contract for the steel for the new road bridge. I left in 1972 because the oil industry was paying more. A lot of the skilled men went around this time because of the pay and conditions.
>
> When I first started there were no doors on the toilets, no tea breaks and no place to hang your coat. It was atrocious. At that time there were around 2,000 men at the yard but by the time I left it was down to 500.

But although times could be tough in the shipyard, the workforce took

Dundee whalers *Active, Balaena* and *Diana* in the Antarctic *by W.G. Burn Murdoch (courtesy of Dundee Art Galleries and Museums)*

enormous pride in their work. Eddie Bree still does: 'Despite everything, I loved my job and would not have missed it for the world. It was a good career and we took a pride in what we were doing. When you saw a ship getting launched it was a great feeling.

'In fact the whole of Dundee took pride in the Caledon. Everybody was sorry to see it go. The economy was hit badly when the shipbuilding slumped. A lot of local companies supplied the Caledon and there was quite a slump in Dundee during the 1960s.'

The nationalisation of the Caledon in 1977 was followed by its closure in 1980, a victim of European edicts that demanded the reduction of shipbuilding capacity. The deep waters of the Tay still make Dundee ideal for shipbuilding. Oil-rig fabrication continues at the shore and shipbuilding design carried out by Marine Design Consultants is the last echo of a once-great Dundee tradition.

But the lasting monument to Dundee's shipbuilding tradition is the Royal Research Ship *Discovery*, a vessel that has emerged as the symbol of modern Dundee, the City of Discovery. The *Discovery*'s fame stems from its role in the National Antarctic Expedition of 1901–04, led by the 33-year-old Captain

A lifetime of shipbuilding: shipyards built men like Eddie Bree, not just ships (courtesy of Ian Jacobs/Scottish News Agency)

Robert Falcon Scott, during which the ship survived two years imprisoned in the crushing vice of pack ice.

The *Discovery* was commissioned for the expedition, the first ship to be built specifically for scientific research. Its remit was to explore the South Pole, taking magnetic surveys and biological and oceanographic data. Because of its unique role, the ship had to be constructed almost entirely from wood at a time when wooden shipbuilding had become almost obsolete. Only a handful of the world's shipyards had the skills to build a vessel capable of withstanding the rigour of the Antarctic, and Dundee's reputation for building whaling ships was a key factor in landing the contract to build the vessel. The ship was constructed at a total cost of £51,000 by the Dundee Shipbuilding Company.

The construction was a phenomenal feat of marine engineering with 25 different woods used in total. The hull, made up of three layers of wood around double frames, is never less than 26 inches deep. Pitch pine and English elm form the outer layer; six-inch-thick green heart from Guyana, the second hardest wood in the world, is the second layer; and a lining of pitch pine, originally Riga fir, makes up the inner hull. The closely spaced frames are made of Scottish oak.

In his memoirs, *Breaking the Fetters*, Bob Stewart, who went on to become a Prohibition Party councillor in Dundee, recalled his time working on the *Discovery*.

> It was most interesting work . . . There were no rivets, no steel plates, no iron nails. With the exception of the funnel, the ship was entirely constructed of wood. It was said at the time that they had to dig men out of the Howff to get the right labour for the construction. The wood was steamed to get it bent into proper position and wooden nails called trunnels were used and battered in to hold the beams in position.

It was this feat of marine engineering, coupled with a bow of 11-foot-thick solid oak, that assured the survival of the ship and the 47 crew during her two years in the icy wastes of McMurdo Sound. The ship was eventually freed by the combined efforts of the *Terra Nova* and the *Morning* on 16 February 1904.

Caledon Yard (courtesy of Marine Design Consultants Ltd)

Ironically, the *Terra Nova*, the last whaling ship to be built in Dundee, carried
Scott on his ill-fated polar expedition of 1910–13.

After returning from the National Antarctic Expedition, the *Discovery* was
sold to the Hudson Bay Company of Canada and converted into a cargo vessel.
During the First World War she ran munitions to Russia and was later involved
in the BANZAR expeditions to the South Pole. From 1931 she was used as a
training ship for Sea Scouts before she was transferred to the Admiralty as a drill
ship for the Royal Naval Auxiliary Reserve. The huge cost of essential repairs
placed the *Discovery*'s long-term future in threat until the Maritime Trust
stepped in and converted the ship into a museum and tourist attraction on the
River Thames.

The *Discovery* was offered a new home in Dundee in 1985 and returned to
the city on 3 April 1986. She finally berthed at midnight, cheered by thousands
of people who lined the banks of the Tay to witness the historic return of the
famous ship. The return was immortalised by Dundee band The Lowland Folk
in the song 'Pride o' the Panmure Yaird', which was released as a single in 1986:

An early-morning waterfront scene

'Build us a ship,' said the men fae the south,
'A ship we can trust with a crew
In seas of ice that grip like a vice,
And winds that cut a man through.'
So the Dundee lads thocht o' the ships
That sail where the whale fish blow,
That they'd built in their time
O' the oak and the pine,
Like 'The Bear' and the 'Esquimaux'.
Here's tae the lads, the lads o' the Tay,
Wha built the ships that dared;
Here's tae Scott's 'Discovery',
The pride o' the Panmure Yaird.

Since 1993 the ship has been the centrepiece of Dundee's top tourist attraction, Discovery Point, which attracts 85,000 visitors each year. Ownership of the *Discovery* was transferred to the Dundee Heritage Trust in 1995. A one-pound note dating from 1901, the year of her launch, was gifted to seal the handover.

While the *Discovery* has been a recent addition to Dundee's maritime history, her less well-known cousin HM Frigate *Unicorn* has been in the city's harbour since 1873. The *Unicorn* was built in the Royal Dockyard at Chatham, Kent, and was launched in 1824. Today the 46-gun frigate is the oldest British-built ship afloat, and the third oldest ship afloat in the world. After use as a powder hulk from 1857 to 1862, she was towed to Dundee in 1873, where she served as a drill ship for the Royal Naval Reserve.

General manager of the *Unicorn* Andrew Fox explained, 'The *Unicorn* was launched on 30 March 1824, which makes the ship 175 years old. Many people do not realise that she was never fully completed. The Royal Navy built a great number of ships with just a hull and a roof on top. The *Unicorn* was ten days from completion but was never used as a warship. Ninety-five per cent of the original timber is still intact. What people are seeing is the original ship. The uniqueness of the *Unicorn* is its purity of construction.'

Today the *Unicorn* sits quietly in Victoria Dock, largely in the shadow of its more famous neighbour. The Unicorn Preservation Society was formed with the aim of restoring the ship to her original design and in 1968 Prince Philip accepted the vessel from the Navy on behalf of the society. Now, more than 30

The launch of the Discovery, *'pride o' the Panmure yaird' (courtesy of Dundee Art Galleries and Museums)*

The Mona *disaster of 1959 (courtesy of Scottish News Agency)*

years later, the ship has undergone extensive refurbishment and attracts 11,000 visitors each year.

Alongside the *Unicorn* is a more recent arrival, the *North Carr* lightship, which came to Victoria Dock in 1997. The *North Carr* was built in 1933 and was used not only for safety but also to guide ships into the harbour. Today lightships have been replaced with fixed buoys and this ship is the only survivor in Scotland.

The *North Carr* lightship has a poignant association with Dundee, as the eight-strong crew of the Broughty Ferry lifeboat *Mona* drowned while on an emergency call to the lightship in 1959. Quietly moored off the shore at Broughty Ferry, in the shadow of the castle museum which keeps a now peaceful vigil over the estuary, the Tay lifeboat today presents a tranquil scene. A memorial plaque on the north wall of the lifeboat shed, however, serves as an ominous reminder of the power of the sea and of that awful night on 8 December 1959.

On the night of the disaster weather conditions were severe, with a strong south-easterly gale blowing across the entrance to the River Tay. Navigational buoys had been driven from their positions by the storm and the crew were called to rescue the drifting *North Carr* lightship. But when daylight broke, the volunteer crew were found drowned in the wheelhouse of the *Mona*, which was beached on Buddon Sands, the final resting place for the vessel which had saved 118 lives in 24 years of service. The deaths stunned the local population. But when the Royal National Lifeboat Institution called for new volunteers in the wake of the disaster, 36 people came forward, testimony to the spirit of the Tayside people.

David Martin, mechanic of today's vessel, the cumbersomely named *Joseph Rothwell Sykes and Hilda M*, explained, 'There are 18 crew, who are all volunteers apart from the full-time coxswain. We are usually called out about twice a month. Perhaps the *Mona* has made people here more aware of the lifeboat and maybe that is why we are so well supported by the local people. But we also have an excellent fundraising team. Lives are not saved by us, they are saved by people out in the street shaking a tin.'

The RNLI took over the service in 1861, and for the last 140 years the volunteer crew and boat have been funded by public donations. Annually the station raises £70,000, among the highest in the country. In 2001 the station will take delivery of a new 25-knot boat to replace the present *Joseph Rothwell Sykes*. The new craft will cost £1.3 million but the investment is important, said David. 'The extra speed will make a difference in response times, which could ultimately save lives.'

Since the lifeboat station was first established in Broughty Ferry in 1830,

The last 'Fifie' crosses the Tay (courtesy of Dundee Art Galleries and Museums)

The Sailors' Home, Dock Street, Dundee (courtesy of Gordon Douglas Photographic)

more than 530 lives have been saved. Students, architects, joiners and lab technicians are among those who have made up the lifeboat's crew. The youngest member, aged 17, is still at school, while recently the crew took on board their first woman member, Fiona Johnston. Mother-of-two Fiona has been involved with boats since she was ten years old and felt joining the crew was a natural continuation of her love of the sea. She explained, 'It's not for everybody. We are on call 24 hours a day and always carry our pagers. My kids are now nine and 12 and my neighbour takes them if there is a shout.'

One catastrophe that the lifeboat could not prevent was the Tay Bridge Disaster of 1879. When the Tay Bridge opened on 1 June 1878, there was great pomp and splendour, with guests, including former US president Ulysses S. Grant and the emperor of Brazil, travelling vast distances to view the marvel of Victorian

Piers of the old bridge – an ominous reminder of the power of the river

engineering. The following year Queen Victoria herself crossed the bridge on a return trip from Balmoral, and she later knighted Thomas Bouch, the bridge's designer. Bouch had conceived the idea of a bridge in 1854 but it had taken years for the plan to overcome opposition. Civic leaders in Perth had been particularly concerned that the bridge would block navigation.

Altogether ten million bricks, 15,000 casks of cement and 4,000 tons of cast iron were used in the construction of the two-mile-long structure, which at the time was the longest bridge the world had ever seen. Aside from the huge financial cost, the bridge claimed the lives of 20 workmen during the six years of construction.

On 28 December 1879, the single-track bridge was to claim another 75 lives when the evening train from Edinburgh to Dundee plunged into the icy waters of the estuary. The train's engine, six carriages and all its passengers plunged into the river as winds of more than 70 miles per hour whistled through the broken bridge. No one survived the terrifying fall and for months afterwards bodies were washed up along the river in a grisly reminder of the failed structure.

In the wake of the disaster, with the screams of victims still reverberating on the Tay, the bridge's designer Sir Thomas Bouch was officially blamed. An inquiry found that the bridge had fallen due to a combination of poor workmanship and failure to allow for the high winds. The tragedy was immortalised in several poems by William Topaz McGonagall, including 'The Tay Bridge Disaster' and 'Address to the New Tay Bridge'. The piers from the original bridge are still visible, and one of the girders is now on show in the new National Museum of Scotland in Edinburgh.

The tragedy was a massive setback for Dundee. But, with the city still enjoying the jute boom, the local business community persevered with their dream to span the Tay and within eight years a new bridge had been built at a cost of £670,000, twice that of its ill-fated predecessor. Incredibly, 118 girders from the original bridge were used in the new structure. Thirteen men died in the building of the second Tay Bridge, but this proved not to be an unlucky omen and the bridge opened on 20 June 1887. It still provides a service today.

Before the construction of the Tay Road Bridge, the only means of crossing to Dundee other than via the rail bridge was the ferry service. The ferries, which have linked Dundee and Fife, in one form or another, for hundreds of years, have, like the bridge, suffered their share of disasters at the hands of the 'Silvery Tay'. In 1815, 19 passengers drowned in a storm, resulting in an investigation and changes to the safety arrangements for the ferries, which at that time were powered by sail and oar.

In 1821 a regular steam-ferry service was introduced between Dundee and Newport with a smaller capacity but a similar frequency and speed of service as the diesel-engined vehicles which were operating up until the Tay Road Bridge opened. In the 1840s the Edinburgh and Northern Railway developed Ferryport as a transit station. Goods trains were transported across the Tay on wagon steamers with passengers on separate paddle-boats; it was one of the first rail-ferry services in the world.

The rail-ferry service was lost forever when the present Tay Rail Bridge was opened in 1887, and for the Harbour Trustees who operated the ferries the bridge was a symbol of a bleak future. Ironically, it was a further stage of transport development, the motor car, which earned the ferries a reprieve. Although the second Tay Rail Bridge was opened in 1887, the phenomenal growth in motor traffic kept the ferries busy as they were the only way cars could cross without a detour via Perth. New ferries were introduced to meet the needs of the motorist and the ports themselves were modified to meet the demands of cars and vans.

The death knell for the 'Fifies' finally came in March 1963 when building began on the Tay Road Bridge. The bridge was completed on 18 August 1966 at a cost of £6 million. The ferries were immediately withdrawn.

Much of Tayside's maritime history, including the history of the bridge and the 'Fifies', is now available on the Internet and CD-Rom thanks to the vision of Douglas MacKenzie, managing director of DMC Ltd, a multimedia software company. Douglas decided to launch the project after he realised the area's maritime history was being ignored. There are now 400 pictures on the site and 6,500 mariner and voyager records as a result of his efforts.

'The reason for doing this is really educational,' he explained. 'It really is done as a labour of love. It provides an advert for what we do but in reality there are more profitable ways of doing that. As always with the introduction of computers, there are those in the museum world who feel that their jobs and institutions are under threat, but this is not the case. A virtual museum does not try to replace the physical museum, nor is it just a flat representation of what is there. It tries to provide something different. We can show objects which are rarely seen and in the virtual museum objects are not limited to appearing in one exhibit.'

While the virtual future of Dundee's maritime history seems secure, the reality is in the hands of Dundee City Council and the owners of the docks, Forth Ports plc. It is still a working port, handling occasional cruise ships and commodities such as grain, cement, steel and potatoes. Among the more unusual imports is the Venezuelan crude oil that is shipped to Nynas UK AB. The plant produces bitumen as well as a range of fuel and oil products.

At the busy Prince Charles Wharf, oil-fabrication companies and subsea operators are at work in a business that has grown steadily since the North Sea oilfields were developed. Nearby, the Robert Gordon Institute of Technology maintains its oil-rig safety-training and rescue centre.

While much of Dundee's modern port still operates successfully, a large section remains unused and Forth Ports believe the future of the docks lies in residential, retail, leisure and tourism uses. They are currently promoting a new scheme called 'City Quay' which aims to bring the waterfront back to the people by making use of a 30-acre site. One of the aims of the development is to build a maritime quarter in the city centre where people live, work and spend leisure time. The plan includes 60,000 square feet of retail space, half of it built out over Victoria Dock, with two pedestrian courtyards, external walkways and a bridge link to the dock's southern side. It also includes a heritage centre adjacent to a dry dock that will house the frigate *Unicorn*, presently moored in Victoria Dock.

Life, it seems, is returning to the very spot that first gave birth to Dundee.

Dundee doorways

5

Every Picture Tells a Story

Dundee's Vibrant Visual Arts

Alison Balharry and Brian Lindsay

On 20 March 1999 a new era dawned for Dundee and its relationship with the arts. With the opening of Dundee Contemporary Arts, a brand new visual arts centre in the city's Nethergate, another piece of Dundee's regeneration jigsaw was put in place. In a city which has often been seen by the rest of Scotland as a cultural backwater, the opening of a centre for the contemporary visual arts may seem at best ambitious and at worst foolhardy. But now that it is in place, few would argue that the building itself is not a welcome addition to the Dundee skyline.

Designed by Edinburgh architect Richard Murphy and funded by a combination of Lottery and European money along with contributions from Dundee City Council, Scottish Enterprise Tayside and Dundee University, the centre is built on five levels. Dipping from its street-level entrance on the Nethergate down to the old Greenmarket, the back of the building comprises part of the city's old sea wall. With two galleries, two cinemas, a print studio, a café, a shop and activity rooms, the centre is bound to attract the artistic *cognoscenti* of Dundee. Does it, however, have a broad appeal to Dundonians at large and will it attract visitors from outside the city? The director of DCA, Andrew Nairne, is confident about the fledgling centre's future on both counts. 'It's not just about a few people who know about it already,

*The interior of the striking DCA
(courtesy of Dundee Contemporary Arts)*

but actually for every citizen in Dundee and for people from much further afield as well,' he says.

If DCA's first show is anything to go by, the centre will succeed. By being able to attract prestigious works ranging from Andy Warhol screenprints to the paintings of Callum Innes and the prodigious organic sculptures of Anya Gallaccio, Nairne certainly got things off to a good start. The challenge will be in sustaining the quality of exhibits and thus creating a lasting interest. In order to be truly successful DCA has to become an established venue in the eyes of potential visitors, and a welcoming and exciting place to be for everyone in Dundee.

As well as the public space, though, the new building also houses the city council's arts and heritage department and, perhaps more importantly, Dundee University's visual research centre. This unique space has been designed to develop further the work of the university's fine-arts school in the field of contemporary visual arts by providing the facilities for new work to be created. The plan is for the visual research centre to dovetail with the kind of work already being carried out at the university, where cutting-edge work has been taking place in the departments of film and TV imaging and, more recently, time-based art, which incorporates modern technology into the artistic process.

A decade ago such a venture would probably have been unimaginable in Dundee, but a series of coincidental events have culminated in the creation of the arts centre. The aforementioned University of Dundee's Faculty of Fine Art

The latest addition to Dundee's multi-media arts scene, Dundee Contemporary Arts (courtesy of Dundee Contemporary Arts)

may be a confusing title for erstwhile residents and students as well as those who have lived in the city all their lives, whereas if you mention 'Duncan of Jordanstone College of Art' or, more simply, 'the Art College', everyone will know what you mean. In August 1994 the University of Dundee and the Art College merged, a move which benefited both institutions but which also left the Art College with its own distinct identity, albeit a rather cumbersome moniker in 'Duncan of Jordanstone College of Art and Design, a faculty of the University of Dundee'. To most people, though, it remains 'the Art College'. Being part of a bigger institution has meant that Duncan of Jordanstone has increased its profile both within and outside the city and it is now one of the top choices for potential students from throughout Britain. This merger created the right environment for an expansion of the arts in Dundee, and the introduction of the Lottery meant that funds could be accessed for a truly ambitious project.

With the arts centre in place Dundee will certainly draw attention to its contemporary cultural activities, and a spot in the limelight may well go a long way towards altering the image of a city recovering from the ravages of post-industrial decline and turning into one which looks confidently to the future with an economy based more on education and arts and culture. Amid all the excitement and shock of the new, however, it must not be forgotten that Dundee does have a substantial artistic past and that the city and the Art College have brought through a number of important, exciting, innovative, eccentric and truly brilliant artists down the years.

Recently Dundee has lost three of its most distinguished artists. James McIntosh Patrick (1907–98), Alberto Morrocco (1917–98) and David McLure (1926–98) all worked in slightly different but overlapping eras. McIntosh Patrick was probably the most straightforward painter of the three, and although the subject matter and style of his paintings may seem a little old-fashioned in these days of abstraction and concept, his landscape oils and watercolours of Dundee and the surrounding countryside are extremely popular in the city itself and beyond. His reputation has been confirmed by the inclusion of works in the Royal Scottish Academy and numerous private and public collections throughout the world. McIntosh Patrick is synonymous with Dundee and will be remembered not only as a fine painter but also as an enthusiastic teacher whose Saturday morning classes at the Art College were enjoyed by hundreds through the years.

As with many artists before him, the value of his work has shot up since his death. The caprices of the market, though, are only one indicator of the true value of an artist's work. John Berridge, of the long-established Dundee Art Society, believes that McIntosh Patrick 'will always live in Scotland's memory as a landscape painter. He was one of the greats, up there with McTaggart, Peploe and Hunter.'

Autumn, Kinnordy, *one of Dr James McIntosh Patrick's best-loved landscapes, 1936, and* A City Garden *by Dr James McIntosh Patrick (both courtesy of Dundee Art Galleries and Museums)*

Still Life on a Red Cloth *by Alberto Morrocco (by kind permission of Mrs Vera Morrocco)*

David McLure (courtesy of Alan Richardson)

The heat which visibly radiates from the paintings of Alberto Morrocco may seem a million miles from Dundee's cool northern climate but the city is where he spent most of his life. Born in Aberdeen of Italian extraction in 1917, he moved to Dundee in 1950 to take up the post of Head of Drawing and Painting at Duncan of Jordanstone. (At this point the Art College was still situated in Bell Street, before it moved in 1953 to the site it now occupies on the Perth Road.) Despite holding such a distinguished position in the college for over 30 years, his own output was prolific. Throughout the '60s, '70s and '80s he was much in demand as a portrait painter, the Queen Mother being one of his more famous subjects, but he was perhaps more renowned for searingly colourful scenes of Mediterranean life.

In terms of influence and originality, David McLure is arguably the most distinguished painter to be associated with Dundee. Like McIntosh Patrick and Morrocco he had close associations with the Art College, having lectured there in the 1950s when he came to live and work in Dundee. He was a distinctive member of a group of talented young painters who emerged from Edinburgh College of Art in the early '50s, and his work is very recognisable for its colour and degree of conceptualisation. McLure was highly committed to his work and continued to paint right up until his death in February 1998.

For a city the size of Dundee, the loss of three such renowned artists in the space of a year is considerable. However, the vibrancy of the city's artistic output in recent decades is often underestimated. In the deaths of McIntosh Patrick, Morrocco and McLure we certainly witnessed the end of an era, but in more recent times there have been many artists who have upheld and enhanced Dundee's reputation. Painters such as James Howie, Will Maclean and David Cook, the sculptor David Mach and the photographer Albert Watson, to name but a few, all have international reputations, and although Mach and Watson have long since flown from Dundee, it is worth remembering that they were trained in the city. Mach is a particularly interesting character in that he has been able to meld a large degree of populism with serious artistic statement. Many of the ideas he uses in his huge sculptures were developed in Dundee when he studied at Duncan of Jordanstone in the 1970s.

The people of Dundee were treated to some of Mach's work in 1986 when the Seagate Gallery showed his work as part of their inaugural exhibition. As an alternative take on the three 'J's, the show was called 'Jute Bobbins, Jam Jars and Journals – Seen As Never Before'. A total of 4,000 jute bobbins, 2,500 jam jars and three tons of journals were used in a variety of works. Mach gave the Seagate Gallery just what it needed in an opening exhibition: a sense of the spectacular, work which had a comprehensive appeal and the status of showing an artist who had already made a big name for himself.

The opening of the Seagate Gallery was an important event in Dundee's art history. Without it, it is doubtful whether the new centre would ever have come about. Mach's time in Dundee looks, in retrospect, fleeting, but it is interesting to look back and acknowledge that his exhibition gave the Seagate management the opportunity to declare its aims and objectives:

> We will originate exhibitions and events of the best-quality contemporary art from home and abroad and provide a stimulus for greater awareness of visual arts within the community. The programme will be tailored to relate closely to the life of the city and at the same time open up new areas of visual experience for its broad public.

Prophetic words, perhaps, and it is doubtful whether the director of Dundee's new arts centre, Andrew Nairne, would argue with that ethos for DCA.

The Seagate, to many people's displeasure, was sacrificed as part of the plan to build the new centre and now lives on only in the memories of those who used the facilities and went to the exhibitions. Although it managed to attract exciting and innovative work to the city, it also provided a platform for local artists to exhibit and, perhaps just as importantly, meet and exchange ideas. Many of the artists involved with the Seagate came to it with a sense of collective spirit and an acknowledgement of the importance of encouraging the arts through grass-roots action. Dundee Printmakers Workshop was an important facility within the Seagate and provided a free and easy atmosphere along with inexpensive access to printmaking equipment that was used by a range of people, from the enthusiastic amateur to renowned artists such as the late Lil Neilson.

Another significant element of this collective ethos was the setting up of the WASPS studios in a converted jute mill called Meadowmill, in the Blackness area of the city. WASPS, or Workshops and Artists Provision for Scotland, is a Scottish-wide organisation which gets funding from the Scottish Arts Council. Meadowmill provides cheap studio space for artists of all kinds and is a hive of diverse activity; there is no doubt that it has been a vital element in encouraging artists in Dundee.

It is not, however, only struggling artists who have found Meadowmill conducive to creativity. James Howie, one of Dundee's most important painters, still works away in his studio in Meadowmill. He first made a big impact in the art world in the 1950s with his highly original and beautifully finished abstract landscapes, and he retains a reputation outside the city that would surprise many Dundonians. Howie, also famous in certain circles for his agility and style on the dance floor, has lived and worked in Dundee throughout his illustrious career and is perhaps one of the city's best-kept secrets. Because of his reluctance to seek the limelight, and because of a fiercely independent spirit which has brought him into conflict with the Establishment on more than one occasion, he has not always enjoyed the recognition in his own city he undoubtedly deserves.

The very fact, though, that someone as eminent as Howie chooses to work in Meadowmill is testimony to the place itself and the regard it is held in by the artists who use it. As anyone who knows a little of Dundee's history will tell you, radical left-wing politics have featured heavily. It is therefore fitting that a scene of previous industrial struggle should now be a place where the collective ideal is central to its ethos. In a city the size of Dundee, studio space such as that in Meadowmill is every bit as important as the new contemporary arts centre in the nurturing and sustaining of creative activity. As James Howie says, 'One of the things that was needed in Dundee was good, simple, well-lit space, and that's what Meadowmill provides. If we are to keep artists and art graduates in the city, we need more spaces like this.'

Perhaps because Dundee is a small city, there have been many connections between different ventures. Little exists in isolation. Bob McGilvray is one man who exemplifies this connection between different arts initiatives over the past two decades. As well as being instrumental in the establishment of the

Anchorite Triptych *by Professor Will Maclean (courtesy of Colin Roscoe)*

Professor Will Maclean in his studio,
April 1999 (courtesy of Colin Roscoe)

James Howie (courtesy of Ian Jacobs/
Scottish News Agency)

Printmakers Workshop and the WASPS studios, he was also the first director of the Seagate Gallery. Perhaps his most important work, however, has been as director of the Dundee Public Art Programme, which began in 1983 as a three-year project to complement refurbishment work taking place in the Blackness area of the city. With funding from the Scottish Arts Council and support from the local authority, this project was the beginning of a public art programme which not only thrives today but is the envy of towns and cities all over Britain.

From a large gable-end mural in St Peter Street to the whale's-teeth sculpture in Polepark to the street furniture which has appeared in the city centre over the past few years, Dundee Public Art Programme has sought to enhance the urban environment with over 90 pieces now in existence. For some artists the programme has provided a vital opportunity to create work which, because of its nature and scale, would otherwise never have seen the light of day. Alister White's aluminium kinetic sculpture which stands at the bottom of the Marketgate is a prime example, because without the kind of commission he was offered he would never have been able to realise his artistic vision.

Although providing work for artists is one of the objectives of the programme, its primary *raison d'être* is to provide an aesthetic dimension to Dundee's urban landscape. The aim of the Public Art Programme is to establish an ongoing series of carefully integrated projects which are designed to be site-specific and to contribute to individual buildings, the environment and the community of the area. The art input will be 'built in' to improvement schemes at the planning stage and will be perceived as part of the overall design.

Public consultation is an important part of any piece of work that is undertaken by the programme and it is testimony to the quality of the art pieces that they have largely brought positive reactions in the communities which house them. Few have been damaged or vandalised and they have come to represent an expression of civic pride, confidence and humanity in a city which has not always demonstrated a keen eye for the aesthetic when it comes to planning and building.

Although the programme has given opportunities to unknown artists in the city, it is worth once again mentioning David Mach, perhaps one of the greatest exponents of public art sculpture in the world today. Bob McGilvray remembers how the Dundee Public Art Programme brought Mach to the Central Library: 'After Mach's exhibition in the Seagate in 1986 we sold one of the magazine columns to the Scottish Arts Council and then installed it in the Central Library, which consequently had the first Mach column, long before anybody else. And it was there for months and months before eventually it began to settle and people started picking out the magazines. David was also brought back to work on the original designs for the city square, but unfortunately it all came to grief because no one could agree and I think people thought his designs were a bit risky.'

Looking back, this appears to have been an opportunity missed and, given the city council's conversion to contemporary art, perhaps one which would be more readily seized today. McGilvray welcomes the new arts centre but, with an ironic smile, likes to state the case for much of the work that was done in the past. 'All of these things, the WASPS studios, the Seagate, the Printmakers Workshop, the Public Art Programme, that's how we got an arts centre. That's how it came about. People tend to forget that from time to time.'

With new projects planned for the city centre and the new science centre, the future for the Dundee

Leaping Deer *by David Annand (courtesy of Dundee Tourist Board)*

Zeki Agacan (courtesy of Ian Jacobs/Scottish News Agency)

Public Art Programme looks bright as we enter the new millennium. McGilvray for one is excited about what lies ahead. 'With our move to the new arts centre, what we're expecting is an increase in work, and I think the programme is now becoming more proactive. The long-term plan is that as the new arts centre develops, we'll develop with it, more work will come along and we'll be in a position to employ more people.'

There is no doubt that the Dundee Public Art Programme has been instrumental in providing work for artists in Dundee. From David Annand's 'Leaping Deer 'which greet motorists as they enter the West End of the city to Chris Kelly's 'Gate Sculpture' which welcomes visitors and workers to the Dunsinane Industrial Estate, there are scores of examples of the success of the programme. But what about the artists whose work is difficult to present in that way or who prefer to work alone and outside the kind of ethos which operates in public art? Edinburgh, Glasgow, Aberdeen and many smaller places have numerous independent galleries which give working artists the chance to show and sell their work. Dundee, until now, has been bereft of such places – with the exception of one very special venue which has always been regarded with great fondness by painters in the city.

Since 1982, near the top of the Perth Road there has been an unlikely and unique gallery space, which also doubles as a Turkish restaurant. Zeki Agacan, who owns the Agacan, would probably not take too kindly to that description and insist that what he has is a restaurant which he decorates with the work of local artists. However, in the last 20 years or so, the Agacan has been one of the few places in Dundee where you can see new, original work.

Originally from the Marmara coast near Istanbul, Zeki has lived in Dundee since 1974 and has come to regard the city as his home. His open-armed and generous attitude towards Dundee's art community has enamoured him to them. 'I like the people,' he says. 'That's what keeps me here. There are no poseurs in Dundee. I like that. I think Dundee has a lot to offer.'

The restaurant itself is an Aladdin's cave of artwork, from the entrance, with its brightly coloured figures and motifs, to the toilets, which have been 'decorated' by a number of different artists. In the body of the restaurant the tables are all original, hand-painted creations, as are the menus. This visual feast ensures that a visit to the Agacan is likely not only to satisfy the taste buds but also to satiate those with a hunger for visual stimulation. 'A lot of people come in and look around in amazement, and when they leave they leave with a smile.'

No mean painter himself, Zeki's work, which largely depicts his homeland and his memories of childhood, can also be seen on the walls of the Agacan. The main walls, though, are kept for a perpetual round of changing exhibitions featuring local work, and unlike conventional galleries he takes no commission. Although he has, down the years, been a source of benevolence, his attitude is very matter-of-fact. 'I didn't intend to start out as an art gallery but I suppose it's kind of turned out that way. But I'm not judge and jury of what is good. If you bring a picture along I'll hang it.'

In recent years Zeki has given many sculptors and painters the chance to exhibit and add bits of themselves to the restaurant. Morag Muir, Ruth Saxon, Jonathan Hood, Vincent Rattray and Nael Hanna have all painted tables as well as exhibited. Stephen Bird, Dennis White, Derek Guild, Tommy Crooks and Charlie Walker are just a few of those who have shown on the walls of the Agacan. Zeki insists, only slightly tongue in cheek, that turning his restaurant into an art gallery has actually saved him work. 'I never need to decorate this place because every time I change the pictures it's like new decoration.'

David Cook in his studio (courtesy of Michael Boyd/Scottish News Agency)

Caishlan Herd at Generator (courtesy of Michael Boyd/Scottish News Agency)

One artist who has figured prominently in the story of the Agacan is another very significant Dundee painter whose work is scattered all over the world and who has recently featured in exhibitions at the McManus Galleries. David Cook is hard to fit into any category. Born in Dunfermline in 1957, he spent his childhood in Lochgelly before arriving in Dundee in the late 1970s to attend Duncan of Jordanstone. A student of Alberto Morrocco, Cook quickly made an impact as a highly committed and prolific painter. 'I remember that at Easter Morrocco had sent us away with the task of doing one painting and I'd come back with about half a dozen,' he said. 'Because I was so into it I'd come back with a big pile of them. I seemed to be working all the time. It had taken me a while to get into art college, so when I was there I didn't waste any time.'

Twenty years on and Cook is just as committed as ever, but he sees his art-college days as a bit more anarchic than things are now. 'There was a lot of humour when I was there, people playing pranks. There was one guy who actually bricked up a corridor. Another time we got a fridge, tied it up and put a tape recorder inside with banging and screaming noises and someone shouting 'Let me out!' and left it at the top of the stairs. I think if you did that now they'd probably have discussions for weeks on end about whether or not it was art . . .'

This anarchic spirit has stayed with Cook through the years. At one time his work was visible up and down the streets of Dundee's West End when he took to painting on the walls. Close brushes with the law led to a curtailment of these delves into graffiti, but even today the unmistakable motifs of Cook's 'outside' work pop up from time to time.

His inspiration comes from nature and he tends to create, with varying degrees of abstraction, big, colourful, vibrant paintings with objects and shapes which emerge from thickly applied layers of paint. His individualism and single-mindedness, though, have often brought him into conflict with the commercial side of art and he has probably not profited as much from his work as he should have. However, Cook is a painter who works because he has to. His art is inseparable from who he is, unavoidably his reason for being.

Although he has always returned to the city, he does not see himself as a Dundee painter, rather as a painter who happens to have spent a fair amount of his life in Dundee. His attitude to the place is pragmatic. 'It's cheap to live here and I've got a close-knit group of friends who've always been supportive.'

With a highly singular approach, Cook believes that his best work lies before him. His suspicion of group work, though, would probably be challenged by many young artists working in the city today. Two new groups have been set up recently which have sought to bring contemporary visual art to the people of Dundee in a bold and imaginative way. Generator and Unit 13 have emerged over the past couple of years and made a big impact with their unconventional methods of presenting artwork.

Unit 13 has predominantly been concerned with showing local artists' work in such diverse locations as a nightclub, a supermarket and Dundee University's botanical gardens. With a mixture of visual, sound, dance, written, performance and experimental art, Unit 13 is keen to take art out of the gallery and present it in more unusual and challenging locations. Their exhibitions in the Produce Direct supermarket and botanical gardens were particularly successful, attracting considerable coverage in the national media. 'Checkout', their supermarket exhibition, brought art to the public in a way which, on the one hand, they could not ignore and, on the other, they could enjoy without the self-conscious inhibition people sometimes feel in art galleries. Tony Nolan of the group feels that 'People are often suspicious of contemporary art. Hopefully with exhibitions like "Checkout" we can break down that suspicion.' Douglas Philips, owner of Produce Direct, agrees. 'I think most of our customers were amused and stimulated and it was complementary to their shopping.'

Generator has been in existence since 1996 and is based in premises between the Rep and Dundee University, a stone's throw from DCA. The emergence of such a group is indicative of the changes that have taken place recently in Dundee. As Caishlan Herd of the group explains, 'Generator arose out of the need for artists in Dundee to feel comparable with those in other cities in Scotland by having a group which is not part of any establishment or institution.' With ambitions to open their own gallery and artists' studios already in place, the group has also been involved in the kind of exhibitions never before seen in Dundee. 'Radar', which took place in the summer of 1998, was a truly international show, pulling in contemporary work from around the globe and showing it in the atmospheric setting of an old warehouse in the Blackness area of the city. Significantly, though, it gave Dundee artists the chance to exhibit alongside international ones. Local collaborators Lorna Bryson and Willie Clark took this chance to present their intriguing and spectacular mixture of electricity and alchemy within the context of an international art show. It certainly did not look out of place as it sparked through the ghostly gloom of the old warehouse.

Generator's success in attracting exciting new art work to Dundee was further illustrated in the week DCA opened, when they staged an exhibition called 'Fade Away and Radiate'. At a variety of locations in the city, a series of light-projection-based works were displayed in public places with the intention, once more, of taking art out of the gallery and directly to the people of Dundee. Generator took this opportunity to declare, 'Our role as an independent, artist-led organisation is increasingly important in Dundee, helping to sustain and encourage the production of contemporary art in the city.'

There is no doubt that the success of DCA will be measured not just by how it performs itself but by how much more is generated in the arts in the city as a whole. With the existence of groups such as Generator and Unit 13, things are certainly looking promising in terms of creating a hub of artistic activity to complement the established institutions.

With all the recent excitement surrounding the arts in Dundee it is sometimes easy to forget the city's already existent art heritage. The McManus Galleries house and store one of the biggest art collections in the country, from European and English art to key Scottish painters such as Ramsay, Raeburn and Scott Lauder. With its numerous works by contemporary Scottish painters such as Bellany, Will Maclean, McIntosh Patrick, Morrocco and McLure and its stunning collection of fine art photography, it certainly contradicts the sometimes fusty image of municipal art galleries.

Much of the development of the McManus in recent years is due to the vision and enthusiasm of Clara Young, who works for the city council's arts and heritage department. 'When I came here in 1980 we had three galleries devoted to European old masters and eighteenth- and nineteenth-century British art, yet no permanent gallery for modern art. The first thing I did was to get the Scottish painters displayed. This was both nationalistic and contemporary.'

This enthusiasm for the new as well as respect for the old is a feature of the McManus and provides an excellent complement to the new arts centre. Already a part of DCA's inaugural exhibition, 'Prime' has become part of the McManus's permanent collection with Catherine Yass's spectacular photo-

Lochaber No More, *a scene familiar to millions worldwide who have ever purchased tins of Walkers' shortbread, but the original by John Blake MacDonald resides in Dundee (courtesy of Dundee Art Galleries and Museums)*

Disbanded *by John Pettie (courtesy of Dundee Art Galleries and Museums)*

A Lowland Church *by one of Scotland's favourite colourists, John Duncan Fergusson (courtesy of Dundee Art Galleries and Museums)*

graphic light-box depictions of the Tay Rail Bridge being purchased by the city. Clara Young, meanwhile, is confident that the McManus will continue to move with the times. 'We will be collecting a variety of works by contemporary Scottish artists, and DCA will be commissioning international artists to produce works in Dundee which may possibly become part of the collection.'

With DCA and the McManus in place, there's no doubt that Dundee has plenty to offer those who want to experience a range of visual art. And one mustn't forget the galleries which exist inside Duncan of Jordanstone, which are open to the public. These facilities, though, cannot operate in isolation if a truly lasting economic generation is to be achieved. Perhaps an indication of the future can be seen in a new independent gallery recently opened in the building which houses the Queen's Hotel, a few yards up the Nethergate from DCA. The Queen's Gallery is run by Joyce McGlone, and one of their first exhibitions exemplified the diverse and often forgotten range of work which has been going on in Dundee over the years. The late Ian 'Scoop' Bryson (1946–97) was an enigmatic and notoriously exhibition-shy painter whose work never reached the audience it should have while he was alive, and it was a great joy for those who were familiar with his work to see it brought to a wider audience.

It would be impractical to cite every notable artist who has emerged from Dundee, and no doubt excellent cases could be made for those who have been omitted. However, that only demonstrates the richness and diversity of art in the city today. The new arts centre has certainly put the focus on Dundee as it moves into the new millennium and a new era for itself. Andrea Stark, Dundee's chief arts and heritage officer, said on a radio programme broadcast just before the centre opened that she hoped it 'would be a landmark regionally, nationally and internationally but would be firmly rooted in Dundee'.

Let us hope that this ethos can be applied to the city itself and that its attempt to reinvent, regenerate and, most importantly, rejuvenate itself through the arts is successful.

City of Poets

Dundee's Literary Scene Explored

Carol Pope

If you want to take the pulse of a place, sample its current literature. Builders gauge a city's buoyancy by counting the tower cranes on its skyline, traders by calculating sales figures and property prices, but when it comes to the heart and soul, the very spirit of a place, statistics are sterile in comparison to the writing coming out of it. Poetry, novels, plays and stories uniquely capture the quirks and nuances, the strengths and frailties that characterise a city and make it throb with a life all its own.

Writers have the power to give voice to a city, to breathe life into its history, to revive and inspire citizens and visitors, to help them discover the rich layers beneath the High Street veneer. It's rare that they'll champion the pillars of the place – the bosses and the bureaucrats – but their alchemy can capture so much more, crystallising a city in incidents, characters and images for readers to hold up to the light like ancient insects caught in amber. James Kelman's Glasgow, Roddy Doyle's Dublin, Irvine Welsh's Leith, Ian Rankin's Edinburgh – these urban novels get under the skin of a place. Although it has produced some fine contemporary novelists, Dundee has not yet been the subject of such an urban novel, although with the first Dundee Book Prize winner poised for publication, that could come soon. Present-day Dundee, however, could be described as a city of poets, with claims to no fewer than four of the UK's 20 best young contemporary poets as named by the Poetry Society in 1994: John Burnside, W.N. Herbert, Kathleen Jamie and Don Paterson.

It is a measure of Dundee's growing confidence that the city is awakening to its most fertile literary period. In addition to the four poets named, Douglas Dunn, A.L. Kennedy and Kate Atkinson are among the 'glitterati' who have drawn on the City of Discovery for their inspiration over the last two decades. The year 1999 alone saw the publication of two new Dundee-based novels, by John Burnside and Whitbread Award winner Kate Atkinson, and a new collection from Don Paterson, as well as witnessing a rising poetry talent in

Dundee's famous four clockwise: John Burnside (courtesy of Gordon Douglas), W.N. Herbert (courtesy of Alex Black), Don Paterson (courtesy of Dundee Contemporary Arts) and Kathleen Jamie (courtesy of Phil Butler). A fifth of the UK's best contemporary poets are connected with Dundee

Rosamunde Pilcher, Dundee's international best-seller (courtesy of Hodder Headline)

Tracey Herd. All have called the place home, some more cheerfully than others, and accordingly given voice to 'their' Dundee.

These are the literary figures, but there is also a healthy layer of commercial or popular writers based in the environs including best-selling author Rosamunde Pilcher, whose back titles alone earn her an astonishing £4.4 million per year. Originally from Cornwall, she came north some 50 years ago as a young bride to join her husband, a company director involved in the jute industry. Best known for *The Shell Seekers*, Rosamunde Pilcher has developed her career from selling stories to magazines, through Mills and Boon romances to more serious fiction for women, drawing an international audience. Not one who enjoys public occasions, she lives quietly at Invergowrie with her family, including son Robin, who launched his own first novel in 1998.

More recently, locally based novelists Ann Swinfen and David Wishart have made their mark, Ann with a handful of outstandingly crafted works of evocative fiction. The fourth, *Mere Incidents of War*, came out in late summer 1999. David Wishart has used his knowledge as a Classics scholar to great effect in his fiction. His fictional autobiography of Virgil, *I, Virgil*, in 1995 put a new spin on the circumstances of the poet's death and led to a series of novels bringing to life ancient Greece and Rome. His latest is *The Horse Coin*, set in Roman Britain at the time of Boadicea. Work by well-respected writers such as James Meek and poets John Glenday, Margaret Gillies-Brown, Andrew Fox and Kate Armstrong, amongst others, also attract wide attention. And you cannot talk about writing and Dundee without mentioning the immortal stable of cartoon characters from D.C. Thomson, which over the last 60 years have become part of the fabric of Scottish childhood. Which one of us has not been touched by Oor Wullie, The Broons, The Bash Street Kids, Minnie the Minx or Dennis the Menace?

If Dundee has neglected its writers in the past, there is a growing recognition that now is the time to put that right. The city has grown sufficiently in stature, sophistication and resilience to value its poets, playwrights and authors on merit rather than fearing the content of their work. This was vividly demonstrated in 1996 by the reception accorded to Alan Spence for *On the Line*, his award-winning stage portrayal of the Timex dispute, a subject of immense sensitivity to the guardians of the City's image. It had taken many months of protracted persuasion to convince the board of the Dundee Rep Theatre that the play should be staged. When Spence tapped into that old workers-versus-bosses vein that throbs through Dundee's past life, drawing full houses and reviews in the national papers, there was a concerted civic fingering of the jugular. That the city leaders showed the constraint, the courage and the vision to congratulate a fine piece of drama rather than condemn the play for raising bad ghosts is a measure of how far Dundee has travelled in recent years. The second recent instance was the setting up of the £6,000 Dundee Book Prize for an unpublished novel set in the city by the City of Discovery Campaign and the University of Dundee. The winning book, *Tumulus* by Andrew Murray Scot, announced in April 1999, is to be published by Polygon.

For many years, virtually the only literary figures of any stature associated with Dundee were Reformation writers the Wedderburn brothers, whose plays and morality ballads were popular in the sixteenth century. Today they are unread and all but forgotten. Early literary references to Dundee have been almost uniformly unflattering. From his Mearns base, Louis Grassic Gibbon famously referred to habits of gin and infanticide. And Hugh MacDiarmid, who for some years edited the *Montrose Review* in nearby Angus, gave the city the literary blowtorch treatment, comparing it to Dante's Hell. But, to be fair, MacDiarmid was not a man for gentle words and praise from him was rare indeed. Charles Dickens might be regarded as one of the kindest since, after visiting on a reading tour, he described Dundee as 'an odd place . . . like Wapping', though he was less generous about its citizens, who failed to flock to his performances in the town. About the best that could be salvaged from this reputational wreckage was the suggestion that Mary Shelley had found some of the original inspiration for her *Frankenstein* on childhood visits to the city. The 'monstering' of the city was rife even then.

It could only have been compounded by the contributions of that 'incomer' from Edinburgh, William Topaz McGonagall. The self-styled 'poet' cuts a tragi-comic figure as much for his appalling verse as for his extraordinary self-belief in the teeth of all the evidence. Had he just been a doggerel-monger he might have carried it off as some early Pam Ayres incarnation. But it is McGonagall's self-certainty, his insistence on taking himself seriously that brings out the full spectrum of reactions in his audience. His long literary shadow has hung over the city like a curse down the years. No one, it seems, could talk or write about poetry or literature in Dundee without raising his ghost. He offered every tired hack the easy jibe, the cheap joke against the city. And it is ironic that while Dundee can claim several of the UK's leading contemporary poets, most Dundonians are quite unaware of the richness of their contribution. It is McGonagall, the King of Crass, who continues to be associated with the place and whose lines on the Silvery Tay are most often quoted in relation to the city.

Time then to exorcise the ghost? Not exorcise, perhaps, so much as subsume. McGonagall is a diversion which for too long has been allowed to take the eye off the main picture. His is a small, tartan and badly woven part of the Dundee literary tapestry which elsewhere is threaded with silver and gold.

The reactions of today's Dundee writers typify the extremes of feeling brought out by the tragi-comic figure. Douglas Dunn is passionate in his view: 'I detest McGonagall. I've never even seen him as a joke. I think he shows what is wrong with Scottish culture . . . making a monument out of a mediocrity.'

Don Paterson believes, semi-cynically, semi-seriously, that McGonagall set a great benchmark against which today's poets can only look good. 'I'm sure writers in other towns must be quite jealous of that. After all, it's impossible to be any worse than him.' Even so, he admits McGonagall has the capacity to infect the imagination. Indeed, the poem which gives its name to his second collection, *God's Gift to Women*, starts with a line from McGonagall, although it is one that might just as easily have been lifted from a Dundee street guide: 'Dundee, and the Magdalen Green'.

Kate Atkinson, mistress of the black comedy, feels quite defensively sorry for him: 'I like McGonagall, and why not? He was persistent and tried hard and he had a great belief in himself, which is a real gift for a writer.'

For Bill Herbert, McGonagall strikes a chord. And the chord has enough resonance to inspire poem after poem. What Herbert sees first is not McGonagall's doggerel but the reaction to it. He is appalled by the contempt shown by the public, the mocking and the open nastiness directed at McGonagall. But any suggestion that he sees in this an echo of his own early experiences as a poet in Dundee is quickly dismissed. Nevertheless, the bathos of McGonagall's situation has taken on such significance for Herbert that he has dedicated an entire book to him, *Cabaret MacGonagall* (*sic*).

John Burnside is uncomfortable about squandering too much attention on what he regards as essentially a 'shortbread-tin figure'. 'There's a kind of apologetic quality that says McGonagall wasn't that bad, or he was great, or

On the Line, *Alan Spence's award-winning stage portrayal of the Timex dispute (courtesy of Dundee Rep Theatre)*

he's really a bit of a hoot, isn't he? But if you start getting serious theses written on McGonagall this and that, it's definitely going too far.'

It is cheering to note that the city's rising poetry star at the end of the millennium, Tracey Herd, whose first collection, *No Hiding Place*, was published by Bloodaxe Books in 1996, has come through a Dundee upbringing almost unscathed by McGonagall. She claims never to have read his poetry and harbours no great interest in or feelings for or against him. There is a translucent quality to both Tracey and her poetry as if she flits invisibly through the city. Like John Burnside, her gaze focuses beyond the Tay, often beyond Scotland, to the worlds of the Romanovs, Eva Perón and Jacqueline Kennedy.

It is only now, at the end of the twentieth century, that Dundee is truly beginning to flower in a literary sense. But, it could be argued, the seeds of those blossoms were planted some 20 years ago. No doubt there have been many previous talents that failed to survive. What made this generation different? Maybe the seeds were particularly vigorous, or maybe the climate was right and the ground a little more receptive. One contributing factor seems to have been the establishment of the post of creative writing fellow at the University of Dundee in 1971. The introduction of a recognised literary figure to the local scene was a tonic to latent and budding talents. From some of the earliest days, particularly with poet Anne Stevenson, the standard was set. The list of succeeding fellows were gifted individuals, mostly poets, who had the capacity to inspire and nurture other writers. Somehow the university had a knack of selecting fellows on the rise, often just as their talent truly flourished. Most have maintained a connection with the university. According to the head of the department of English at the university, Dr David Robb, 'The result is that the post of creative writing fellow at Dundee is one of the most sought-after of its type. We have tried to foster and to draw strength from as many different sorts of writers from a variety of backgrounds as possible. It has been a genuine two-way process. We have been able to help a number of important writers at significant points in their careers. They have put Dundee in touch with the crosscurrents of contemporary writing in Britain and abroad. It has been a major success story.'

The early 1980s was a watershed period for writing in Dundee. Bill Herbert, Don Paterson and A.L. Kennedy were all living in the city and the university's creative writing fellow was poet Douglas Dunn. Brought up in Renfrew and Paisley, he had studied English at the University of Hull, where he later served as a librarian with poet Philip Larkin. In 1971 he became a freelance writer, continuing to live in Hull with his artist wife. He arrived in Dundee in 1981 at a time of tragedy in his life. His wife had recently died and he was not, by his own admission, in the best frame of mind. But a desire to return to Scotland had led to his taking up the post at the University of Dundee. He knew the place, of course, having given readings there in the past, and he went through the motions – seeing students, talking to writers' groups in the town and writing. It was while in Dundee that he composed the fine collection of *Elegies* in memory of his wife, and the city later featured in *Northlight*. Above all, it seems, it is the estuarial aspect of the place that appeals to Dunn.

It was a sad year for Dunn and perhaps a cathartic – if not a very comfortable – one. 'I was in a small rented flat in Roseangle. It had no curtains, was badly furnished and bloody cold.' He carefully describes Dundee today as a 'characterful place', drawing parallels with Hull. 'Both are built on estuaries, with road bridges and former whaling industries . . . I like the location of it, its views . . . the Scottishness of it.' Speaking of the city in 1999 from his position as head of English at the University of St Andrews across the water, one senses that his bond with the place, never strong, is increasingly distant. But he did find pleasure, and inspiration for some fine poems, while living there. 'I liked the long views, for example, from Dundee Law when you catch sight of little bits of Dundee you might not otherwise notice – like the small green patch next to the funeral parlour on Perth Road . . . And, particularly, the estuarial views – the sort you get when you're going into or leaving Dundee by train.'

It is the sort of view, in fact, that is captured in a poem from *Elegies*, published by Faber and Faber, which strikes a chord with so many Dundee writers.

LEAVING DUNDEE

A small blue window opens in the sky
As thunder rumbles somewhere over Fife.
Eight months of up-and-down – goodbye, goodbye –
Since I sat listening to the wild geese cry
Fanatic flightpaths up autumnal Tay,
Instinctive, mad for home – make way! make way!
Communal feathered scissors, cutting through
The grievous artifice that was my life,
I was alert again, and listening to
That wavering, invisible V-dart
Between two bridges. Now, in a moistened puff,
Flags hang on the chateau-stacked gables of
A 1980s expense account hotel,
A lost French fantasy, baronial.
From here, through trees, its Frenchness hurts my heart.
It slips into a library of times.
Like an eye on a watch, it looks at me.
And I am going home on Saturday
To my house, to sit at my desk of rhymes
Among familiar things of love, that love me.
Down there, over the green and the railway yards,
Across the broad, rain-misted, subtle Tay,
The road home trickles to a house, a door.
She spoke of what I might do 'afterwards'.
'Go, somewhere else.' I went north to Dundee.
Tomorrow I won't live here any more,
Nor leave alone. My love, say you'll come with me.

For Dunn, Dundee was essentially a station on the way back from somewhere and to somewhere else. He spent only a year there but his time coincided with the start of what we might now look back on as the first real literary stirrings in the city, and many of today's writers feel they owe him a debt.

One of these is Bill Herbert, who has probably written more than anyone else about his native Dundee. A writer with a razor-sharp mind and a soft voice, he still retains a hint of the local brogue in spite of many years of exile. Born in 1961 and raised in the city, first in the archetypal tenement, then in the 'multis', before his family moved to a bungalow in 'the Ferry', he left for Oxford University in 1979, where he gained a first and went on to pursue a PhD on Hugh MacDiarmid. In 1989 he founded a literary magazine, *Gairfish*, with co-editor Richard Price, which in one of its first issues published an essay by Dunn,

'Dundee Law considered as Mount Parnassus'.

Herbert keeps a complex relationship with the place. Sometimes he is its champion, sometimes its chief assailant. 'It's not that I dislike the place,' he says. 'Quite the contrary. I am obsessed with it. I stalk Dundee.' It is a love-hate relationship, he admits. The love is something born of familiarity as much as the simple pleasures afforded there. Ask him what he loves about the place and he'll talk about the coastline, the quality of the light, the architecture, taking his daughter to Broughty Castle and 'the wind that blows you half-way to Fife'. He'll mention lunch in an Italian café, the perfection of a tiny seaside bay, the bandstand at Magdalen Green and 'a wander through the pends and closes in the town'. He claims, 'You can define the city by its architecture and the gaps in that architecture. It's a strange mixture of old and new . . . a very particular fingerprint that in places has been stubbed out.'

The Poets' Box bookshop in the Overgate. c. 1920s. Lowden McCartney is at the door (courtesy of Dundee Art Galleries and Museums)

But Herbert drew too from the sounds of the place. His *Dundee Doldrums*, written during one week in the summer of 1982, was a turning point. Up until then he had been writing in English, as he describes in the foreword: 'The poems were written by going to the places they describe, sitting down and scribbling them out. As the week progressed, I found that my focus on sound was producing some odd effects. Very little of this was due to other voices: I tended to be either alone or given a wide berth . . . What I mean is the sounds, some clearly Dundonian, some more inarticulate, were apparently coming from an internal source.'

The other side of the coin has its root in his experiences in early-'80s Dundee and a deep-seated frustration with what he perceived as the city's lack of interest in culture. Aside from Dunn's influence, there was little support for literary talent. Dundonians turned their collective back and all but smothered the bright young sparks under a blanket of apathy. Herbert, however, was a survivor. He went on to establish himself as the leading Scots-language poet of his generation and for some years has been based at Newcastle. He still returns to Dundee to visit family and confesses he would be back to live if his wife could be persuaded . . .

The first verse of 'Seagull Blues' in *Cabaret MacGonagall*, published by Bloodaxe Books in 1996, gives a feel for Herbert's sensitivity to the Dundee sounds.

> *Well Eh luked up at grey gulls shriekan*
> *Eh luked doon at peopul speakan*
> *and Eh swerr therr wiz nae diffrence in thi soond*
> *as Eh daunnert thru thi streets*
> *lissnin til thi girns and greets*
> *O thi sowels that flew an waulked thru Dundee Toon*

Don Paterson believes Dunn's influence cannot be overestimated. 'He organised readings, encouraged young poets and brought big names into Dundee like Paul Muldoon.' The fact that Dunn drew on Dundee for his poems also had a profound influence on the young Paterson, who was at that time just flexing his writing muscles. Born in Dundee in 1963, he was brought up in St Mary's, attending Macalpine Primary and what is now Baldragon school in Kirkton before leaving at 16 to join D.C. Thomson as a comics sub-editor.

It's not a well-trodden path, *Commando* comic to Faber poet, but Don Paterson is not one for the usual routes. In 1993 he achieved every tyro's dream by having his first collection, *Nil Nil*, published by Faber. It hit the literary world with astonishing impact, since which time he has followed up with *God's Gift to Women* and collected an impressive collection of awards. He has left Dundee several times but is a regular

The poet William McGonagall, a tragi-comic figure, as painted by W.B. Lamond (courtesy of Dundee Art Galleries and Museums)

James Thin bookshop manager Gordon Dow surrounded by some of the prodigious output of Dundee's authors. According to him, 'Dundee can be proud of the number of writers and poets it produces. Their output forms an important part of our stock, and I'm very pleased to say that Dundee folk support local authors' (courtesy of Ian Jacobs/Scottish News Agency)

visitor and still regards the city as 'imaginatively the primal territory'. He explains, 'Most writers have an Oedipal thing with their mother city. Dundee is my "default mode". It is where, for example, I'm likely to set the action of a poem.' And, like as not, that action will take place in the landscape of his childhood: the derelict Newtyle–Dundee railway line, the Gellyburn, the Law Tunnel, a bus journey up the Hilltown . . .

Paterson claims that his relationship with Dundee has changed over the years. When he returned in 1993 after ten years away, he found it a different city. In an interview in *Scotland on Sunday*, he exclaimed with some surprise, 'There are things going on! I wouldn't go so far as to say there's a buzz, but there is something.' And in his spell as creative writing fellow at the university he added energetically to that 'something', encouraging writers' groups and organising regular readings with top names in the poetry world above Waterstone's bookshop. Since then, like most writers, he has been obliged to find a living where he can, in London or Edinburgh, although unlike most he has another string to his bow, in this case the guitar. He is also a professional musician with jazz band Lammas.

Asked for three adjectives to characterise 'his' Dundee, he hardly hesitates: 'Hellish, purgatorial and heavenly.' It's a well-rounded place, then.

Don Paterson's third collection, *The Eyes: A Version of Antonio Machadio*, was published by Faber in October 1999.

We leave him with a poem that vividly draws on his '60s boyhood:

BALDOVAN

Base Camp. Horizontal sleet. Two small boys
have raised the steel flag of the 20 terminus:
me and Ross Mudie are going up the Hilltown
for the first time ever on our own.
I'm weighing up my spending power: the shillings,
tanners, black pennies, florins with bald kings,
the cold blazonry of a half-crown, threepenny bits
like thick cogs, making them chank together in my pockets.
I plan to buy comics,
sweeties, and magic tricks.
However, I am obscurely worried, as usual,
over matters of procedure, the protocol of travel,
and keep asking Ross the same questions:
where we should sit, when to pull the bell, even
if we have enough money for the fare,
whispering, Are ye sure? Are ye sure?
I cannot know the little good it will do me;
the bus will let us down in another country
with the wrong streets and streets that suddenly forget
their names at crossroads or in building-sites
and where no one will have heard of the sweets we ask for
and the man will shake the coins from our fists onto the counter
and call for his wife to come through, come through and see this
and if we ever make it home again, the bus
will draw into the charred wreck of itself
and we will enter the land at the point we left off
only our voices sound funny and all the houses are gone
and the rain tastes like kelly and black waves fold in

very slowly at the foot of Macalpine Road
and our sisters and mothers are fifty years dead.

A third writer to emerge in Dundee around that time, and now regarded as one of Scotland's greatest literary talents, is A.L. Kennedy. An author of fierce intelligence and international standing, Kennedy is not one to dwell on her Dundee roots – but this is hardly surprising in one who famously chose to write under her initials in order to avoid being classified as a woman and a Scot. Born in the city in 1965 and brought up there, Kennedy's earliest experiments with writing took place in Dundee. In fact it was a story which she first read publicly there in the early '80s that brought her to the attention of the literary world. The public side of the literary path has never come easily to this complex and sensitive character. Well over a decade later, returning to Dundee as a celebrity to read from her novel *Original Bliss*, she vividly remembered that first public reading: 'It was embarrassing . . . it's still embarrassing, but this time I don't think I'm about to die. The people were nice – that's what you remember.'

While Kennedy could never be described as an urban novelist (her vision is widescreen, her subject matter universal), in a rare interview in 1998 on STV's *Artery* programme she explained Dundee's fundamental influence on her writing: 'Because it is somewhere that you grow up there are very, very deep images, very, very deep feelings which I'd be surprised if I don't eventually use.'

A different kind of novelist is Whitbread Award winner Kate Atkinson. While not a native of Dundee, she has spent more than a decade in the city, as a student – undergraduate and postgraduate – and as a lecturer at the university. And it is these student years in the early 1970s that she draws on for her latest novel, *Emotionally Weird*. The hero Bob, a student at Dundee University, lives in a tenement attic in Paton's Lane, 'former residence of Dundee's dreadful but noble-hearted poet William Topaz McGonagall'.

According to Kate, 'It's not really about Dundee, that's just the place where it happens. When you're writing a novel you choose a place that's either real or made up. With the first, *Behind the Scenes at the Museum*, I chose York because I knew it so well. With the second, *Human Croquet*, I wanted to make somewhere up. This takes place in Dundee because I suppose I spent most of my life in and out of Dundee University.'

How does she feel about the city? 'Like most people who have left I feel this enormous fondness for the place. Nobody outside it understands Dundee. It is the great forgotten city . . . It's the friendliest town I've ever lived in by a mile. But at the same time it has this very dark underside. I arrived in 1970 just after all the demolition and ruin. That's Dundee's greatest tragedy – to have been robbed of its architectural history. But one of the city's great characteristics is its

A.L. Kennedy, a new literary force bred in Dundee (courtesy of the University of Dundee)

Kate Atkinson with her prize-winning book (courtesy of The Scotsman*)*

resilience. Dundee has reinvented itself and that's a very brave thing to do. It has put the old jute days behind it very decisively now.'

She is enthusiastic about the new city centre, the imaginative use of public art and the opportunities being used to bring in great new modern architecture. 'I think it would make a fantastic film location . . . every time I go over the bridge my heart jumps. I think, "Oh, Dundee!" From the train you can see seals on the sandbanks and heron and hawk . . . it's an amazing place. I'm surprised it hasn't been used more.'

Award-winning poet John Burnside, who served three sessions as creative writing fellow from 1995 to 1998, is another who talks enthusiastically about the qualities of the city. He too has set his latest novel, *The Mercy Boys*, in Dundee. 'It's not about Dundee and it's not an urban novel. It crystallised because I was living here . . . because it seemed to me that the environment focused lots of issues.' Among these were what he refers to as the 'miracle side' to urban life. In a direct reaction against what he perceives as the current gritty formula for the Scottish urban novel with its preoccupation with drugs, violence and the working class, Burnside looked around him and saw something else. He saw, personified in Dundee, what he calls Scotland's 'key civic values' – education for all and medical achievement. It is a subject on which he grows passionate. It may sound absurd, he says, but he sees Dundee as a very proper city with a great sense of civic consciousness. Witness the Mills Observatory: 'There's no place like it. It's a great idea that somebody, because they wanted to share with the people the beauty of space, should have built this beautiful building.' So passionate is Burnside about the Mills Observatory that he wrote a scene around it for *The Mercy Boys* but in the end took it out 'because I was too much in love with the observatory'.

Ninewells is another manifestation of Dundee's 'miracle side', according to Burnside. 'For a city the size of Dundee, the achievements in the medical field are amazing. The idea of professional health care, and doing it properly and caring about it – it seems to me that these are the kind of things that are important about Scottish civic life, and they are embedded in Dundee.'

In the city itself he sees 'a kind of openness. Dundonians don't act as if they've got anything to lose . . . they have no airs or graces, no pretensions.' He recalls an incident on his first working day in Dundee. 'It was a horrible day in October. I was walking along the street when a woman looked up at me with a broad smile on her face and said, "Dreich day." She was so much enjoying the fact that it was a dreich day. Glaswegians and Dundonians both have that relishing of dreichness.'

That openness to which he refers is touched upon in Burnside's 'Dundee', published in *Dream State: The New Scottish Poets 1994*.

DUNDEE

The streets are waiting for a snow
that never falls:
too close to the water,
too muffled in the afterwarmth of jute,
the houses on Roseangle
opt for miraculous frosts
and the feeling of space that comes
in the gleam of day
when you step outside for the milk
or the morning post
and it seems as if a closeness in the mind
had opened and flowered:
the corners sudden and tender, the light immense,
the one who stands here proven after all.

As one who has kept a close relationship with the place, especially over the last few years, Burnside sees tremendous change and optimism. The essence of that new Dundee has yet to be captured by its writers. The corner will truly be turned for the city when the first poems, plays or novels emerge where its life sciences, design excellence or futuristic computer technology form part of the plot.

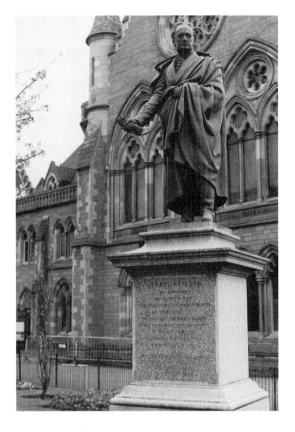

JAMES CARMICHAEL

ENGINEER

BORN 1776 DIED 1853

ERECTED 1876

Dundee statues

7

The Dundee Song
Popular Music in Dundee

Rob Adams

'Made in Dundee'. These words have famously gone across the world, on marmalade jars, on cash registers, even on the tarpaulin that covered the Prairie Schooners, or covered wagons, that took civilisation into America's Wild West. With less fanfare – we Dundonians are not the greatest blowers of our own trumpets – these same words have also travelled just as widely in connection with the Dundee song.

A song of many tunes and diverse styles, the Dundee song has been sung and played from folk club to jazz club, from Lochee church hall to Californian concert auditorium, and from the *Top of the Pops* television studio to a Mongolian village square. Its singers and players have rubbed shoulders with Kings of Swing and Rolling Stones, soul gurus and Eurythmics.

Sometimes, in Dundee, we didn't know the Dundee song was being sounded out there – even when 'out there' was no further away than darkest Broughty Ferry. But then, as well as being congenitally overmodest about Dundee's achievements, we've also been guilty of letting Dundee's prophets go without honour in their home town. I hold my own hand up on this charge with regard to Mary Brooksbank, the woman who arguably launched the Dundee song on its journey and who stands now as an inspiration to all those who wish to add their own versions of it.

There used to be a tea-time programme on Grampian Television on which local characters – war

Mary Brooksbank, originator of the Dundee song (courtesy of Dundee Art Galleries and Museums)

Sheena Wellington, who has taken the Dundee song to the Scottish folk scene
(courtesy of Michael Boyd/Scottish News Agency)

heroes, sportsmen and women, collectors of all sorts, people with almost any claim to fame – were interviewed about their lives. One night an elderly woman was introduced as a great songwriter, a description which, in my early teenage ignorance, I greeted with disdain. I'd seen great songwriters on TV before and they looked like Ray Davies of the Kinks, or the Beatles, or Bob Dylan, or my then latest discovery Joni Mitchell. This woman looked like somebody's granny.

As is often the way with these things, a blush-making realisation wasn't long in setting me straight: not only was Mary Brooksbank the writer of at least one classic song, the 'Jute Mill Song', but the things she wrote about and the simple, direct and honest way she wrote about them made her the Dundee equivalent of America's blues singers. Back-breaking, unrelenting, poorly rewarded work was as prevalent in the Dundee jute mills as it was in the Mississippi cotton fields and Mary Brooksbank's songs and poems recorded her fellow workers' experiences in the same way as her near-contemporaries Victoria Spivey and Maybelle Hillery had chronicled hardship in the American south. And although by the time of her TV appearance she may well have looked like somebody's granny, Brooksbank in her younger years had been a forerunner of 1960s protest singers like Joan Baez, and probably more fearless.

Brooksbank was actually born in Aberdeen in 1897, but the family moved to the Overgate in Dundee when she was eight. At the age of 11 she was discovered working underage as a shifter in the Baltic Mill and was sent back to school. On leaving school officially in 1911, she worked in the Craigie Mill, where the seeds of her 'Jute Mill Song' were sown:

Oh dear me, the mill's gaein' fest
The pair wee shifters canna get their rest
Shiftin' bobbins coorse an' fine
They fairly mak ye work fur yer ten an' nine

Brooksbank's musical protests didn't actually come to light until she had retired from the mills when, during a concert appearance in the city, radical folk singer and song collector Ewan MacColl requested songs about Dundee for his work-song series. Before that, her protests were of a more physical and very public nature. A Communist Party activist who founded the Working Women's Guild, Brooksbank served three terms, albeit short ones, in Perth prison for her part in Dundee street riots during the '20s and '30s. She gave up work in 1950 and wrote in secret until MacColl's intervention took the 'Jute Mill Song' and with it the Dundee shifters' lot to an international audience.

Although she died in 1978, Mary Brooksbank's name lives on in the local library, which was named after her. As well as through her songs and poems, her words live on in her books, including her autobiography *No Sae Lang Syne*, and in two plays whose titles directly quote the 'Jute Mill Song', the Dundee Rep productions *Coorse An' Fine* and *They Fairly Mak Ye Work*. (Few songs, surely, can claim to have spawned two plays out of a single chorus – and from consecutive lines at that!)

Dundee-born folk singers such as Sheena Wellington and Jim Reid have carried on Brooksbank's message in their own songs. Wellington, indeed, could also be said to possess the Brooksbank trait for speaking her mind. She is a staunch and very public advocate of Scotland's traditional songs and music – and, in her younger days, wasn't afraid of protesting. Her jousts with authority, however, cost her no more than a five-shilling fine following her arrest in Dunoon during the Polaris demonstrations of the early 1960s

Making music in Laing's Beer Garden

when she was still a pupil at Harris Academy.

Born in Lochee, Sheena was encouraged to sing at family gatherings and she won the Leng Medal, that holy grail of the Dundee Schools Music Festival, for her singing of Burns's 'The Winter It Is Past'. Her love of folk song, bolstered by her regular attendance at folk clubs and concerts in the city as a teenager, sustained her through her dozen years in the Women's Royal Naval Service (an odd choice for a former anti-Polaris demonstrator) when she would sing – proudly and in unadulterated Scots – for audiences in the south-west of England, where she was posted.

In 1989, by this time an established figure on the Scottish folk scene and the host of Radio Tay's weekly folk-music programme, Sheena toured America coast-to-coast. Playing sell-out concerts with singer-songwriter Dougie Maclean, she captivated the Americans with her warm, heartfelt singing, her genuine presentation and her songs of Scotland in general and Dundee and its environs in particular.

'Eh'll Bide a Wiver-o', a traditional weaver's song learned from her aunt Lydia, embodies much the same experiences as Brooksbank's writing, while Sheena's own 'Newport Braes' and 'The Dandy and The Beano and The Sunday Post' pay tribute, with varying degrees of reverence, to the 'Fifies' of fond memory and to Dundee's journalistic tradition.

These days Sheena, an adopted Fifer for many years, works with typical energy as Fife Council's Traditional Arts Officer. But as one of Scottish folk music's finest ambassadors, she is still in demand to sing all over the world, and since her first American visit she has added Nova Scotia, Barcelona and Singapore to her list of conquests, among others. Sheena was also asked to sing Robert Burns's 'A Man's a Man for A' That' at the opening of the new Scottish Parliament on 1 July 1999, an honour she was proud to accept.

Less doughty than Sheena Wellington, perhaps, Jim Reid is nonetheless a strong carrier of the Dundee song. A singer of disarming couthieness as well as an able mouth-organ player and piper, he got into folk singing, appropriately enough for a singer whose group, the Shifters, were to help further popularise Brooksbank's 'Jute Mill Song', through the trailblazing American group of the 1950s the Weavers. In the late 1960s and early 1970s Jim sang with the Taysiders, a popular group in the Clancy Brothers mould, before a move to Arbroath led to him joining the house band of his new local, the Foundry Bar Band. Their dance tunes and general knees-ups in many ways anticipated the ceilidh-band boom of the late 1980s and 1990s.

Although he obviously feels at home with his Foundry Bar chums and his other group, the ceilidh band An Teallach, it's during his solo performances, when accompanied by his simple guitar playing and his trusty 'moothie', that Jim really shines. He doesn't so much sing as simply give his audiences a song.

The artful blowing of Jimmy Deuchar

His settings of Angus poet Violet Jacob's poems, particularly 'Wild Geese', and his own songs about the Dundee he remembers, such as 'Catherine Street' – with its sideways swipe at Dundee's favourite by-product, the car park – can draw an emotional response from people who have never even been to Scotland.

A great admirer of the late Belle Stewart, singer, maker, song collector and matriarch of the world-renowned travelling family from Blairgowrie, Jim was honoured to step in for Belle at short notice in 1988 at a festival at the Pine Trees music camp in Massachusetts, where his contributions of daily song and piping workshops and nightly concerts won him many friends. He is also well thought of in Denmark, through his appearances at the massive Tonder Folk Festival, and in Ireland, following his many visits to folk events there. Yet if you stopped the average person in Dundee High Street and asked about Jim Reid the folk singer, the response would almost certainly be, 'Who?'

The never-a-prophet – or, indeed, profit – in-your-home-town syndrome has afflicted jazz musicians as well as folk singers in Dundee. The trumpeter and flugelhorn player Jimmy Deuchar was a musician of world class. Born in

Allan Neave

Dundee in 1930, he moved to London aged 20 and soon found work with the Johnny Dankworth Seven, then the Jack Parnell Orchestra. In the 1950s he toured the USA with the bands of American vibraphonist Lionel Hampton and saxophonist Ronnie Scott, owner of the famous Soho jazz club. Deuchar's playing alongside Scott in the Jazz Couriers in the 1950s and with the brilliant saxophonist and vibes player Tubby Hayes's 1960s quintet was still glowingly inventive when it made the transfer to CD in the mid-1990s. As an arranger, too, for the Radio Orchestra in Cologne and for the blistering Kenny Clarke/Francy Boland big band of the late 1960s, he was spoken of in awe.

Stories about Deuchar sketching out highly involved arrangements on the back of cigarette packets while travelling to gigs aboard the band bus may or may not be apocryphal. This is, though, the man whom Rolling Stone Charlie Watts enlisted as arranger and trumpeter when he put together his extracurricular big band to tour America during a break from the Stones in the mid-1980s.

One story that verifies Deuchar's musical standing is certainly true. It happened after he'd moved back to Dundee in the early '70s. In those days Deuchar had a regular Sunday lunchtime gig in the Sands nightclub on Broughty Ferry beach, and one Sunday an American gentleman, in town on oil business, came in to hear the music. Noting the sparse attendance, he remarked that Dundonians were lucky indeed to have such a musician as Deuchar in their midst. Did people round here not realise, he asked, how good this guy was? The American, when he sat down to play during the interval, proved to be a fine

The Average White Band (courtesy of Alistair Brodie collection)

pianist himself, although he pooh-poohed all compliments by saying that his sons were the real musicians in his family. His sons turned out to be Randy and Michael Brecker, two of the greatest jazz musicians of their generation who between them have played with everybody from Charles Mingus to Yoko Ono and from Frank Sinatra to Steely Dan. So their father, Bob, knew a good musician when he heard one!

The connection between a Deuchar trumpet solo and Mary Brooksbank may be difficult to draw, but in his own way, particularly on flugelhorn, Deuchar was undoubtedly, like Brooksbank, a poet. And although his chosen art form has its roots in America, when he died in 1993 he left behind at least one celebration of his home town which had travelled with him to concerts and gigs as far afield as Hong Kong, a composition which managed the remarkable feat of romanticising a local waterway which has long been infested with discarded shopping trolleys, old prams and other jetsam, 'Moonlight on the Dichty'.

Jimmy Deuchar wasn't the only top-quality jazz trumpeter to have come out of Dundee. (Indeed, nor does the trumpet hold a franchise on Dundonians' jazz creativity, violinist Nobby Clarke and accordionist John Huband both being examples of musicians whose public appreciation, or maybe just their ambitions, languished some way behind their talents.) John McLevy, whom jazz authority Digby Fairweather has described as 'a jazz original in any language' and whose cousin Harry was a well-known trade-union organiser in Dundee, has enjoyed a similarly illustrious career to Deuchar. Having featured in clarinet Swing King Benny Goodman's British big band in 1970, McLevy then toured Europe – on the recommendation of leading American trumpeter Bobby Hackett – with Goodman's smaller group, which included such jazz legends as pianist Hank Jones, bassist Slam Stewart, guitarist Bucky Pizzarelli and trombonist George Masso. As a session player on the London scene, McLevy has also recorded some 21 albums with singer/comedian Max Bygraves – but we can overlook that in favour of his representing Dundee at major European jazz festivals such as Nice and for his enduring partnership with the brilliant accordionist Jack Emblow.

Whereas Deuchar and McLevy could be said to represent jazz musicians who just happen to have come from Dundee, the music of drummer Ken Hyder could only have been born of a Dundonian. The often uncompromising blend of pipe tunes, muckle sangs and the free jazz expression pioneered by Americans such as Albert Ayler, as performed by Hyder's band Talisker, took its root from Hyder's theory that, since the *ceol mhor* (or 'big music') of the bagpipe, pibroch, was based on improvisation, jazz was, at least partly, a Scottish invention. A record deal with Virgin Records' Caroline imprint in the mid-1970s didn't prevent Hyder from taking a fair bit of ribbing for this assertion. Yet the proliferation of folk/jazz fusion groups during the 1990s – among them Lammas, the brainchild of another Dundonian and former Talisker member, guitarist Don Paterson – could be seen as proof that Hyder's ideas weren't as far-fetched as his detractors claimed.

By that time, however, Hyder had incorporated another folk-music strain into his music. Into the saxophone macmaelstroms powered by drum rhythms that Mary Brooksbank might just have recognised from her jute mill days came Mongolian throat singing, an art form that wouldn't have got many repeat bookings on the Dundee club scene but one which earned Hyder great acclaim in the throat-singing capital of Tuva.

A guitarist whose inventive playing has won him the respect of at least one of his heroes, Oregon's Ralph Towner, Don Paterson and his musical partner,

Talented and tragic, the late Billy MacKenzie, pictured with Naomi Campbell (courtesy of Alan MacKenzie)

saxophonist Tim Garland, took a more overtly melodic, less uncompromising approach to the folk/jazz synthesis. Through Lammas, Paterson introduced audiences across Europe to a highly individual take on 'The Road and the Miles to Dundee' as well as giving them musical impressions of Tayside localities such as the Dundee–Newtyle railway and Oathlaw and teaching them expressions like 'Skitters', which is a much better tune than its name might imply.

Paterson is also an acclaimed poet. His *Nil Nil*, with its tangerine-and-black cover confirming on which side of Tannadice Street his football allegiances lie, won the Forward Prize for the best first collection of 1993. He comes from a generation of Dundonians which has also produced the much-lauded classical guitarist and founder of the burgeoning Dundee Guitar Festival Allan Neave, and the classically trained accordionist and maverick composer Gordon MacPherson. It is a Dundee musical triumvirate to look out for in the twenty-first century, for sure.

While the achievements of folk singers and jazz musicians may go largely unnoticed, a feature which is by no means restricted to Dundee, Dundonians are generally strong in their support of local bands who swim in music's mainstream. Indeed, in Dundee, the traditional Scottish put-down of 'kent his faither' for those who have made it by moving away can just as easily be a boast.

Ricky Ross performing at Tay Square, 1997 (courtesy of David Martin/Fotopress)

The sense of pride among local musicians and music fans alike that greeted the Average White Band's massive success in America in 1974 – one of the music business's most audacious examples of taking coals to Newcastle – was almost palpable.

There had been Dundee connections with chart bands before, the late Jim Kelly with Honeybus ('I Can't Let Maggie Go') and Johnny Lynch in Cupid's Inspiration ('Yesterday Has Gone') springing immediately to mind. In the Sleaz Band, made up of brothers Clark and Phil Robertson, Jimmy Ross and Jim Bodie, Dundee had a group whose hard-rockin' live show never quite translated into the chart recognition which their friends Nazareth and Deep Purple enjoyed and which had seemed inevitable following their immense popularity at gigs up and down the country.

But the Average White Band, who achieved the unusual feat of topping the American singles and album charts simultaneously, were a blazingly successful band whose very heart and soul was a product of the Dundee music scene. While Alan Gorrie (actually from Perth but an adopted Dundonian) fronted the band with great style alongside Glaswegian Hamish Stuart and the Dundee Horns, saxophonists Molly Duncan and Roger Ball, the groove, the drive and the undercurrent of rhythmical exuberance in the band's sweet soul music came from the magnificent drumming of Robbie MacIntosh. Even 25 years on, the quietly emphatic snare and floor-tom intro to the *White* album's 'Work to Do' can cause goosebumps in anticipation of MacIntosh's expert percussive flow and accentuations, not to mention Onnie MacIntyre's brilliantly concise guitar solo, which give the band's version of the Isley Brothers' song its compelling bounce. And the virtuosic skelpity skelp – a kind of meeting between Buddy Rich, American session drummer Steve Gadd and the pipe-band discipline that is the Dundee Boys' Brigade's contribution to rock music – of MacIntosh's drum break on the band's dance-floor hit 'Pick up the Pieces' remains one of the glories of vinyl history.

Tragically, MacIntosh died following a party to celebrate the *White* album's elevation to the US number one spot, having apparently refused to be sick after swallowing chemicals by mistake. After having worked so hard – the *White* album's producers, Atlantic Records legends Arif Mardin and Jerry Wexler, were notorious perfectionists – MacIntosh missed out on the success that his efforts over the previous three years had played such a major part in creating. Although small consolation to those he left behind, it is gratifying that the records sit at the heart of pre-Average White Band, as part of jazz/rock organist Brian Auger's Oblivion Express, were being snapped up and appreciated by a whole slew of new fans as part of the late-1990s Hammond Organ renaissance.

The Average White Band's authentic soul sound might have persuaded black American radio audiences that they were listening to a black American band, but 'Work to Do' held clear evidence of the group's origins. The resigned, wearisome chant of 'wurk, wurk . . . wurk, wurk' as they funked towards the song's coda represented a sentiment and a pronunciation with which Mary Brooksbank's shifters would have been only too familiar.

As the Average White Band rode the crest of their wave, according to some press items there appeared to have been a rhythm-and-blues influence in their music that, to the uninitiated, might have been confusing. In those rather trite 'meet the band' features, alongside favourite foods, colours and cars the members invariably spoke of wishing they were able 'to sing like Dougie Martin'. Record-company execs hoping to follow up on the band's popularity by trawling the catalogues for recordings of this mysterious figure to reissue, or checking with contacts to see if he was still around, would have had to look no further than the Cleppie Road, where Martin and his band Mafia were 'giein' it a' that' in the Ambassador at weekends.

A survivor from a time when Dundee had more bands than you could have shaken a rolled-up copy of the *Evenin' Tele* at and when every Dundee church hall seemed to throb with a youth-club dance on a Saturday, Martin is the epitome of the local boy who never quite made good – at least, not nearly as good as his talent deserved. With his gruff but tender vocals, honed in four generations of bands including the Mystery Men, Cleo's Mood and the Poor Souls, Martin has become a Dundee legend whose 'Rainy Night in Georgia' threatens to outBrook Brook Benton and whose 'Evenin'' carries all the lonesome desperation of Jimmy Witherspoon's original.

In light of the Average White Band's success and the Dundee connection, several record-company execs did, in fact, check out Mafia. Quite what was missing only the Big Ears of London's A&R land can tell, especially in the wonderfully self-contained trio edition where Gerry McGrath nailed the bass part and Donnie Coutts drummed superbly while all three sang like harmonising soul-fired linties.

As the 1970s headed towards the 1980s, a veritable platoon of Dundee hopefuls made the trek to London in search of the all-important record deal. Some would return disillusioned, others to refine or completely redefine their music. Others, such as Billy MacKenzie, bided their time, convinced that they had something special and that London would catch up with them sooner or later. To shoppers in his Crypt boutique, MacKenzie was the arbiter of style with his fingers on the fashion pulse. But when those fingers snapped to the beat and he exercised his vocal cords, he became one of the greatest soul singers Britain has produced.

MacKenzie and his songwriting partner, guitarist Alan Rankine, wrote 'Party Fears Two' five years before it became a massive hit in 1982, transforming the Associates from cult band to post-New Romantic pop stars whose ideas U2's Bono has subsequently admitted the Irish megaband ripped off. The MacKenzie story thereafter, however, is one of peaks and troughs, with the singer appearing to sabotage his own success by singing a different melody to his hit song 'Breakfast' on *Top of the Pops* and disappearing back to Dundee to roam the Sidlaw Hills with his beloved whippets rather than take care of musical business.

Collaborations with electro-poppers Yello and Eurythmics' Annie Lennox failed to sustain MacKenzie's interest in his own career and he was declared bankrupt in 1995. Ironically, by this time he had begun working with his friend and fellow Dundonian, keyboardist Steve Aungle, and, as evidenced by the 40 songs they co-wrote in their final three years together, he was beginning to regain his appetite for music. However, unable to accept his mother's death from cancer six months earlier, MacKenzie committed suicide in January 1997.

At the same time as MacKenzie and Rankine had been devising the Associates in London, in his Dundee bedroom Ricky Ross was developing the songwriting skills that would result in his leading the Glasgow band Deacon Blue to massive chart success with songs like 'Fergus Sings the Blues'. Word was also emanating from Dundee's first proper recording studio in the Seagate of a

Danny Wilson in the studio (courtesy of David Martin/Fotopress)

17-year-old laddie with more talent than 17-year-old laddies were legally entitled to, Gary Clark.

Whereas Deacon Blue only appropriated their name from a Steely Dan song ('Deacon Blues' from the Dan's *Aja* album), on his emergence on to a stage following his first Seagate sessions, Clark seemed to have acquired the Steely Dan sound of sophisticated chord changes, classy tunes, oblique lyrics, blistering yet intelligent guitar solos – the lot. On an early support gig, his band Clark's Commandos, a name which lent sensible shoes an unlikely rock'n'roll credibility, impressed no less an authority than the father of British blues, Alexis Korner, and it seemed only a matter of time before a major record company confirmed Korner's assertion that 'this guy has it'.

As it turned out, it took quite a long time and a lot of frustrating trips up the music business's blind alleys before Clark, his younger brother Kit and his schoolfriend and long-time bass guitarist Jed Grimes enjoyed success. Now known collectively as Danny Wilson, they finally reaped the rewards for years of woodshedding, poorly paid gigs and dire London flats with their hit 'Mary's Prayer' at the second time of asking in 1987. Further high-quality pop and rock songs were to be heard on the band's debut album, *Meet Danny Wilson*, but after completing another album, backed up with some excellent, well-received live dates in Britain, Europe and America, the trio went their separate ways – Kit Clark to another Dundee band, Swiss Family Orbison, Jed Grimes to studio ownership and session work with Eddi Reader, and Gary Clark to a solo career which began auspiciously with *Ten Short Songs About Love*. When last heard of, Clark was living and writing in Los Angeles with, one suspects, his definitive musical statement still ahead of him.

One of Gary Clark's early champions, offering him support gigs and music-business contacts, was the man who brings the Dundee song full circle, Michael Marra. In his evocations of local characters and vignettes, nobody brings Dundee – and some would argue Scotland – to three-dimensional musical life more clearly and more masterfully than Marra. And although his chosen subject matter might be perceived as parochial, even small time, nobody has taken the Dundee song to a wider audience (Marra's CV stretches to films, theatre productions and television drama) – or, it has to be said, through more unlikely mediums.

This writer can't be alone in finding priceless the idea of the curly-powed purveyor of anodyne pop, Leo Sayer, eulogising former Dundee United goalkeeper Hamish MacAlpine's ability to blooter the ba' from Tannadice into Invergowrie Bay. But by covering Marra's 'Hamish the Goalie', Sayer did just that. The fact that Sayer, Frankie Miller and Barbara Dickson, regular chart visitors of the '70s all, covered Marra's songs is more than a little ironic as, following his highly polished debut album *The Midas Touch*, the songs Marra was preparing, the very songs these artists covered, were deemed of no commercial potential.

Marra's retreat, following this rejection, into the Scottish psyche and into Scottish literature such as Louis Grassic Gibbon's *Scots Quair* (whence songs such as 'Monkey Hair' and 'Happed in Mist' from his second album, *Gaels Blue*, emanated) may have been seen as confirmation of his unsuitability for the music mainstream by London's music moguls. But it was the making of him as an idiosyncratic song stylist. Besides, if London couldn't hear that Marra's tribute to Dougie Martin, 'Julius', as seen through Martin's jealous dog's eyes and sung in Marra's trademark benign foggy growl, was a brilliant song, that was London's problem.

Marra's career path, from his days as a regular performer at Woodlands Folk Club in Broughty Ferry through the often irreverent rock of Skeets Bolivar to his position as one of Scotland's most respected songwriters, has often appeared haphazard. Yet from his earliest days as a performer there has always been a strong thread of song craft, as well as an appreciation of music in its widest sense, at his work's core, even in his contributions to the exploits of Dundee's patron saints of mayhem, St Andrew and the Woollen Mill. His ability to observe and encapsulate scenes and characters with the most concise, witty choice of words has won him an army of admirers which stretches across Europe and America and which includes Loudon Wainwright III, Billy Connolly and that most careful of song choosers, English folk diva June Tabor, who covered 'Happed in Mist' to stunning effect.

Michael Marra

Described variously as 'a poet in blue-suede shoes' and 'the Randy Newman of the north' due to his easy-rolling, Newmanesque, boogie-woogie piano style, Marra made the transition from solo performer on the music stage to team player in theatre productions such as Wildcat's *Border Warfare* with remarkable ease, although he has always likened singing to acting in that in order to do either well you have to be believable.

Some might argue that many of Marra's songs are not at all believable. Did General Ulysses S. Grant actually visit Dundee and proclaim its newly built but ultimately doomed railway marvel 'a mighty long bridge for a mighty little old town'? Did the legendary Dr John really play in Blairgowrie once? Of course they did. Marra's songs deal only in truth, at any cost – which may be why a co-writing project with Bjorn Ulvaeus of Abba broke down when Marra's hard-wrought lyrics and Ulvaeus's computer-corrected, market-driven music couldn't quite match up.

The search for truth and authenticity that Marra sees in all his favourite songwriters and strives for so painstakingly in his own work surely would have endeared him to Mary Brooksbank, whose working world Marra inhabited in the music he provided for Billy Kay's play *They Fairly Mak Ye Work* at Dundee Rep in 1986. Whether Brooksbank would have associated with Marra's depiction of the average Scot as the 'never nae bather fae me', room-tidying chiel in his song 'Hermless' is less certain.

But as the twentieth century drew to an end, 'Hermless' was still being widely touted as the putative national anthem for an independent Scotland. The Dundee song – at least, one of its many guises – as Scotland's national anthem? Now that would be something for Dundonians to shout about – in our own quiet way, of course.

*Dundee is unique in having two football grounds in the same street, Dens Park and Tannadice
(courtesy of D.C. Thomson and Co. Ltd)*

8

With Style, Courage and Fair Play
Dundee's Sporting Life

Sandy McGregor

In a land about as far removed from Dundee as it's possible to be, and at a time when most Dundonians were sound asleep, a slim, crew-cut 21-year-old put himself and his home town on the sporting map in a way unparalleled before or since.

Yet up to that moment on 1 December 1956, most of those back home had never even heard of him. Dick McTaggart, a tenement lad from Dens Road, had joined the RAF a few years earlier and was a corporal butcher. He was also an amateur boxer, and that day, in far-off Melbourne, Australia, he became a legend. By outpointing Harry Krurschat, the German champion of Europe, McTaggart became Olympic lightweight champion, an astonishing feat for someone who had practically no international boxing experience and had never won a national title before, or even boxed for Scotland. More was to follow. At the conclusion of the Melbourne Olympics boxing finals, McTaggart was again called to the rostrum, this time to receive the Val Barker trophy awarded to the most stylish boxer at the Games. It was the first time a European had won the trophy and was something not achieved even by Floyd Patterson or Cassius Clay (later to become Muhammad Ali), who went on to become professional heavyweight champions of the world.

Back in Dundee that winter morning, news of McTaggart's awards began to filter through to the awakening population. Among the first to hear were the newspaper offices, and a reporter from *The Evening Telegraph* was immediately despatched to interview the new champion's mother, who promptly burst into tears when told of her son's achievements. (Mrs McTaggart herself almost qualified for the record books, in her time giving birth to 18 children!)

When the triumphant Dick returned home two weeks later, thousands turned out to greet him off the London train and he was carried shoulder high from the railway station to a waiting open-top vintage car. Then, led by a pipe band, the procession wound its way through town to Dick's house, which was bedecked with 500 flags, where hundreds more had gathered to welcome him home.

Dick McTaggart in action (courtesy of D.C. Thomson and Co. Ltd)

Despite his destructive power in the ring, McTaggart was a mild-mannered, unassuming young man, and from that day forth Dundee took him to its heart as only Dundonians can. In a career that lasted another nine years, the elegant southpaw amassed a string of titles which was quite unprecedented, establishing himself as the greatest amateur boxer Britain had ever produced. His extraordinary achievements gave him Olympic gold and bronze medals, European gold, Commonwealth gold and bronze, five ABA titles, seven Scottish championships and four Imperial Service titles. By the time he hung up his gloves in 1965 he had taken part in 634 bouts, winning all but 24 of them, an astonishing feat considering his opponents numbered the very best in the world. His reputation, and his distinctive white boots, were known around the globe and the very thought of meeting him in the ring was enough to overawe even the bravest of fighters.

Although McTaggart's Olympic championship came suddenly and his other successes were so phenomenal that they were in that sense also unexpected, no one should really have been too surprised that the city had produced a boxer fit to take on the world, for in the years leading up to 1956 the noble art and the name Dundee had become almost synonymous. As in other industrial towns that had experienced high unemployment, proud young men took to the ring to feed their families and the city produced a succession of gutsy and talented pugilists who found fame in varying degrees.

In the early days most of the bouts took place in Premierland, a stadium operated by promoter George Grant, a city bookmaker, in a lane between Victoria Road and King Street, an area later occupied by the Ladywell Avenue housing complex. The first 'stadium' to bear the name was in fact a large marquee, which had seats around the ring and standing room behind. After the Second World War a more permanent construction, looking like an aircraft hangar, was built by Grant and remained in place until its demolition in 1972. Every boxer who was anyone in Scotland made an appearance in Premierland.

Dundee's own fighting sons, such as Mickey Summers, Jim Cowie, Mickey Malone, Jim Brady, Gilbert Johnston, brothers Norman and Freddie Tennant, Jockie Smith, Ken Shaw, Bobby Boland and Jimmy Croll, were only some of those who between them brought a string of titles to the city. Freddie Tennant probably epitomised the generation of professional boxers who were around in the poverty-stricken '30s – they didn't fight for glory but simply for the purses which would help to feed and clothe them. Tennant turned pro at the age of 15, making him not only the youngest but, at just five foot tall, also the smallest paid fighter in the country, and he went on to take part in an astonishing 1,000-plus contests. Tennant himself admitted that he never really kept count but reckoned it was in the region of 1,300, 'give or take a hundred or two either side'.

His first paid bout took place in a fairground boxing booth in Aberdeen. To get there the destitute youngster walked all the way from his home in Dundee, taking two days to complete the journey. He arrived only a few hours before the contest and despite his weary legs earned a draw. More importantly, he also earned ten shillings (50 pence in today's money). To the little Dundonian that was a king's ransom, and rather than waste any of it on transport, he tucked it in a pocket and walked home again!

Tennant never really got away from the booths during his long career, and as a fistic mercenary he was prepared to go anywhere if there was money on the table. Within weeks of his hike to Aberdeen he was on the road again, this time walking to Edinburgh for a purse of one pound. After 30 or so contests he wanted more security and pleaded to be taken on as a boxer with one of the boxing booths which toured the country. After some hesitation, because of his youth and his diminutive stature, the promoter hired him at the princely weekly wage of 15 shillings (75 pence) regardless of the number of fights he had. Sometimes he was in the ring as often as ten times a week, and on one memorable occasion at a fair in Nottingham he boxed 12 different opponents in a single day, starting at 10 a.m. and finishing at 11 p.m. By this time the battle-scarred Tennant was earning two pounds a week, plus 'nubbings' – the collection he made around the crowd with his cap after a bout. That day he was so busy boxing and collecting his nubbings that he didn't have time for a meal, surviving between bouts on snatched cups of tea. But it was all worth it. For his 13 hours of work he made ten pounds, perhaps a trivial sum for what he had done – but to Tennant it was a fabulous figure.

Eventually he tired of booth boxing and began seeking class opponents and the consequent higher purses. On one night in May 1933 Freddie Tennant stamped his name in the Scottish boxing history book by beating Benny Lynch, the little Glaswegian who was to become one of the greatest flyweights of all time. The contest took place in Glasgow and to get there the Dundee man once more chose to walk rather than spend his hard-earned cash on transport. However, he was lucky and managed to hitch a lift for most of the way. Tennant fought Lynch four more times after that but never beat him again; the best he could manage was to draw once.

The highlight of his career came at Dens Park in 1938 when he knocked out Abe Tweedie in the tenth round to lift the Scottish flyweight championship and a purse of fifteen pounds. A year later, at Dundee's ice rink, he lost the title to an 18-year-old from Glasgow, Jackie Paterson, who later won a world title and became another of Scotland's all-time greats. Ironically, that crushing defeat saw Tennant collect his biggest ever purse, ninety pounds. The tiny Dundonian might have been small in stature but he had one of the biggest hearts in the land, in and out of the ring.

Jim Brady, who was British Empire bantamweight champion from 1941 to 1945, entered boxing by mistake. As a 14-year-old he set off one evening to join the Boys' Brigade which met in Dudhope Castle but took a wrong turning and finished up in the room above, which was the home of Dundee Amateur Boxing Club. He was fascinated by what he saw and remained there for the rest of the night. Master Brady's poor sense of direction that night set him off on a path of fistic glory few in Scotland could emulate.

During a 180-fight professional career he fought the best in the business, including Benny Lynch, whom he met on four occasions, drawing once and losing the others. Unlike many of his contemporaries, Brady loved to train and could skip for hours on end, astonishing onlookers with his speed and grace with a rope. After turning professional at the age of 19, he left his job in a city jute mill and eventually found his way to London, where the most money was to be made.

Brady won the distinction of being the only Scotsman ever to fight for an English area title in Scotland. It happened after local promoter George Grant put up the most cash for the contest, and on a July evening in 1938 Brady KO'd Pat Palmer in the eighth round at Dens Park to take the title. Three years later, on New Year's Day in 1941, across the road at Tannadice Park, he beat the tall, gangling Kid Tanner from British Guyana during a blizzard to win the British Empire crown. Coincidentally, he lost that title in much the same way as he won it – in the face of one of Mother Nature's uglier moods. This time it was in a thunderstorm at Hampden Park in a fight against Jackie Paterson when Brady was aged 33, long past the age for defending titles. But it wasn't his advancing years which beat him that night, it was the atrocious conditions. The contest started in heavy rain and the weather worsened as the bout progressed. By the half-way stage the ring had been transformed into a pond and the 28,000 crowd scuttled for cover as lightning flashed across the sky. Brady, the nimble-footed bobber and weaver who liked to hit and run, was slowed down by the inches of

Freddie and Norman Tennant, the only brothers ever to hold the Scottish title. Both were Scottish flyweight champions (courtesy of D.C. Thomson and Co. Ltd)

water around his feet and never really struck form and Paterson, who had years earlier taken Freddie Tennant's title, won on points to take another Dundonian's proud crown.

Brady became a newsagent in the city after hanging up his well-travelled gloves and later returned to amateur boxing as a coach back at Dudhope Castle.

McTaggart's stunning success inevitably eclipsed the efforts of every other amateur boxer to come out of Dundee, but others, like Frank McQuillan, who won a Commonwealth silver medal at the Games in Vancouver, also made their mark. McTaggart and McQuillan were products of Dundee Amateur Boxing Club based in Dudhope Castle, where they were trained by Frankie Quinn, but across town at the Hawkhill club in Park Place, others were carving their own brand of fistic glory. Headed by Dennis Gilfeather senior, the club produced a steady stream of top contenders, including the stylish sons of Gilfeather, Danny (later to become a bit-part TV and film actor in London), Dennis junior and Frank. Their Scottish heavyweight champion Jock McVicar put himself into the spotlight for two reasons: he was lighter on his feet than most flyweights, gliding around the ring like a broken-nosed ballerina, and he was also banned from boxing for life for hitting the wrong person. Ironically, that happened when the city put on its greatest ever celebration of amateur boxing with a tournament in the Caird Hall sponsored by *The Courier* to mark McTaggart's Olympic victory.

Staged within a month of his return from Melbourne, and with the great man himself topping the bill, 2,500 people packed the hall to see the finest unpaid boxers in the country. McVicar was among those on the programme and for reasons never fully understood he took it into his head during his bout to punch the referee, the unfortunate Willie Mason from Perth, himself something of an exhibitionist. The life ban remained in place for some time but was eventually lifted, and McVicar went on to form his own club.

'Wild' Bill Bannon, a light-heavyweight, was without doubt the most fearsome boxer of his generation, renowned not for his skill but for his ability to shrug off the hardest of blows and plough on, head down, teeth bared, regardless. In training he once hit the heavy bag so hard that he burst a hole in it. Completely oblivious to the sawdust pouring from its innards, he continued to rain blows on it and only stopped after being dragged away by his trainer. A coalman in his day job, Bannon was reputed to have once carried a settee half-way across town on his back to save removal costs.

His crowning achievement in the ring came during the Commonwealth Games in Wales when he faced the captain of the English team, Joe Leeming, a blond Adonis with film-star looks and a physique to match. The much taller Leeming was tipped for the gold medal and the bout in the quarter-final against Bannon seemed little more than a formality. The Beauty versus the Beast encounter lasted less than two rounds. Unleashed from his corner, Bannon sprang immediately into the fray and shrugged off everything his stylish opponent could produce. Then he delivered a mighty up-and-over haymaker left hand that everyone in the hall – except Leeming – saw coming. The Englishman dropped like a stone, rose at the count of nine, then moments later hit the canvas again after another telegraphed left from Bannon. Leeming struggled to his feet and was still trying to come to his senses when the round ended. His respite was short-lived. Immediately after the restart Bannon laid into him with another succession of windmill blows and sent him crashing to the deck once more. Somehow Leeming beat the count but when he was put down for the fourth time seconds later the referee stepped in and ended the contest. The folk in Dundee lucky enough to own a TV set at that time went delirious at the greatest upset of the Games, which gave Bannon an unexpected but well-deserved bronze medal.

Amateur boxing maintained its popularity for a number of years after the McTaggart era ended but gradually went into decline as young men looked for softer options as hobbies. The sawdust-and-sweat nights in darkened halls gave way to boxing dinners in plush hotels where dinner-jacketed businessmen enjoyed expensive meals and drinks while watching young gladiators battle it out. These types of bouts weren't to everyone's taste and took boxing away from the ordinary fan, who couldn't afford the high cost of a place at the table, but there is little doubt that without them the sport might eventually have vanished without trace. The man who introduced these types of events to the city was Frank Hendry of St Francis Boxing Club, under whose banner the boxing dinners were staged. Hendry rose to become a powerful figure in the sport and as the president of the Scottish Amateur Boxing Association for many years officiated at major championships throughout the world. His style didn't please everyone, however, and his opponents formed a breakaway association. Not for the first time in amateur boxing circles was there just as much fighting going on outside the ring as in!

Although McTaggart left Dundee a few years after his magnificent triumph to live in the west of Scotland, his name lives on in the McTaggart Centre, the council-owned sports centre in the north of the city. A similar tribute was paid to the Lynch brothers, Ned, Andy and John, who founded Lochee Boys'

Jim Brady, who began his 180-fight professional boxing career by mistake (courtesy of D.C. Thomson and Co. Ltd)

Club and introduced scores of youngsters to boxing, football and gymnastics.

It took more than 30 years before any other Dundonian came even close to emulating the achievements of Dick McTaggart, and when it happened it couldn't have been more unexpected. From a town with absolutely no pedigree in athletics, a little slip of a lass exploded from nowhere on to the nation's running tracks, beating all who came her way. Liz Lynch, later to become Liz McColgan, didn't know a thing about boxing, but she turned out to be one of the greatest fighters Dundee ever produced.

Like McTaggart, she came from humble origins. A product of the uncompromising Whitfield estate, she went into the jute mills after leaving St Saviour's High School, but that was simply what she did when she wasn't running. She had been obsessed with running from her early teens, and it was an obsession which would ultimately lead to enormous glory and riches for the slightly built mill girl.

Her life changed for ever on the evening of 21 December 1982 when she received a telephone call from Bob Woods, a recruiting officer for Ricks College in Idaho, who, after explaining how impressed he was with her rankings in British junior athletics, said he wanted to offer her a scholarship to enrol at the Mormon college, where she would train with other young athletes while undertaking a course in business studies. The 18-year-old McColgan declined, saying she didn't know anyone in America and had never been away from home before. Woods called back on the next two nights with the same offer and received the same emphatic response – 'Thanks, but no thanks.' After the third call Woods phoned McColgan's coach, Harry Bennett, who managed to persuade her father that it was too good an opportunity to miss, and finally McColgan accepted.

That created an immediate problem – how could she find the £1,200 required for return air fares and new clothes? As she was by then, like her father, unemployed, it seemed an impossible figure. When her plight became known, friends and clubmates at Hawkhill Harriers rallied round and a series of raffles, jumble sales and other donations from well-wishers raised the cash. She was on her way, and in more senses than one.

Within months of her arrival the single-minded McColgan had established herself as one of the college's brightest stars and began setting new State middle-distance records. After two years she was emerging as a major force in American college athletics when it suddenly all went sour. She accepted $3,000 for taking part in a race and a row raged for weeks about whether her amateur status had been infringed. In British terms it hadn't. The money had gone into her trust fund and she had broken no rules. But she had violated US college regulations and had effectively ended her career in their events. She returned home wiser but richer. It was to be just the first of a number of controversies involving money which were to surround her in the years ahead.

Most people in Scotland first became aware of McColgan in 1986 when, overnight, she became the nation's pin-up after storming round and round the track at the Commonwealth Games in Edinburgh to win the gold medal in the 10,000 metres, setting Scottish, British and Commonwealth records in the process. The TV pictures of her running into the outstretched arms of her father at the trackside immediately after her win were one of the indelible images of the Games, and Dundee's heart swelled with pride at her achievement.

Within a year of that memorable day in Edinburgh she had amassed more money than she had thought she would see in a lifetime. In two races alone, held within days of each other in Bali and Florida, she picked up £40,000. Apart from the winner's cheques she was collecting, she was also able to command high appearance fees and commercial firms were queuing up for her to endorse their products.

Nothing stood in the way of her career. With a single-mindedness that didn't always endear her to those she came into contact with, she mercilessly ground out the miles day after day, sometimes clocking up more than a hundred miles in a single week. She ran on the morning of her wedding and she ran again on the morning of the following day. Then she went on honeymoon to America and won £25,000 in two races there. All the time she was setting new records for events around the globe.

McColgan seemed destined to follow McTaggart and win Olympic gold, but in the end she had to settle for silver. She started as favourite in the 10,000 metres in the 1988 Games in Seoul and led from the half-way stage. Just when the most treasured prize in sport seemed to be hers she was outkicked in the last lap by the diminutive Olga Bondarenko, a feisty Russian with just as much determination as the Dundonian, and try as she might she couldn't catch up. Many theories were advanced about why McColgan had been outclassed that day. Some said she had simply tried too hard by overtraining in the week leading up to the Olympic final, clocking 83 miles. Others argued, and not for the first time, that she was a single-pace runner, unable to respond to any fast finisher who could hang on to her to the final bend.

Whatever it was, it had nothing to do with courage. Even her detractors, and by this time there were a few, recognised her as the toughest on the track who never knew when she was beaten, and that was demonstrated in stunning fashion at the World Championships in Tokyo in 1991. In temperatures of 90 degrees McColgan ground out a sensational victory, totally pulverising the opposition. While she was in the process of doing so, BBC commentator Brendan Foster, himself a former world-class distance runner, said that, win or lose, it was the bravest run he'd ever seen by a British runner. Later, on air, he described it as 'the greatest performance by a male or female British athlete in the history of long-distance running'. Few who witnessed the ruthlessness with which she ignored the searing heat to demolish the finest runners in the world will disagree with him.

McColgan's personal fortunes, professional and financial, had never been better and later that year she turned to what many felt had been her true destiny in athletics – the marathon. For someone who was a glutton for mileage and who couldn't really produce a sprint finish, the event was made for her and she for it. It was, happily for the money-conscious former jute worker, also the event where the most cash could be made. Her first attempt at the distance was in the famous event through the avenues of New York in 1991. She won in a time of two hours, 27 minutes, 32 seconds – the world's fastest first-time marathon by a woman. She also won £25,000 and a £20,000 Mercedes, plus a secret bonus and appearance money.

More marathon successes – and more money – followed, but she never again came close to Olympic gold. In the Barcelona Games in 1992 she could manage

The loneliness of the long-distance runner: Dundee's own Liz McColgan outpaces Yvonne Murray (courtesy of D.C. Thomson and Co. Ltd)

only fifth in the 10,000 metres. But, just as after her defeat in Seoul, she bounced back and six months later won the world half-marathon title, becoming the only British athlete, male or female, to win two world titles.

Inevitably, the punishing routine of high training mileages week after week eventually took its toll and McColgan began suffering more and more injuries which took longer and longer to heal. At one point a surgeon announced that her athletics career was over, but with her usual obstinacy she ignored him and went on to compete at the highest level. Olympic gold, however, continued to elude her, and in the marathon at the Atlanta Games in 1996 she could do no better than finish in eighth place.

Later that year she won the London Marathon, an event which in itself made her one of the richest female British athletes of all time. Just for taking part on three occasions she was paid £500,000. No one apart from McColgan, and perhaps her accountant, will ever know for certain how much wealth her great talent and iron will brought her, but it is thought to be significantly more than £1 million. It gave her a lifestyle she could only have dreamed about when she stood as a teenager at one of the city's jute-mill looms earning £23 a week. Her home is a 14-room baronial mansion and she drives a sleek, expensive car with a personalised number plate.

But it all came at a cost. Her life from her early teens was utterly committed to her sport and she sacrificed the normal youthful pursuits of clubbing and parties for the endless grind of mile after mile churned out in training. The stubborn single-mindedness which was necessary to put her at the very top of women's athletics also cost her dear in personal relationships, and her path through running was littered with those she clashed head-on with or simply irritated.

One of her most public disputes was with her one-time coach John Anderson. It ended in a civil court action he raised against her to recover some £60,000 which he said she owed him as part of their contract, giving him 20 per cent of her earnings during their four years together. Another spat saw her fall out with her club, the Hawkhill Harriers, and ended with her bizarrely joining St Francis Sporting Club, which had no other runners, just boxers!

Comparisons between McTaggart and McColgan highlight strong parallels in certain areas but great distinctions in others. Both came from working-class backgrounds where there was little spare money. Both had unique talents in athletic ability, sharing courage and determination and never knowing when they were beaten. They each put Dundee on the world sporting map.

Beyond that, however, they were about as opposite as it's possible to be. McTaggart, the self-effacing quiet man, made virtually nothing in terms of hard cash out of his special gift, turning down £2,000 (a considerable sum at the time) to turn professional. He was liked by everyone and after retiring went on to coach others in his spare time, going back to the great international arenas of amateur boxing as a corner man for the Scottish team. McColgan, never short of confidence or a willingness to speak her mind, was variously described as arrogant, aloof and abrasive. Yet despite – or perhaps because of – these characteristics, she became the richest sportsperson ever to come out of Dundee. Those who criticised her for being too motivated by cash were a little ungenerous and should have asked themselves if they would have rejected the opportunity to make themselves and their family financially secure when the alternative might have been a career in the jute mills. Nor did they understand the psyche of the woman who above all else just loved to run. If she hadn't been getting paid, she would have done it anyway.

The city council made its own distinction between the two. They named a sports centre after McTaggart but did not honour McColgan in the same way. That probably didn't rankle very much with the runner, but in any event she built her own with £600,000 out of her winnings. The Liz McColgan Health Club opened to paying customers in the summer of 1999.

Ironically, several thousand Dundonians had, somewhat bizarrely, decided to take on the toughest event in the entire programme of athletics several years before McColgan, with all her natural ability, got round to it. They had been part of the mad but marvellous craze that swept the nation in the early 1980s – the mass marathons, where no-hopers shared the roads with some of the finest athletes in the world.

Dundee got around to staging their first event of that kind in April 1983, when 1,343 of the most unlikely runners ever lined up in the city centre before embarking upon a 26.2-mile run stretching from one end of town to the other. Until a few months earlier, most of them had done nothing more strenuous than push a supermarket trolley on a Saturday afternoon. Suddenly they were trudging their neighbourhoods after dark, slowly getting fitter and boring their families and friends with stories of epic feats of endurance and vast distances covered.

It seemed that half of Dundee turned out to witness their madness in the race itself and on every corner there were rows of people willing them on with non-stop applause and a flow of encouraging shouts. Some of those in the crowd handed out sweets and lemonade, banners were held up for dad, people hung out of windows and music played on corners. Nobody, except the handful of real runners away up at the front, cared how long it took to get around. Just finishing was winning. One competitor, truly indifferent about record performances, stopped off to visit his mother in King's Cross Hospital when he was passing. Some of those lucky enough to live on the route went home for a cup of tea. Meanwhile, down in the High Street, the crowds were gathering in their thousands. They stood six deep on both sides, perched on the flower beds and standing on their tip-toes at the back. The crowds cheered and cheered and people who meant to stay for just half an hour were still there four hours later.

The official winner that day was Donald Macgregor, who had finished seventh in the marathon at the Munich Olympics. His winning time was two hours, 17 minutes, 34 seconds. The last person home that day took six and a half hours. People still lined the street to see him come shuffling home, and when he was presented with his finisher's medal he was every bit as proud as Don Macgregor, who by then was back home in St Andrews with his feet up. Remarkably, in between those two crossing the line, all but 30 of the courageous band who had started the race made the memorable journey along Nethergate to finish at City Square. Some were in fancy dress, some limped in and one crossed the line playing the bagpipes – but every one of them had a memory to last a lifetime.

Dundee staged another eight marathons after that, the highest number of entries being just over 4,000 in 1985, when snow fell before most of the competitors had finished. Organised by Dundee Sports Council, the events quickly gained a reputation for being among the friendliest and best-organised in the country. Other shorter races developed from the marathons and almost overnight the streets were full of joggers. It also gave the city an unexpected world-beater, for among those taking part in the events was a sprightly former local councillor in her 70s. Jenny Wood Allen beat the world age-group record for a septuagenarian with a remarkable time of four hours 21 minutes in the 1985 event. Long after most of her youthful contemporaries had given it all up, she was still competing in marathons and other distance races and became something of a national celebrity, particularly in the famous London marathon, which she took part in 13 times, the most recent in 1999 when aged 87. Most of her runs were for charity and altogether she raised in excess of £30,000 for worthwhile causes.

As the twentieth century drew to a close Dundee's two senior football clubs faced their greatest challenge – not on the park, but trying to compete on level terms with big-city clubs in a sport increasingly dominated by money. After 100 years of see-sawing fortunes which saw both clubs soar to the heights in the heady, glamorous arena of European competition, they found themselves wondering precisely how they would fare in the new millennium.

Sadly, what happened on a Saturday afternoon was no longer the final arbiter of whether Scotland's soccer clubs were judged as being truly successful. Beating the opposition was fine, but in reality meaningful achievement was a club keeping its head above the perilous financial waters they all swam in. Every club in the country save two faced the same agonising and unfamiliar ritual of trying to transform what began as a beautiful game into a viable business. The two best at it, and by definition those responsible for the heartaches of the

149

others, Rangers and Celtic, had marched ruthlessly through the closing decades of the century, grinding the opposition towards the bankruptcy courts, not always because of their superior tactics in competition but also because of the spending power of their vast legions of supporters. Inevitably, as Celtic and Rangers prospered, the others struggled, first to keep their stars, then on the park, and ultimately just to stay open for business.

After a series of ownership changes, some more controversial than others, the city's oldest club found itself staring extinction coldly in the eye in the closing months of the 1990s. Faced with the need to provide an all-seater stadium to meet the requirements of the Scottish Premier League and with insufficient funds with which to do it, the principal directors of Dundee FC, brothers Peter and James Marr, were said to have spoken to their counterparts at Dundee United in a conversation along the lines of 'Individually we might not survive but together we can'. The exact terms of the talks were never publicly disclosed and it was never revealed whether they were discussing the prospect of a full-blooded merger (or, more likely, a takeover by the Tannadice club) or a ground-sharing deal. In any event, both scenarios were swiftly ruled out, with first the Scottish Premier League declaring that every club in the SPL required its own ground, then the clubs announcing that there would be no merger.

Fans of both clubs were delighted. Common sense and financial logic, it seemed, should be ignored for the blind emotion of undivided loyalties. After flirting with the controversial idea of a sell-off of at least part of the club to a foreign investor but rejecting the proposition in the face of a hostile reaction from a large section of supporters, the Marrs set about finding the cash for the new stands by themselves. They did it within weeks of a deadline set by the Scottish Premier League, and the season taking football into the new millennium opened with the club proudly boasting a 10,000 all-seater stadium. Now, for the time being at least, there will be no unified Dundee City FC and the two clubs that uniquely share a street and the same love of a sport will defiantly fight the Glasgow giants separately.

How different it all was at the turn of the previous century. Dundee United, who ended the millennium as much the stronger financially of the two clubs, didn't even exist and Dundee, formed in 1893, had had it all their own way for 16 years until the Irish community in the city were successful in forming a new club which they called Dundee Hibs, renaming it Dundee United in 1923. As if to establish their superiority over their new rivals, Dundee lifted the Scottish Cup in 1910, the year after Dundee Hibs came into being. It was to be another 37 years before the team which had worn dark-blue shirts almost from their birth put themselves back into the record books, this time with amazing back-to-back 10–0 victories over first Alloa, then Dunfermline, in March 1947, a high-scoring best which has never been bettered by the club.

Arguments will always rage about who Dundee's most distinguished player was, for the criteria have never been set. Is it the player who scored the most goals, the one who played the most games, the one who was sold for the greatest amount of money or the one who played most often for his country? Can a defender or a goalkeeper ever be compared with a high-scoring forward?

Billy Steel, who joined the club from Derby County in 1950 for a fee of £23,000 (or '£11,500 for each leg', as Dundee fans always maintained), never really fulfilled any of these criteria, yet his mesmeric skill and ability to read a game were still topics of conversation in pubs more than 40 years after he left the club to try his luck in America just three years after going to Dens. Steel was not the most popular of men in the dressing-room but some of his team-mates are among those who think he was the greatest player ever to have turned out for the club. One member of the same side was another 'great', half-back Doug Cowie, who made a record 445 appearances for the club before bowing out in 1961. Both players were in the side which played Rangers in a Scottish Cup second-round tie at Dens Park in 1953 before 43,024 fans, still an attendance record for the club.

The most glorious chapter so far in the history of the club began in the 1961–62 season, when they won the Scottish League Championship for the first and only time with a team put together by Bob Shankly, arguably the best manager the club has ever had. The title race went to the last Saturday of the season and Muirton Park down the road at Perth was jammed with 26,500

Football in Dundee, a sport for all ages and both sexes

151

spectators to see Dundee trounce St Johnstone 3–0 and lift the championship. Their closest rivals that season were Rangers and on the way to the title Dundee thrashed them 5–1 at Ibrox, a result still considered by many to be among the most notable ever achieved by the Dark Blues. The scorers that day were two of the club's finest players, Alan Gilzean, who netted four times, and Andy Penman.

All who watched Dundee that season have their own memories of that wonderful run of victories, but one Dundonian who didn't see a single ball kicked has more reason than most to remember the occasion. He was born a short time after the title was won and his delirious father, a rabid fan, decided to name his new son after the entire championship-winning team: Liney, Hamilton, Cox, Seith, Ure, Wishart, Smith, Penman, Cousin, Gilzean and Robertson.

That championship win set the club up for a place in the European Cup the following season and in an incredible giant-killing sequence of wins they went all the way to the semi-final, going out to eventual winners AC Milan, whom they managed to beat at Dens Park in the second leg after going down 5–1 in the first game in Milan. On their way to the semis Dundee beat Sporting Lisbon, Anderlecht and favourites Cologne, whom they sensationally trounced 8–1 at Dens Park.

The club's marvellous performances in the early '60s naturally turned the spotlight on their players, and two of the championship-winning side went south to top English sides, Ian Ure to Arsenal for a fee of £62,500 and Alan Gilzean to Tottenham Hotspur for £72,500, at the time the highest transfer fee ever received by a Scottish club. Gilzean had enjoyed an outstanding goal-scoring run and in the 1963–64 season, just before his move to London, he scored a record 52 league goals. His most goals in a single game for the club was in December 1962 when he equalled Bert Juliussen's record by netting seven times against Queen of the South. 'Gillie' remains the Dark Blues' top scorer overall, with 163 goals in 181 games for the club.

That championship-winning side contained another record-breaker in left-back Alec Hamilton, who was also turning out for Scotland at that time. His total of 24 international jerseys between 1961 and 1965 is the most awarded to a Dundee FC player.

A long run of managers came and went in the years after Bob Shankly's departure, but none came close to producing a side capable of matching the squad which had won the championship. How much of that was down to a lack of spending power rather than a lack of talent will never be known, but a management change in the '70s had far-reaching consequences for the club in their continuing rivalry with neighbours Dundee United. In 1971 former Rangers manager Davie White replaced John Prentice as the man in charge at

The legendary 1962 Dundee FC side which brought soccer glory to the city with the League Championship win (courtesy of D.C. Thomson and Co. Ltd)

Dens. The following day it was announced that coach Jim McLean was leaving to take over as manager of United. The next 30 years of football in Dundee might have been very different indeed had McLean made his move into management with Dundee FC, as many felt was his due, instead of crossing the road to Tannadice . . .

Ironically, given the controversy surrounding the suggestion of a merger between the two clubs as the twentieth century neared its end, Jim McLean might have found himself in charge of a club called Dundee City – the name suggested as that suitable for a unified team – much earlier in his managerial career. After Dundee Hibernian had been in existence for 14 years, it was felt the club needed wider appeal and a change of name was proposed. Dundee City was the preferred new title but those then in charge of Dundee FC protested and Dundee United was eventually chosen. The club officially took that name in 1923.

Managed at the time by former international goalkeeper Jimmy Brownlie, the club yo-yoed between the first and second divisions for a number of years and endured considerable financial hardship as they struggled in the backwater of Scottish football. One of their most notable achievements in that era was probably the afternoon they recorded their highest ever win, humiliating Nithsdale Wanderers 14–0 in the first round of the Scottish Cup in 1931.

It was to be the 1950s before United, by then playing in black-and-white

*Alan Gilzean, a Dundee FC favourite, uses his head against St Mirren in 1962
(courtesy of D.C. Thomson and Co. Ltd)*

hoops, began to emerge as the powerful club it ultimately became. Two of the
players who set them on their way were Peter McKay and Johnny Coyle. The
former, a curly-haired centre-forward, scored 158 goals for the club, still a
record. He eventually lost his place in the side to the bustling Coyle, who netted
41 times in season 1955–56 to establish the record for the most league goals in
a single season.

Without any doubt at all, however, the man who did the most to transform the fortunes of the club around that time was Jerry Kerr, who took over as manager in the middle of 1959. He immediately guided the club back to the first division and remained at the helm for 11 years. Kerr was among the first Scottish managers to introduce foreign players into his side, going to Scandinavia to make a succession of signings in the '60s. Names like Orjan Persson, Finn Dossing and Lennart Wing were at first difficult to pronounce for United fans who were more used to team lists with fine-sounding names such as MacKay, Briggs and Gillespie, but they soon learned after the new imports started to make their mark on the Scottish game.

It was during this renaissance period that the Terrors first entered the European arena, and they did it in spectacular style by beating the mighty Barcelona, the holders, in a Fairs Cup tie. The home leg, played in November 1966, attracted a crowd of 28,000, the biggest ever attendance at Tannadice.

When Jerry Kerr stepped down after his lengthy and distinguished reign at Tannadice, he was replaced by a man who was to remain manager for twice as long and have an even greater impact on the fate of the club. Jim McLean came from up the road at Dens Park without any managerial experience, but by the time he gave up the job in 1993 to concentrate on his other role as chairman, he had established himself as one of the best club managers Scotland has ever produced.

Frequently the centre of controversy by doing it his way, McLean brought the club to its most successful era in its entire history. He introduced a youth policy that ultimately produced an unprecedented flow of talent and gave the club some of its finest players. It also brought United startling success and saw them march triumphantly through Europe, conquering some of the finest teams in the world. Holidaymakers from the city no longer had to explain where precisely Dundee was when they conversed with Spanish and Italian waiters. 'Ah, you have Dundee United,' was the impressed response from the football-mad Europeans and no further explanations were needed. It even helped Dundonians negotiate their way more quickly through some customs posts!

The pinnacle of the club's magnificent performances in Europe was unquestionably in 1986–87 when they battled through to the final of the UEFA Cup, the first Scottish side to do so. They lost narrowly to Gothenburg of Sweden but won high praise from FIFA for the sporting way the United fans conducted themselves in the second leg of the tie at Tannadice. Despite the agony of seeing their team draw 1–1 but go down 2–1 on aggregate, the disappointed supporters generously applauded the Swedes and made friends with their travelling support. It eventually led to FIFA bestowing a first ever Fair Play award on the club and the cash which came with the honour was spent on the Fair Play Enclosure, which has since been replaced by a stand occupying a proud corner of Tannadice.

Numerous players came through during these exciting times and carved out distinguished careers in the game, and the club established itself as a major force at home and abroad. Prior to 1977 no one from the club had ever played for Scotland, then a host of them finally burst through, among them Dave Narey, Paul Hegarty, Paul Sturrock (who went on to manage the club at the close of the '90s), Eamonn Bannon, Davie Dodds, Richard Gough, Maurice Malpas, Kevin Gallacher, Jim McInally, Dave Bowman, Duncan Ferguson and Billy McKinlay. Of that talented group, two names stand out. One is Dave Narey, who made a record 612 league appearances for the club in a 21-year career spanning 1973 to 1994 and another 76 in European ties, a record for a Scottish player. The other star in a glittering galaxy was Maurice Malpas, who was capped for Scotland 55 times, earning him a coveted place in Scotland's Hall of Fame. Duncan Ferguson also made it into the club's record books when he was transferred to Rangers in 1993 for £4 million, the highest fee ever received by the club for a player.

Despite his huge success with United, one honour eluded McLean – the Scottish Cup. He took the club to the final at Hampden six times but watched them lose on each occasion. The so-called Hampden hoodoo was finally laid to rest as soon as McLean stepped down as manager. In his first season in a short managerial career with the club, Yugoslavian Ivan Golac brought the cup back to Tannadice after a memorable victory over Rangers. In a fairytale ending to the final, Dundee-born Craig Brewster scored the only goal of the game to give United the one trophy they needed to achieve the complete set of domestic honours.

McLean was rightly recognised as the man who gave the club its best ever team and brought them to undreamed-of heights. But his influence in putting United on a sound financial footing cannot be overstated either. With the help of predecessor Jerry Kerr, he built a support which allowed Tannadice to be transformed from a humble ground with a ramshackle wooden stand into one of the finest stadiums in the country – and left them with money in the bank.

Curiously, the two Dundee clubs have never really prospered simultaneously and the rise of United seemed almost to be mirrored by the decline of Dundee. After 100 years together Dundee United, so long the poor relation, reached the new millennium in comparatively good heart, while the very future of Dundee had at one stage been seriously in doubt. Ironically, although in the midst of fighting for their very survival off the park, Dundee had remarkably achieved fine results on it and finished the last complete season of the twentieth century in fifth place, with a significantly better tally of points than their neighbours down the road. Tough times lie ahead for both clubs, as they do for other sides, as they try to match the Old Firm off the park. But as their records demonstrate, fighting and winning are things both Dundee and Dundee United have been good at in the past.

Although far removed from the rugby-playing heartlands of the Scottish Borders, Dundonians, mainly attached to Dundee High School FP, have made a minor but significant impact on the oval-ball game. High's first international was prop George Ritchie in 1932, but it wasn't until the '80s, when the club established itself as the major force in the game north of the Tay, that the FPs began to produce talent consistently for the international set-up in all age groups. That development was largely down to the influence of David Leslie, certainly the leading figure in Dundee rugby over the last 30 years, as player, coach and catalyst.

Leslie the player was a dynamic and aggressive open-side wing forward who never won British Lions recognition like his fellow FP Chris Rea just a few years before but was maybe the best in his position in the entire history of Scottish rugby. First capped in 1975, he was limited by injuries to only 32 appearances for his country. His greatest season was 1983–84 when Scotland won their first Grand Slam for 50 years and Leslie was voted European Player of the Year. He captained Scotland the following season.

The next Dundonian to make it into the international side was Andy Nicol, the grandson of Ritchie. A scrum-half of great pace and lightning-quick delivery, Nicol uniquely captained Scotland at all levels, culminating in the senior side on two tours in 1995 and 1997, also winning a Lions place in New Zealand in 1995. Like Leslie, a succession of injuries probably robbed him of a number of caps, but he blossomed again towards the end of the decade with top English club Bath and was the first Briton to lift rugby's European Cup as their captain in 1998.

No cyclist from Dundee has found success in Europe, far less won the prestigious Tour de France, probably due in part to the fact that no one from the city has ever entered! That is not to say that Dundee is without a strong representation in that particular sport. Every Saturday and Sunday morning a peloton of members from the three main clubs in town set off from the gates at Camperdown Park for what starts as a friendly run of some 60 miles but invariably ends in a race. Among the assorted bunch of riders are a group who admit they are long past the age when they should know better than to spend their weekend mornings trying to ride a bike faster than men half their age. Common sense has never got in the way of competitive spirit for the veteran riders of Dundee Wheelers, however, and in their own eccentric way they too have put their home town on the sporting map. Always among the leading clubs in the country for producing veterans, they surpassed themselves in 1994 by taking the first three places in the Scottish Veteran Time Trial Association all-

The Europe-conquering Dundee United FC, 1986–87 (courtesy of David Martin/ Fotopress)

round championship, a unique achievement for a cycling club. The trio, Dave McCallum (56), Bill Shewan (69) and Jim Lyon (63) spent that particular season shattering personal-best times and age-group records and with the assistance of Jim Brewster (53), father of Dundee United centre forward Craig Brewster, also won every team event open to them save one – the one they didn't compete in.

McCallum had broken records from an early age and set the Scottish ten-mile best time and the Dundee-to-Perth record (which still stands) before turning veteran at the age of 40. Shewan won the veterans' championship six times and had international titles, as well as a world age record, to his credit. Lyon made a comeback to the sport in his 50s and lost five stone in weight before winning the British Over-60 championship in 1994. Each of the group was capable of cycling for two hours at an average speed of around 25 miles an hour, impressive at any age but remarkable for men within sight of travelling on buses for a reduced fare.

A dozen members of the Wheelers, half of them veterans, set an offbeat record in 1998 when they crossed Scotland coast-to-coast from Oban to Broughty Ferry and completed the 122-mile run in well under six hours. Among the riders that day was Donald Langlands, who 40 years earlier had represented Scotland in the Cardiff Commonwealth Games.

For a city that is surrounded by more golf courses per head of the population than probably any other place on the globe, Dundee might have been expected

Dundee Wheelers keep alive Dundee's great cycling tradition (courtesy of D.C. Thomson and Co. Ltd)

to produce a regular flow of world-class players. For unexplained reasons, things haven't quite worked out that way – so far. The leading local players have been produced by the Downfield club where the long, parkland layout was described by former Open champion Peter Thomson as one of the best inland courses in Britain. The most celebrated golfing figure to come out of Dundee was prodigy Bobby Walker, son of Downfield pro Fred. He qualified for the 1959 Open at Muirfield when he was just a 15-year-old, turned pro before his 16th birthday and won the Scottish Professional Championship at only 18. Sadly, a serious injury in 1967 meant that his huge promise was never fulfilled, and he died in 1995 aged only 52.

In the amateur game the city can just about lay claim to Ian Hutcheon of Monifieth, since that seaside burgh was at least part of Dundee for local-authority purposes at the time when he was still winning trophies. A twin whose brother Fred was also a fine player, 'Hutch' was Scottish champion on four occasions between 1971 and 1979. He also represented Great Britain and Ireland on 12 occasions, including four Walker Cups, and won the individual event at the Eisenhower Trophy, effectively the world amateur title, in Portugal in 1976.

Dundee's swimmers figured prominently in international waters during the second half of the 1900s. Among the first to find fame was Bob Sreenan, who broke innumerable Scottish and British records and went on to swim in two

159

Olympic Games, Helsinki in 1952 and Rome four years later. Sreenan also contested Commonwealth and European Championships. Others followed in his wake, Ian Blyth, Paul Marshall and brothers Dougie and Iain Campbell all gaining selection in various Olympic competitions. A third Campbell brother, Kenneth, represented Scotland at water polo. Another name of note was Billy McGoldrick, who won a Commonwealth Games bronze medal in the relay.

The city's best-known 'water babe' is Ruth Gilfillan, whose sisters Elaine and Sharon also made their mark. Ruth started swimming at the age of ten and broke the first of an astonishing 86 Scottish and British records five years later. She competed in two Commonwealth Games, winning a bronze medal in the 200 metres at Edinburgh in 1986, and reached the Olympic finals in Seoul in 1988.

Impressive though that record is for a place of Dundee's size, it was in one of the world's toughest swimming events that the city bettered any other town in Britain. No fewer than five people, including two from the same family, succeeded in swimming the English Channel, a remarkable feat for a quintet coming from a population of less than 200,000. The first Dundonian to cross the hostile 20-mile stretch of water – although not the first to attempt it – was Ian Reid. He was followed several years later by Kevin McIntosh and Mary Yates. Then, in 1992, at the age of 18, Shannon Blair made the crossing to complete the first part of a unique family double, her sister Colleen (20) repeating the achievement in 1998.

Teams representing Dundee clubs in various other sports have also had their share of triumphs. Hockey clubs Menzieshill and Wanderers have consistently been among the best sides in Scotland and the two have won numerous national indoor and outdoor crowns between them. Menzieshill gained international distinction when they lifted the B division title in the European Indoor Championship in Prague in 1999.

Another type of hockey, the kind played on ice, has been hugely popular in the city and the mighty Dundee Tigers, and later the Rockets, thrilled crowds all over the country as well as those who packed the former ice rink on Kingsway. At their peak in the early 1980s, the Rockets travelled to England to win the British championship. Several fine players came out of Dundee but none rivalled Marshall Key, who eventually played for London, then Swiss sides. He competed on the same stage as the classy imported Canadians and invariably outperformed them.

As the new millennium beckoned, the city was well placed to see its triumphs of the twentieth century at least equalled and probably surpassed. The McTaggarts and McColgans of tomorrow will find their paths to glory easier to negotiate than their predecessors. In addition to the clutch of neighbourhood sports centres which were constructed in the closing years of the '90s, complementing the swimming and leisure centre, athletics stadium and cycle track already in existence, the town imaginatively transformed the site of the former Maryfield Hospital into the Dundee International Sports Complex at a cost of £4 million. The development caters for a wide range of activities and its sports hall hosted the Men's Indoor European Club Hockey Championships just three months after its opening late in 1997. Building work on a new ice rink to replace the demolished Kingsway building began just as the century came to an end, and its completion will doubtless see the return of the packed arenas of a bygone era when thousands enjoyed ice sports.

This has been just a glimpse of Dundee's distinguished sporting history. Others in sports not even mentioned have brought honour to the city and themselves and their absence from these pages is in no way a reflection on how their successes should be measured. They have devoted much time and effort to their particular interest and can justly take great pride in what they have achieved. And these unidentified champions and record-setters, like those singled out throughout this chapter, will be the first to acknowledge the assistance they have received from another group of anonymous sports-minded people – the trainers, coaches and watch-holders, whose names never make it to the sports pages and who may never have had a single trophy to polish. Their sacrifices are in some ways greater than those of the people making it to the podium, and Dundee should be as proud of them as of its sporting sons and daughters who have found fame.

A Dundee riot in 1851: as police attempt to arrest a drunken sailor, they are set upon by the crowd

9

The Palace of Scottish Blackguardism
Dundee's Battle for Law and Order

William G. Boyle.

Over the last 300 years Dundee has carved out a sensational legal history. The city has had trials for witchcraft, rebellion, treason, sedition and espionage, not to mention arson, murder, rape and pillage. It was the scene of one of Scotland's most historic murders, when a young William Wallace murdered the son of the English governor of the town. We have rooted out corruption of magistrates and police. We have broken the law by preaching equality and advocating the rights of man. We have never given in to laws of oppression and we freed the slaves before Lincoln was born. We may even have tried and hanged Jack the Ripper.

Dundee has had a head of police who turned out not to be a policeman but a wanted fraudster (William Mackison, 1844), a head of police censured for cowardice in the face of the enemy, i.e. the ever-active Dundee mob (Robert Home, 1834), and, in recent memory, a chief constable who voluntarily took the place of hostages held at gunpoint (John R. Little, 1977). Dundee also provided in Dame Margaret Kidd Scotland's first woman sheriff, who went on to become Scotland's first woman QC and subsequently Scotland's first woman sheriff principal, and, most recently, Scotland's first female advocate general in the shape of Lynda Clark QC.

John R. Little (courtesy of Tayside Police)

163

This idiosyncratic city, once famously described by Lord Cockburn as 'a sink of atrocity that no amount of moral flushing seems capable of cleansing', may have had its share of villains but it has been cast as hero sufficient enough for the author's civic pride. The brightest star in the legal firmament is when we (yes, I claim the credit as a born-and-bred Dundonian) outlawed slavery 30 years before Abraham Lincoln was born. It appears in the law books as the case of Joseph Knight, a Negro, against John Wedderburn. Mark the date. It took place on 15 January 1778, a remarkable 55 years before Wilberforce's Abolition of Slavery Bill was given royal assent and long before Lincoln freed the slaves in America.

Joseph Knight was taken as a slave from Africa as a child of 12 or 13 and imported to Jamaica, where he served John Wedderburn, a scion of the powerful Dundee family, who himself had fled Scotland because of certain difficulties over the Jacobite rebellion. When Mr Wedderburn returned to Scotland he was wealthy enough to set himself up with an estate and he brought with him Joseph Knight, by then his house slave. After several years' service and marriage to a local girl, Mr Knight decided upon leaving his master's service. After he asserted his freedom, however, Wedderburn had him arrested and brought before the magistrates in Dundee, who found Wedderburn entitled to his services and that Mr Knight's state of slavery should continue.

With the support of the local populace, Knight appealed to the sheriff, according to the court writs 'praying the Sheriff to find that he cannot continue in a state of slavery or be compelled to perpetual service and to discharge Mr Wedderburn from sending the petitioner abroad'. The latter plea was of some importance to Mr Knight. If the court found for Wedderburn, the loss of freedom was the least of his worries. Wedderburn had the power and was threatening to return him to Jamaica, where the penalty for being a runaway slave was being roasted alive on slow-burning coals. The dry legal argument about whether slavery was legal obscured the human drama, because what was at stake was nothing short of Joseph Knight's life.

Mr Knight, a man of some intellect and astounding physical courage, won at the first instance, but Wedderburn appealed to the Court of Session. The arguments in the Court of Session, though couched in terse legal terms, are worth rehearsing. It was argued for Wedderburn that a state of slavery had been universally received. It took place in all ancient nations and in all modern European nations and the right of the master ought not to be annihilated. His counsel stated, 'In this case the master is not insisting for the exercise of any rigorous powers, he only demands that he shall be entitled to the personal service of the Negro in this country during his life. His right is not immoral or unjust.'

Knight's counsel argued that just because slavery was recognised in the colonies and other countries it did not mean it was legal in Scotland. He declared, 'Whether the slave was ensnared or bought from his parents, the iniquity is still the same; that a state of slavery has been admitted in many of our nations does not render it less unjust. Child murder and crimes of a deep dye have been authorised by the laws of different states. Tyranny and all sorts of oppression might be vindicated on the same grounds.'

In a passionate finale he concluded, 'Oppression and iniquity are not palliated by the gain. The institution of slavery deprives men of their most essential rights that attend to their existence.' He asked the judges for an order freeing the slave and protecting Mr Knight from being sent out of Scotland without his consent, just as the sheriff had granted – and they agreed. While watching *Amistad*, Steven Spielberg's film that recounts a similar struggle taking place in the United States' Supreme Court in 1839, I thought, 'Dundee first, Dundee first.'

A century earlier and Joseph Knight might not have fared so well. There does not seem to have been any coherent, organised system of justice in Dundee apart from that enforced by the sword or Privy Council. Modern Dundee's first dose of order, if not law, came with General Monk, who, having put most of the city to the fire and sword in 1651, subdued what remained. The vacuum was easily filled by the church. The churchmen, who had held considerable judicial influence with a range of sanctions over moral offences including 'ducking' in the harbour for adultery and a spell in the stocks for gossiping, do not appear to have been held in high regard by Dundonians. When Cromwell's forces abducted them and attempted to hold them to ransom, Dundonians refused to cough up any cash and one pronounced that 'the loons are weel awa'. With the departure of Monk's troops the city seems to have avoided any system of law and order until 1679, when the Council formed a 'nightlie guard'. This seems initially to have been a voluntary service but soon five discharged Highland soldiers were appointed town officers by local authority.

They were housed in the Town Guard House. According to a contemporary account, it seems to have been regarded as an unremarkable building, but prisoners must have been made of sterner stuff in those days because one of the cells was described as 'the Thief's Hole, a place horrible and small where only the most notorious criminals are put'. Other amenities included four rooms used as a prison for debtors, an odious practice now thankfully abandoned, and 'an Iron House where notorious offenders are put in irons'. Escapes were not only frequent, they were often undertaken in groups and escapees were usually never seen again.

If conditions in the cells were draconian, the punishments visited by the magistrates could be equally severe. The usual form of punishment for petty crimes was a form of banishment for a specific period with the threat of whipping and branding on the face for early return. Once such a sentence was pronounced the unfortunate was escorted with some solemnity by the town guard and the town drummer to the limits of the town and banished to Perthshire or, even worse, placed in a boat and sent to Fife.

Another common penalty was the pillory or 'being whuppit throo the toon'. The offender was stripped to the waist and fastened to the rear of a horsedrawn cart, then driven through the town. At every principal street the cart was stopped and the cat was liberally applied to his back. Schoolchildren were given time off their classes to see what a life of crime entailed. Capital punishment, too, was so routine that the *Dundee Magazine* of the 1770s wasted barely a paragraph to announce the following:

> George Moncur, a soldier in the Tayside Fencibles, and Thomas Moncur, weaver of Dundee, two brothers, were found guilty of robbing William Duncan, a Hilltown labourer, of a watch, pocket book and bills of a considerable amount. They are sentenced to be hanged.

By the 1820s Dundee was becoming a prosperous and expanding city with an increasing crime problem. The area was lawless at night as the original 'nightlie guard' of 1679 had given way to town officers who only did their duty during the day. During the upheaval of the French Revolution, when Dundee was a hotbed of rioting, sedition and radical conspiracy, the controversial Lord

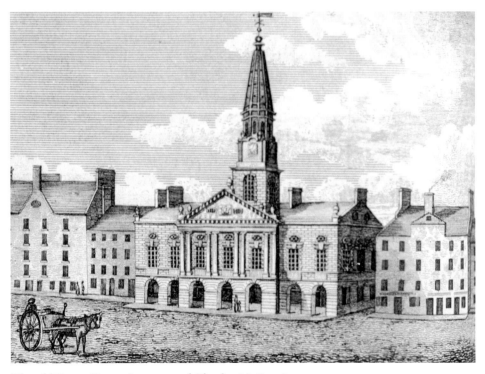

The old Town House (courtesy of Charles McKean)

166

Provost Riddoch applied to the government to have a barracks built in the town. And, on 23 October 1794, he informed the council that 'a number of inhabitants in the town had associated themselves for the purpose of aiding the local magistrates for the preventing and the suppressing of riots, tumults or disorders within the borough'. The council was so delighted at the appearance of the vigilante group that it promptly voted to supply the volunteers with 100 rifles. It was this sort of volunteer force, supplemented by shore porters, that policed the city until the formation of the police proper. In 1821 local businesses got together and established a night watch, paid for by voluntary subscription. So hard were the magistrates pressed at this time that when a visitor who came to the town complained bitterly that he and his friends had been molested in the street by some of the locals and appealed to them for some form of protection, he was tersely told that 'the magistrates were not in a position to protect themselves on the streets of Dundee, let alone worry about visitors to the town'.

After much public agitation, Parliament passed the first bill on Dundee's policing in 1824 authorising a police force for the city. Nowadays the police force is headed by a chief constable but in those days the formal title was superintendent of police. The magistrates' first appointment was of John Low, a local tailor who was simply an interim measure until a 'professional' was found. He occupied the post for a few months before Alexander Downie was appointed. He was said to be a veteran of the Peninsula campaign – perhaps too much of a veteran, because he held the post for only a year before resigning in May 1825. He was followed by a Mr John Hume, whose main act of distinction was to abandon his office and run for his life when heavy-handed policing of a demonstration in support of the Reform Bill led to several days of rioting.

When news of the proposed bill to extend the vote had reached Dundee on Saturday, 26 March 1831, impromptu celebrations had broken out in the High Street. The magistrates wisely agreed to allow a gathering the following Monday to celebrate further. On that night the hills of Fife were lit up by bonfires and thousands crammed the High Street. A large bonfire of tar barrels was set up and effigies of the Duke of

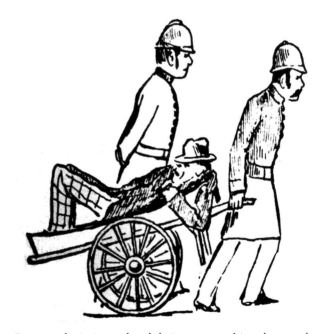

Cartoon depicting a drunk being removed in a barrow by police (courtesy of Dundee Art Galleries and Museums)

Police constables Alick Reynolds and John Tosh (Toshie) in their Alvis two-seater police car (courtesy Dundee City Council)

Wellington, Sir Robert Peel and a former Lord Advocate were burned. As the crowd began to break up, however, the police arrived and began to manhandle some of the demonstrators. A full-scale battle erupted, with 40 of the crowd arrested and the police being stoned.

The next day, all but three of the protesters were released. When this became known, a large crowd gathered outside the Town House demanding the release of their three comrades. The crowd steadily grew as inside the justices of the peace met to discuss the situation. To encourage them in their deliberations the protesters hit on a novel idea. An old boat was procured, covered in tar and hauled to the pillars of the Town House, where it was placed against the doors and set alight. The smoke billowed in, nearly choking the justices sitting inside. In a panic they decided to give in and ordered the release of the prisoners, but the police could not find the keys for the cell. This only further enraged the mob outside, who promptly fought their way into the Town House using a battering ram and freed the prisoners.

The police were taken hostage and the contents of the Town House were thrown out of the windows and set on fire by the jubilant crowd. Fearing for his life, Superintendent Hume fled out through a back door as the crowd broke into the city chambers. He remained in hiding while the crowd marched to his house in the Hawkhill and destroyed it. A shop in the Overgate belonging to a police sergeant was also ransacked.

Eventually two companies of troops were sent to Dundee from Perth Barracks and the police were ordered to keep off the streets. Mr Hume was heavily criticised for what was seen as desertion in the face of the enemy. Hume resigned, but the fate of some of the rioters was more tragic. The original three prisoners who had been freed were quickly recaptured and sentenced to six months each, but four of their rescuers were more harshly dealt with. John Thomson, flesher, and James Findlay, a bottler, were each sentenced to 14 years' transportation. George Haggart, a 17-year-old painter, was sent to Botany Bay for seven years, and a watchmaker called Frederick Scott was sentenced to 18 months. A large petition pleading for mercy was ignored, although some years later Findlay was pardoned. The message had been well and truly sent to the people of Dundee: collective bargaining by riot, a practice endemic in Dundee since the 1780s, would no longer be tolerated.

Following Hume's resignation there were a number of nondescript police chiefs until the appointment of William Mackison in 1844. He was shortlisted for the post along with Donald McKay, a native of Caithness who was a serving police inspector in Dunfermline. Mr Mackison hailed from the county of York, where he stated that he was superintendent with a rural police force and that he had been a non-commissioned officer in a fusilier regiment. Canvassing for both men was energetic, and despite Mr McKay being the favourite, Mr Mackison was described as an outstanding candidate and much impressed the magistrates. Mr McKay's cause was not helped by the leaking of information that while an officer in the City of London police force he had been sent to Fife to assist in the quelling of rioting miners during a strike. He was accused of being a government spy, which did his cause no good at all.

The local authority was obviously impressed with Mr Mackison, however, and they duly appointed him superintendent of police. In announcing his appointment they described him as 'a tall, handsome man in appearance vigorously intelligent and ideally suited for the post'. That judgement needed to be hastily reversed, because in less than three weeks a Superintendent Chalk from the Yorkshire Police arrived and handcuffed Mr Mackison, who turned out to be a well-known con man. Somewhat chastened, the magistrates fled to Dunfermline and asked Mr McKay to take on the job, which was the best thing they ever did. Mr McKay introduced many substantial police reforms and oversaw the transition from a somewhat amateurish, inefficient, incompetent force to a modern police force.

The city's force today has been rightly congratulated for a number of achievements, having introduced a whole range of new technologies and equipment. Dundee is host to Scotland's leading forensic science laboratory, which in May 1996 set up Scotland's only DNA database with links to the UK national database in Birmingham. The force has also led the way in introducing

How police uniforms have changed since the Second World War (courtesy of Tayside Police)

new body armour, CS sprays, asp batons and even revolutionary handcuffs. The current Dundee police force complement is 530, of which 90 are women. The first woman police officer appointed in Dundee was a Miss Annie Ross in 1935.

If Dundee in earlier years had difficulty getting policemen suitably qualified to catch villains, the authorities had difficulty in housing them. By 1820 the inability of the city to prevent prison escapes was becoming a national scandal. Whether prisoners were housed in the Town Guard House or an auxiliary jail at the Old Steeple prison, escape seemed a fairly routine event. At a public meeting in 1831 concerned citizens agitated to have the magistrates build a new jail. The local newspapers took up the matter and ultimately the police commissioners were forced to act. In August 1834 the Jail Bill for Dundee received royal assent. The new prison was completed in July 1837, its construction having been hastened because of continuing escapes. It cost £12,000, and on 6 July some 92 prisoners were transferred from the Town House and the Old Steeple to the new Bridewell. The building was situated adjacent to the rear of the west end of the present Sheriff Court, extending up Lochee Road. The governors' house abutted on to Bell Street. However, this modern building seemed no more successful in preventing prisoners from escaping than the old Town House, and it was some time before Dundee convicts got used to the idea of being locked up for the duration of their sentences.

One of the most celebrated escapes was on the morning of 9 April 1868. Two prisoners – John Milton, serving eight years' penal servitude for theft, and David Jenkins, serving ten years' penal servitude for assault and robbery – removed the boards which formed part of the floor in their cell and crawled along an air flume only 18 inches square. The two men squirmed their way to freedom, climbing on to the roof of the Courthouse Library and over the high prison wall to freedom. Four days later Jenkins was apprehended in Annfield Road, where he had been in hiding, but Milton seems to have been an imaginative character who enjoyed 11 months of freedom, including a trip to Spain, before being arrested in Newcastle.

Another skilful break-out was that of William Bremner, who escaped by picking the lock, abseiling with a rope that was attached to chimney-sweep apparatus and then scaling the wall, enjoying a month of freedom before being apprehended in Inverness.

Not all escapes ended happily. In 1871, three boys drowned while attempting to escape from the *Mars* training ship, the harsh 'industrial school' for 'friendless and destitute boys' that was moored in the Tay for 60 years until 1929. The boys' graves can still be seen in nearby Forgan cemetery. None of the boys had committed any crime but they were treated as if they had. Each was given a number instead of a name, the food was frequently inedible and cold showers with water straight from the Tay were the order of the day in both summer and winter. It was a hard school of which the author's own grandfather was a reluctant graduate. Unsurprisingly, mutinies and attempted escapes were commonplace.

The first sheriff was appointed to Dundee in 1831. Among the most

Mars training-ship boys spell out 'Happy New Year', from a postcard collection (courtesy of Dundee Art Galleries and Museums)

remarkable of Dundee's early resident sheriffs was Campbell Smith, who presided over the Sheriff Court from 1885 to 1911. A man of humble birth, originally a stonemason who gave up his trade to study law, he was eventually called to the Bar, a considerable achievement for the time. Frequently he followed a policy of extreme leniency with respect to offenders. It was not to everyone's taste, and as another distinguished sheriff, John Christie, commented, 'It certainly wasn't in accordance with the sentiments or practice of the date, but his leniency does not seem to have resulted in any increase in lawlessness.'

Post-war, the foundation of shrieval dignity, industry, common sense and good law was provided by Sheriff John Christie, who was installed in Dundee in November 1955. Sheriff Christie had strong Dundee connections through farming, shipping and whaling and dispensed justice with fairness, courtesy and even-handedness until his retirement in 1983. In 1968 he was joined by Sheriff Graham Cox, who had attended Grove Academy in his schooldays. Sheriff Cox served the city until his promotion to sheriff principal at North Strathclyde. It is universally recognised that in these two men Dundee was blessed. More proactive than Sheriff Christie, Sheriff Cox combines an exceptionally sharp intellect with a radar-like ability to address the heart of a legal problem. Sheriff Cox presided over the arraignment of the Libyan terrorist suspects in 1999 and also conducted the investigation into the E-coli fatalities in Lanarkshire. Now that he is sheriff principal at Strathclyde, it is probably safe for me to say it was a bit 'nippy' to appear before him if arguments were not up to scratch!

Sheriff Christie and Sheriff Cox have passed the mantle to yet another remarkable lawyer, the present senior sheriff Alistair Stewart. Sheriff Stewart is of the first rank, recognised by his appointment as a High Court and Court of Session judge, where he presides regularly. Sheriff Stewart is a man of considerable academic achievement and continues to contribute much to the research and the development of the law, and while he too can be 'nippy' when arguments are not up to scratch, his best quality is the fair, courteous and judicious manner in which he, like Sheriff Christie and Sheriff Cox, treats the citizens of Dundee who have business before the court.

The sheriffdom also has three relatively new judges: Sheriff Richard Davidson, Sheriff James Scott (the latter having been appointed following the tragic early death of Sheriff John Young) and, most recently, Sheriff Ian Dunbar, a Dundee-born and Dundee-educated lawyer. History will tell of their involvement, but as I am a frequent pleader before them, discretion compels me to leave the judgement of their contribution to my successor in 100 years' time . . .

Dundee Sheriff Court has seen many poignant moments, not least the inquiry into the Tay Rail Bridge Disaster and the trial and subsequent acquittal of Corporal Stewart Shepherd for the murder of Private John Fitzgerald, who was

A Dundee police Black Maria stands outside the Sheriff Court, driven by D. McIntosh. At the rear is Constable Cruikshanks (courtesy of Dundee City Council)

shot for alleged desertion at Tay Bridge station during the Second World War. Shepherd was lucky to have been tried in time of war.

Someone fortunate not to have been tried in wartime was Jessie Jordan, the woman at the centre of Dundee's own German spy case just before the Second World War. A Scotswoman who had been living in Germany, she returned to her native land in 1937 after the failure of her second marriage and settled in Dundee, where she opened a hairdresser's business. Her cleaner was suspicious of various maps and went to the police. A surveillance operation was mounted and soon other incriminating documents were found, including maps of military locations and coastal defences. Jordan also appears to have acted as post bag for information sent by German spies from the United States. Her attempts were fairly amateurish, and this, together with the fact that the war had not yet commenced, saved her from a fate worse than her four years' imprisonment. She spent the war in an internment camp and in 1945 was deported to Germany, where she died in 1954. During the war her case inspired a Hollywood propaganda film starring Edward G. Robinson.

Behind Dundee Sheriff Court, in a secret place caged in concrete, there is a simple stone with the initials and date 'WHB 1889'. It marks the grave of the last man to be hanged in Dundee Prison. He may have been Jack the Ripper.

In April 1889 a black flag was raised above Bell Street signifying that an execution had taken place. The condemned man was William Henry Bury and

Nazi spy Jessie Jordan (courtesy of Dundee City Council)

his execution caused a sensation. Bury had been in the town for less than three months and his presence in Dundee was something of a mystery. He had arrived with his wife Ellen, whom he had wed the previous year as a passenger on a steamship, the SS *Cumbria*, that had sailed from London. He seems to have been a bit of a wanderer and arrived with few possessions, no connections with the town or any significant employment prospects. Within three weeks, however, he was to end up in Dundee folklore as the man known as 'Jack the Ripper'.

On Sunday, 7 February, at about 7 p.m., Bury burst into the central police office and demanded a private meeting with a police officer. While being interviewed by a Lieutenant Parr, the agitated man made mention of Jack the Ripper and confessed that he had cut up his wife and sealed her in a box. The police hurried to the small house at 114 Princes Street that had been occupied by Bury and his wife for just over a fortnight. In a packing case in the two-roomed house they found the body of Mrs Bury decomposing and mutilated beyond recognition. Justice was swift in those days and a month later Bury appeared before Lord Young in the High Court in Dundee and was sentenced to death. There was a minor hiccup in the proceedings when the jury came back with a recommendation of leniency, to be told by Lord Young that such a verdict was not acceptable and that it was a case of either 'guilty' or 'not guilty'. The jury subsequently returned a verdict of guilty. Although a petition was raised to save Bury from the gallows, it received little support and his fate was inevitable.

The hanging itself was sensational enough but the reference to Jack the Ripper excited even more public interest. The hanging gallows were erected inside the prison courtyard adjacent to what is now Lochee Road and overlooked by the high buildings which came to be known as Tay Rope Works. Dundee has never

174

lacked entrepreneurial spirit and some wag, aware that the private execution could be seen by the public from this vantage point, charged people for the privilege of witnessing the event. There was no shortage of takers and the police were forced to erect hastily made black-cloth barriers to stop the public viewing of a man going to his death.

On Wednesday, 21 April 1889, William Henry Bury, who had occupied the death cell for four weeks, was woken at 5 a.m., whereupon he had a light breakfast and a smoke and commented to his jailer, 'This is my last morning on

A courtroom drawing of William Bury – was he Jack the Ripper?

earth. I fully forgive all those who gave false evidence against me.' The execution solemnities commenced at 9.40 a.m. when the prisoner governor, the bailies of the town, the town clerk and his assistant, a doctor, a city architect, the minister, the chief constable and the warden visited the condemned man and read the execution warrant. Thereafter the hangman performed his deadly duties.

Strangely, until recently Bury never figured in any serious investigation as a likely Jack the Ripper, but his leaving of London and his death were reasonably contemporaneous with the ending of Jack the Ripper's murders, the last of which was on 9 November 1888. Folklore has it that present at Bury's execution were two silent men from the Metropolitan Police sent up with the request to attend his execution. If this was the case, there is no record of why they were there or why they were keen to make certain of his death, but Bury may have been a more likely suspect than the Duke of Clarence, Henry Stephens, The Free Masons, Dr Gull or all the other major suspects. He was buried in the grounds of the prison with a simple stone carving encased in a wall recording his initials and year of death. When the prison was demolished to make way for the new police headquarters, the grave was buried in concrete.

Judicial executions may have been rare from the nineteenth century onwards but they were by no means a unique event in earlier times, and one of Dundee's most infamous was the burning for witchcraft of Grizzel Jaffray, who was sent for trial on 11 November 1669 under order of the Privy Council. Little is known about her trial other than her conviction and the admonition that no confession was to be tortured out of her. It is probably a reasonable presumption that she

Men of substance: Sir Thomas Thornton (right) and Robert Fleming, founder of Fleming's bank and ancestor of James Bond's creator, Ian Fleming, in Meadowside, c. 1790 (courtesy of Dundee City Archives)

was in fact tortured; she certainly confessed. On 23 November the poor soul was executed by burning at the stake. Oral tradition has it that her son, a seaman, arrived at the harbour as the execution of his mother was taking place in the Seagate and on learning the reason for the crowd's agitation he set sail and left Dundee, never to return.

Dundee has never been a particularly respectful city. Lord Cockburn called it the 'Palace of Scottish Blackguardism', but perhaps what he ought to have called it was the Palace of Martyrs. Take the Tayside meal robbers who, to feed the starving populace in the 1770s, ransacked farms and ships laden with meal. Six men were indicted; five of them wisely fled and were outlawed. One, a sailor named Robertson, refused to leave his family and was convicted on the unsatisfactory evidence of paid informers. He made a desperate plea for mercy, asking for any punishment that did not separate him from his family. He said he would rather hang than face transportation to Botany Bay. He was promptly sentenced to Botany Bay for life, a virtual death sentence.

No crime was ever visited with such severe penalties as working for the advancement of the common man, and many Dundee citizens felt those savage penalties. George Kinloch was outlawed in 1822 for daring to suggest ordinary folk should have the vote. Thomas Fysche Palmer, a Unitarian minister, was in 1793 sentenced to transportation and seven years' imprisonment allegedly for writing an anti-war pamphlet – but his true crime was to advocate equality for all and association with the lower orders.

One of the lower orders he associated with was George Mealmaker, a weaver whose own fate was sealed at Palmer's trial before Lord Braxfield when he gave evidence that he had written the offending pamphlet. He dodged the authorities for a number of years but, like his friend Fysche Palmer, was to be sent on the convict ships, never to return. Mealmaker was tried in 1798 and sentenced to 14 years' imprisonment.

Dundonians, or those trained in Dundee, who have graced the law begin with Henry Scrymgeour who, in the mid part of the sixteenth century, after graduating from St Andrews, went to Geneva and became Professor of Philosophy and Civil Law at the University of Geneva, probably at the time the most prominent academic post in the world. The law faculty of Dundee University, situated in Park Place, has named a building after him in honour of his achievements.

There are many who should be honoured in connection with what is now the law faculty of the University of Dundee and formerly part of Queen's College, St Andrews. The faculty's very existence owes everything to the tenacity of Dundee's own citizens and its legal scions. The establishment of a law school in Dundee was accomplished in the face of hostility from academia and indifference from the government. In 1878, a Royal Commission on Universities recommended that university education should be made available to Dundee but the government refused to fund it. Queen's College was founded by way of an endowment by a private individual, Mary Ann Baxter, in 1881 and opened its doors in 1883 without a law school. In 1885 the Faculty of Procurators and Solicitors in Dundee, itself founded in 1820, had upwards of 100 clerks and apprentices anxious for instruction and wrote offering to pay for at least 60 places at seven shillings and six pence but the university refused, offering to provide a room for free instead.

The persistent Thomas Thornton (instigator of the Tay Rail Bridge and its rebuilding and also founding father of the Thornton's law firm still prominent in the town) led the Dundee solicitors in persuading the council of the university to agree to a law class which commenced on 15 October 1890. The first female law student, Mary S. Ferguson, was admitted in 1912. Unfortunately no degrees were granted until 1938 and generations of Dundee lawyers studied without gaining credit for their work until the law teachers revolted at such an iniquity and forced change by threatening to resign. Since 1966, the law faculty has been under the auspices of Dundee University and caters for accountancy students, law students, postgraduates and research in law and accountancy. It operates a world-renowned oil and gas development department and accepts students for their professional exams in both English and Scots Law.

There are too many academics who have contributed to the development of the faculty to mention, but the name Thornton should also be acknowledged because of the service two of its law-firm partners, Professor Alexander McDonald and Stuart Fair, gave the university. Two full-time academics who graced legal teaching and research are James Robertson – 'JJ' to several generations of students – and Professor Ian Willock, one-time dean of the law faculty whose erudite research contributed greatly to the abolition of the old Burgh Court and its replacement by the District Court, an altogether fairer vehicle for delivering justice.

Past lawyers of Dundee seem to have been giants in the fields of law and commerce: Thomas Thornton, who, with another Dundee lawyer, a Mr Pattullo, planned and conceived the building of the Tay Rail Bridge; Hugh Carlton, who taught generations of lawyers; John Ross senior, whose grandson Kenneth carries on admirably the very practice that his grandfather and father John Ross junior established so expertly. Many of the great legal firms of yesteryear are gone but many are still in place: firms such as Ogilvie Cowan, that the Ritchie family of several generations continues to serve, the Robertsons, Norman senior and junior, the Scotts, the Stevens and the Rosses. Some are gone, like the Laverocks, whilst Burns, Veal and Carltons have been incorporated into Miller, Hendry and Blackadder Reid Johnston. And some are simply irreplaceable, like the legendary John Boath, the original 'poor man's lawyer', to whom I was indentured.

Of the present-day judges and lawyers, Dundee more than pulls its weight in terms of numbers and achievements, but a few are worthy of special note, such as Lord Cullen, the Lord Justice Clerk of the High Court of Justiciary and the Court of Session (the Second Senior Judge in Scotland), and his immediate predecessor as Lord Justice Clerk, Lord Ross (Donald), son of the legendary Dundee legal family. Both men are Dundee born and educated.

Among Scotland's crop of advocates, Dundee-trained lawyers abound, such as Donald Findlay QC, educated at Harris Academy and Dundee University – as gifted a trial lawyer as he is lacking in judgement in football and politics! Michael Jones graduated with distinction from Dundee University and is said to be Scotland's highest-earning QC. Vice-dean of the faculty of advocates Colin Campbell QC and David Burns QC also began their careers in Dundee.

Following this short trawl through Dundee's legal history, certain changes are apparent as Dundee looks towards the new millennium, and yet I am tempted to say things may be much as they ever were. A certain amount of criminality will be present in any industrial city. Dundee is no different from other places. Detection of crime due to technological and forensic break-throughs is on the increase; CCTV cameras are more efficient than the night watch. There will be changes in the law and its structures and it will affect our citizens. Challenges lie ahead. The criminal justice system is in danger of falling apart through underfunding, and government parsimony denies many access to justice. But we now have a law-making parliament in Scotland for the first time in 300 years. The fight for civil liberties will continue. And Dundee, as ever, will play a prominent part in meeting these challenges.

Dundee windows

10

Spirits Above and Spirits Below
How Dundee Tamed the Demon Drink

Thomas Peterkin

There's spirits above and spirits below,
The spirits of love and the spirits of woe.
The spirits of above are the spirits divine,
The spirits below are the spirits of wine.

As a young mill girl, the Dundee missionary Mary Slessor used to worship in a church that stood beside the Wishart Arch in the Cowgate. Beneath the church where Slessor passed her love and wisdom on to the infants at the Sunday school, drunkards passed out on to the grimy floor of one of Dundee's most notorious drinking dens, the John O'Groats pub.

The Cowgate building, described in local rhyme, was known colloquially as 'Heaven and Hell', and the stark contrast between the saintly and the sinful is a reflection of Dundee's turbulent relationship with strong drink. For moderation has played no part in the city's consuming love affair with alcohol. Even the antidote to the orgy of drunkenness that once engulfed Dundee was an equally extreme anti-drink backlash. The city saw the rise of an evangelical temperance movement, which was fiercely dedicated to saving lost souls from the evils of drink while advocating a life of total abstinence.

The movement took hold in Dundee with a religious fervour and was to lead to the city achieving the unique distinction of becoming the only constituency in British political history to return a Prohibitionist MP. Edwin 'Neddy' Scrymgeour was the architect of one of the election upsets of the century when he beat the great Winston Churchill in 1922. A dejected Churchill took defeat badly and vowed never to return to the city that he cursed for its 'bestial drunkenness'. Meanwhile, the Dundee electorate toasted their new MP by sinking endless 'hauf and haufs' and mocked the future Prime Minister for being a 'WC without a seat'.

Today some form of compromise between the tedium of teetotalism and rampant dipsomania appears to have been reached and Dundee enjoys a vibrant

They Talk a Power of our Drinking but Never Think of our Drought, *by Erskine Nicol (courtesy of Dundee Art Galleries and Museums)*

drinking culture, reflecting the city's new-found optimism and confidence. But while people relax over a couple of quiet drinks in the congenial surroundings of one of the many fine Dundee public houses, it should be remembered that today's respectable hostelries have risen from the ashes of an almighty hangover caused by the bad old days of truly Herculean debauchery.

In the seventeenth century, overconsumption of the potent ale brewed in the city was blamed for the inhabitants being caught unawares in 1651 when the city was sacked by General Monck. Earlier evidence of this chronic addiction to drink is provided by the Dundee pint measure, which is one of the few in Scotland to survive from the medieval period. The measure, which dates from the fifteenth or sixteenth century, is four times larger than today's imperial pint.

The destruction of the city at the hands of Monck's army failed to dampen the Dundee ardour for alcohol and, in desperation, the astute city fathers decided the only way to repair the damage caused by the English invaders was to capitalise on this fatal weakness. On 23 December 1669 an act was passed allowing the town to raise 14 pennies Scots on each pint of French wine and 20 pennies Scots on each pint of sack, Rhenish brandy wine or tent, a deep red wine from Galicia and Malaga. The act refers to that fateful night in September 1651 when Dundee 'was stormed violently by the usurpers and their town plundered with the losse of many lyffes'. The act also went some way towards recouping losses caused by 'the great storme and tempest of wether' in October

1669 that resulted in the 'utter demolishing' of the harbour.

A change in drinking habits which saw the grape being forsaken for the grain led to the passing of a 1707 act which allowed Dundee to levy two pennies Scots on every pint of ale and beer brewed and sold within the town and its suburbs. Once again, public debts resulting from Monck's invasion and the destruction of the harbour were responsible for the new legislation, which also aimed to raise enough money to sponsor the building of a new gaol. By a strange quirk of history the Tuppenny Act has never been repealed and, if it so wished, Dundee City Council could reintroduce it tomorrow. It would not, however, prove to be such an effective revenue-raising device in the modern age.

Three hundred years after Monck's invasion, alcohol still held the city in its vice-like grip and the appalling drunkenness which was to dominate Victorian Dundee and the early years of the twentieth century earned Dundee the unenviable title of the drunkest city in the British Empire. Before the Lintrathen reservoir started supplying Dundee in the 1870s, drinking beer was considered safer than consuming the insanitary water drawn from the Ladywell, which, ironically, now lends its name to the popular tavern in Victoria Road.

During the Victorian era, the intemperate habits of his fellow Dundonians horrified the teetotal poet William Topaz McGonagall.

> *Oh, thou demon Drink, thou fell destroyer;*
> *Thou curse of society, and its greatest annoyer.*
> *What hast thou done to society, let me think?*
> *I answer thou hast caused the most of ills, thou demon Drink.*
> *Thou causeth the mother to neglect her child,*
> *Also the father to act as he were wild,*
> *So that he neglects his loving wife and family dear,*
> *By spending his earnings foolishly on whisky, rum, and beer.*
> *And after spending his earnings foolishly he beats his wife –*
> *The man that promised to protect her during life –*
> *And so the man would if there was no drink in society,*
> *For seldom a man beats his wife in a state of sobriety.*

Behind the eccentric McGonagall's heartfelt doggerel lies an insight into the misery and brutality of drink. But for many Dundonians there were few attractive alternatives to senseless drinking bouts. Overindulgence provided the only easy escape from the appalling conditions of the working-class slums and the drudgery of work in the jute mills.

Rioting, prostitution, vandalism and violent crime were the unsavoury by-products of this drink-sodden existence and a pious newspaper report of 1863 was quick to condemn the 'insanity' caused by drink.

These two recently discovered photographs show typical Victorian public houses (both courtesy of Gordon Douglas Photographic)

Anyone who has witnessed the brutal ferocity and unscrupulous cowardice with which drunken labourers gash the faces of their fallen antagonists by kicks from ponderously booted feet must have felt that, but for the police, the sickening spectacle of a hanging would be no uncommon event in Dundee.

Despite the frantic efforts of the police to keep some semblance of order, fights between tanked-up sailors and locals were commonplace and violent families, like the Molonys, Mulligans, McFees and McFarlanes, punched, lashed and kicked each other as they sought 'bottle' honours after spewing out of the pubs in the Overgate. The pandemonium was captured by the same newspaper report.

> The nearest policeman, as in duty bound, interfered to stop the fray, upon which certain bystanders 'of the baser sort' interfered to stop the policeman, and threw him down and kicked him when down . . . A prisoner was hurried along to the station, followed by a mob of some three hundred persons, yelling and throwing stones . . . the valiant Belialites [devils] commenced to wreak their rage on the public gas lamps, and on the windows of the Post Office.

Closing-time riots became so severe that by the 1870s it was estimated that it would take a thousand policemen to quell them. The famous Dundee communist and lifelong teetotaller Bob Stewart, who for a time was Neddy Scrymgeour's right-hand man, remarked that there was more fighting in the Overgate on a Saturday night than the Black Watch did in the whole of the Great War.

By 1888 it was estimated that Dundee had more pubs per head of the population than anywhere else in Scotland, with 447 licensed premises plus innumerable shebeens selling illegal liquor. The following year Lord Cockburn branded the city 'a sink of atrocity which no moral flushing seems capable of cleansing'.

Sir R.H. Bruce Lockhart lived in Broughty Ferry as a young boy and he recalled the terrifying experience of wandering along Dock Street on a Saturday night to change trains.

> Every second door opened on to a public house. Drunks of both sexes encumbered the pavement. Brawls were frequent and on one occasion we had to make a wide detour to avoid a bottle fight. Beneath the yellow light of the street lamp I saw a man fall, his head smashed open by a broken bottle. His opponents were kicking him. I should have liked to rush in to

185

Alcohol's terrible toll in Dundee: mug shots were circulated to publicans of people with drink convictions. Most were women (courtesy of Dundee City Archives)

stop this brutality, but my knees trembled with fear. And, indeed, to a small boy the crash of broken glass, the pools of blood lying on the pavement and the vision of the pale, sodden faces of the men and women, more like animals than human beings, were terrifying enough.

As Bruce Lockhart's memories indicate, intoxication was not the exclusive preserve of the male population. Statistics from the last century show that the 'fairer' sex in Dundee struck an early blow for equality by committing just as many drink-related crimes as their menfolk. Of the 201 offenders convicted of between 20 and 150 crimes of drunkenness in 1887, 101 were women. The extent of female drunkenness is further illustrated by the fact that none of the men had been convicted more than 70 times. One woman appeared before the courts 253 times before she was confined to the lunatic wards of the poorhouse. Her list of convictions included 120 breaches of the peace, 112 cases of drunkenness and seven assaults.

The brazen attitude towards drinking displayed by many women could be explained by their role as the main breadwinners in Dundee households. The jute industry was reliant on the female workforce. Feisty Dundee women had more economic independence than their counterparts in other cities, and this gave them the freedom to embark upon drinking sessions.

In the early twentieth century an innovative scheme was devised to weed out the worst offenders. The red-eyed, bucolic and bloated visages of the most notorious drunkards peered out from photographs which were circulated around the pubs so that landlords could turf out the troublesome element before the carnage began.

Mass inebriation was not confined to the dives in the Docks or the Overgate, and Dundee drunkenness even managed to spill over to the genteel pastime of cricket. Railwaymen had to lay out rows of drunks on the platform at Broughty Ferry station after the annual match between Forfarshire and Perthshire. As the flannelled jute wallahs of Forfarshire battled against the upper-crust cricketers of Perthshire, thousands of whisky-soaked spectators poured into Forthill for a fine day's sport of hurling sandwiches, bottles, pies and obscenities at the fielders.

Given the extent of Dundee's drink problem, it is perhaps not entirely surprising that the reaction was ferocious and fanatical, and as the anti-alcohol movement grew, two Dundee men from vastly different backgrounds were to play key roles in the development of the British temperance movement. The Right Honourable Lord George William Fox Kinnaird was a prominent Dundee philanthropist who was one of the first people to introduce the concept of the drink-free working-men's coffee houses, which became common in British cities during Victorian times. Lord Kinnaird was also the driving force behind a piece of legislation which was to play a profound role in alleviating the awful drunkenness that plagued Britain's cities. Meanwhile, as the aristocratic Kinnaird was carrying out his good works, a humble grocer named Thomas Lamb was building up a highly successful business which was to result in Dundee becoming the home of an institution that was to become arguably Britain's most prestigious temperance hotel.

Lord Kinnaird, an old Etonian who lived at Rossie Priory, was a founding father of the Dundee Working Men's Coffee Houses and Reading Rooms Association, which was almost certainly the first organisation of its kind in Britain when it was formed in 1842. It was through the work of the association that teetotal coffee houses were introduced to Dundee 30 years before the national temperance movement brought them to other cities. Kinnaird's greatest temperance achievement, however, was steering the 1853 Forbes Mackenzie Act through Parliament. The Forbes Mackenzie Act was named after the two men who had drafted it, but it was Kinnaird's discussions with the ordinary working men of Dundee and the other Scottish cities that had inspired the legislation.

Prior to the introduction of the Forbes Mackenzie Act, which imposed tighter licensing hours, it was not uncommon for pubs to open at five o'clock in the morning, and bibulous Dundee mill workers often turned up for a hard shift fortified by a whisky breakfast. The new legislation restricted weekday opening times, introduced a ten o'clock last-orders rule and made it illegal for pubs to open on a Sunday.

The problems caused by early-morning boozing were referred to at the opening of the Victoria Coffee House beside the Wellgate in February 1880. At the opening ceremony, the director of the Working Men's Coffee House Association, Mr A.J. Buist, said, 'It was hoped that by opening these houses in the morning people going to the works at an early hour might be induced to take a cup of coffee, which would certainly be very much more wholesome than a glass of whisky (hear, hear). I have also a vivid recollection of the number of public houses from the Hawkhill to Barrack Street that were opened between five and six o'clock in the morning . . . It was hoped that the Working Men's Coffee Shops would have a counteracting effect to the unwholesome habit of indulging in strong drink at such an early hour.'

The parliamentarian's contribution to the temperance movement was recognised two years after his death when a coffee house named The Kinnaird was opened in the West Port in 1880.

A plethora of unlicensed premises sprang up as temperance took hold, but many found life hard in such a thirsty city. Denied the social release and the income provided by a good booze-up, many of these premises had to diversify by offering sidelines in prostitution and gambling. Such seedy activities were certainly not on offer at Lamb's Temperance Hotel in Reform Street, which was a model of moral rectitude. For over 50 years it was a fixture in Dundee and its success can be put down to impeccable standards of service, inexpensive prices and a complete absence of the patronising anti-alcohol propaganda that spoiled some other temperance establishments.

Lamb was a young grocer of 27 and had just acquired his first spirits licence when he underwent a dramatic conversion. The first temperance crusade arrived in Dundee in 1828 and Lamb's reaction was to pour his entire stock of spirits down the drain. His actions nearly bankrupted him, but it won him influential friends in the temperance movement. Two years later Lamb had opened a coffee house above his grocer's shop at 30 Murraygate. The upright citizenry of Dundee were weaned from the pubs by Lamb's high-class confectionery, fine-quality coffee and cheap ginger beer and lemonade. Literary and temperance societies met at Lamb's coffee house, which earned a reputation as a seat of learning, while the proprietor campaigned for shorter working hours for factory workers under the age of 18. His venture was so successful that he moved to larger premises in the Murraygate and his wife opened another coffee house in the West Port. From there he moved to a prime location at 56 Reform Street, and on 30 July 1852 Lamb's Temperance Hotel opened its doors for the first time. Contemporary reports describe it as being almost too grand for a provincial city hotel, but the winning formula of good food served in plush surroundings attracted a great number of commercial travellers and businessmen, who were happy to relax in lavish comfort even if it meant going dry.

Other examples of Dundee temperance hotels included Mathers' in Whitehall Place, Cameron's in Whitehall, The Waverley in South Union Street and Christie's in Whitehall Crescent. Diners settling down over a glass of Chianti and an Italian meal at Visocchi's café in Broughty Ferry today are probably unaware that a 'pub with no beer' stood on the premises until the 1920s. A British Workman's Public House opened in the Ferry in November 1873 and set itself the difficult task of trying to recruit drouthy fishermen. An attempt to set up a similar establishment in the Overgate was not so successful. At first it was hailed as a significant moral victory for the temperance brigade when in 1875 the Dundee Workman's Public House took over premises that had been occupied by a pub for the previous 70 years. But the Dundee Workman's Public House was to last only three years. A product of the national temperance movement as opposed to the local initiatives like those founded by Kinnaird and Lamb, it fell into the trap of adopting an overbearing approach to saving the wayward. Coffee houses, which provided reading rooms as well as pursuits such as draughts and bagatelle, proved to be more popular establishments than those which favoured a preaching and hectoring approach.

Organisations such as the Good Templars, the Rechabites, the Band of Hope, the Blue Ribbon Army and the Teetotal Party all maintained a strong presence

Poster advertising a 'Tee-Total Soirée' in Dundee in October 1851 (courtesy of Dundee City Libraries)

in the city and subscribed to the dogma that drink was the root of all evil. The strength of the movement can be gauged by the result of a poll held in the city in November 1926 under the Temperance Scotland Act 1913. The town-council minutes of that year record that a total of 12,726 people voted for a resolution which would have banned liquor licences from Dundee. Mercifully, the 'no licence' resolution was overcome by the 30,292 drinkers who voted for no change.

Perhaps the greatest hero of the Dundee temperance movement was Neddy Scrymgeour, the Dundonian who founded the Prohibition Party of Great Britain. Denounced as a harmless eccentric at the outset of his political career, Scrymgeour possessed a crusading zeal that was to take him all the way to Westminster. He came from a middle-class family and was the son of a devout

Café society in Visocchi's, Broughty Ferry, formerly the pub with no beer (courtesy of Michael Boyd/Scottish News Agency)

Wesleyan Christian Socialist, James Scrymgeour. From a young age he was instilled with an urge to help those less fortunate than himself which was almost as indefatigable as his hatred of strong drink.

James Scrymgeour himself was described as the best-known person in Dundee through his work organising teetotal trips and social events. He even had the distinction of being commemorated in verse by the incomparable McGonagall:

> *Fellow citizens of Dundee,*
> *Isn't it really very nice,*
> *To think of James Scrymgeour trying,*
> *To rescue fallen creatures from the paths of vice.*

His son Neddy left school at the age of 15 to work as a clerk in a Dundee office. After an unsuccessful spell in London he returned to his home town and took up a succession of poorly paid and unrewarding jobs. Averse to the idea of seeking comfort from the bottom of a bottle, he found solace in local government, where, as a parish councillor, he gained a reputation for exposing real and imaginary municipal scandals. As the editor of *The Prohibitionist*, he dreamed up such headlines as 'Dundee Poorhouse Scandal', 'Heartless Treatment of Patients', 'Doctor Decamps under Prohibitionist Fire', 'Parish Council Stagnant', 'Local Government Board to Be Invoked' and 'Press Silent'. Once described as 'the stormy petrel of municipal politics', he was nicknamed 'the White Star of Purity' by his rivals on the parish council.

Funded by the burgeoning prohibitionist movement, Scrymgeour first stood against Churchill, who had come to Dundee looking for a safe seat for life after defeat in Manchester, in the 1908 parliamentary contest. Scrymgeour's first venture into national politics was not a success. Despite campaigning slogans such as 'Vote for Scrymgeour and death to the drink – have done

Edwin Scrymgeour, the anti-drink campaigner who defeated Churchill in Dundee to become Britain's one and only Prohibition Party MP (courtesy of Dundee Art Galleries and Museums)

How the newspapers saw Churchill's defeat (courtesy of Dundee City Libraries)

with bogus Labour representation and go in for socialism', he polled only 655 votes out of 16,118. Undeterred by such an inauspicious beginning, however, he persevered and his support grew. In the 1910 election Churchill was returned with a reduced majority, with Scrymgeour increasing his share of the vote to 1,825.

Churchill expected to be returned unopposed in 1917 because of the wartime political truce, but the newly appointed Minister of Munitions had not bargained for the dogged persistence of Scrymgeour, who managed to scrape together the £500 necessary to stand against Churchill. Churchill won with a vote of 7,302, but this time the pacifist prohibitionist had polled 2,036 – a 21.8 per cent share of the vote. His anti-war stance was becoming more popular and his public support of Irish home rule following the 1916 Easter Rising attracted votes from the large number of Irish immigrants in Dundee. In the 'coupon election' of the following year he won 10,400 votes and emerged as a real political force.

In 1922 Scrymgeour finally broke through and saw off his illustrious rival in spectacular style, winning 32,578 votes. Churchill came fourth with 20,466. But it was not Scrymgeour's unshakeable conviction that Britain could be converted to a USA-style prohibition that resulted in him leaving Dundee for Westminster with a pipe band and the cheers of 30,000 supporters ringing in his ears. Rather his victory was the result of a number of factors, including the Dundee electorate's growing disenchantment with the 'warmonger' Churchill, who it was felt had neglected his constituency, a deep dissatisfaction with the coalition government, and a newspaper campaign conducted against Churchill by D.C. Thomson.

The year after he took his seat in Parliament, Scrymgeour introduced a hopelessly unrealistic private member's bill which called for the complete abolition of the alcoholic-drinks trade. Not surprisingly, its demands for the immediate closure of all public houses, the imposition of a five-year prison sentence for drinks traffickers, and for alcohol sold for medicinal purposes to be marked clearly as 'poison' were deemed to be too severe by most members of the house. Undeterred by the defeat of the Bill for Liquor Traffic Control by 236 votes to 14, Scrymgeour continued to wage his one-man war against alcohol. In 1931 he submitted an almost identical private member's bill, but it again went down by 137 votes to 18.

'Neddy' Scrymgeour departs for Westminster. He won an election battle for temperance but lost the war when Dundonians voted overwhelmingly in a temperance referendum not to ban the demon drink (courtesy of Dundee City Libraries)

By this time Scrymgeour's political life was coming to an end, but his unshakeable ideals remained as strong as ever. In his last speech to the House of Commons he attacked legislation that increased duty on the poor man's drink, beer, but failed to increase taxation on the spirits drunk by the middle and upper classes. In 1931, at the age of 65, Scrymgeour finally lost his seat. Two years later he became the chaplain to the East House and Maryfield Hospital in Dundee, a position he retained until his death in February 1947.

Scrymgeour's Conservative successor Miss Florence Horsbrugh, later Baroness Horsbrugh, adopted a far more pragmatic approach to the alcoholism that bedevilled industrial cities in Scotland. In 1937 Miss Horsbrugh became the first woman for six years to put her name on the statute book when she secured the royal assent for her Red Biddy Bill.

After the First World War, increased duties on spirits made whisky and gin too expensive for working-class pockets. In order to satisfy their craving for hard liquor, chronic alcoholics resorted to drinking Red Biddy, a lethal concoction arrived at by adding cheap red wine to methylated spirits. Consumption of this dangerous cocktail was first noted in Scotland in 1915 and seemed to be a by-product of the Liquor Control Order. In Dundee it was common by 1921 and 100 cases were recorded in 1923. One year later, pyridine was being added to methylated spirits in order to make its taste too revolting for even the most hardened palate. This innovation appeared to lead to a marked fall in the drinking of Red Biddy, with the number of cases

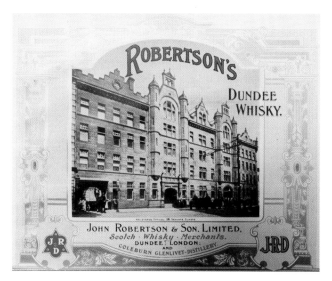

The Seagate Bond in its heyday, pictured in an advertisement for Robertson's Dundee Whisky (courtesy of Dundee City Archives)

dropping to 55 in 1924. Miss Horsbrugh's Methylated Spirits (Scotland) Bill, however, which restricted the sale of meths, also made a major contribution to the battle against drunkenness and proved to be the prelude to a distinguished political career.

The name Ballingall is synonymous with brewing in Dundee and the beers produced by the company until its demise in 1968 gave drinkers a safer and far more palatable alternative to Red Biddy. It seems strange that Dundee no longer has a brewing industry, given the predilection of its citizens for beer and the illustrious history of Ballingall's. Indeed, the 1802 book *Dundee Delineated* gives an indication of the thriving brewing industry that once flourished in the city.

> At one period there was not a town in Scotland where brewers were more numerous or ale more famous than in Dundee. The price was very moderate, and beer was the universal beverage, it being as much the custom for respectable persons to breakfast in the ale-house as it is now to do so in the coffee-houses in London.

According to the statistical accounts in 1800 there were 18 brewers and nearly 50 maltsters in Dundee, which at that time boasted a population of 23,500. But there was a steady decline from this glorious peak of production, which was described in *Dundee Delineated*.

> For sometime past, from the change in manners in the place and from the great taxes paid on malt and worts to the Government, the brewers are diminished in their numbers, and the strength of the ale is greatly reduced, although the price is more than tripled.

In the middle of the eighteenth century there was still a proliferation of breweries in the Seagate, Overgate and Murraygate. But it was at the Pleasance, where there was a ready supply of well water and more room for expansion, that the brewery that was to become famous all over the world was established.

194

Strong ales, table beers and porter were brewed at the Pleasance when the business was taken over by Provost Ebeneezer Anderson in 1790.

The Ballingall family name became associated with the brewery when it was bought by Provost William Ballingall. He was followed by his son Hugh and by the end of the century Ballingall and Son were brewing pale ale, which was drunk throughout Scotland and the north of England. To cope with the growing demand, a new state-of-the-art brewery containing one of the earliest Brewers' Laboratories in Scotland was built on the other side of Hop Street. The storage cellars at the Park Brewery held 5,000 barrels of beer. The Park Brewery concentrated on brewing the popular pale ale, which was now being exported to the Australias, Americas and the Low Countries, while the Pleasance Brewery continued to produce porter, mild ales, sweet Scotch ales and stouts for the local markets. The Victorian brewery historian Alfred Barnard was enthusiastic about the pale ale, saying, 'Without being heady it is highly nutritious, bright and sparkling and tastes well of the hop.' Ballingall's were also doing a line in bottled beers, of which Barnard remarked, 'Although of less strength, [they] possess an aromatic flavour and are most agreeable to the palate.'

As Ballingall's went from strength to strength, its Dundee competitors were failing and by 1890 there were only four other brewers left in the city: W.H. Brown of the Craigie Brewery in Lyon Street, John Neave of the Victoria Brewery in Victoria Street, M. and M. Whitton of the King Street Brewery and William Gray and Son of Fort Street, Broughty Ferry.

The Speedwell Tavern (courtesy of Ian Jacobs/Scottish News Agency)

The interior of Ballingall Brewery

The prohibitionist movement affected trade in Dundee and, according to the Scottish Brewing Archive, Ballingall's even faced competition from producers of non-alcoholic beers, who set up in Dundee at the turn of the century. But the biggest blow to the company at that time was the sudden death in 1910 of Hugh Ballingall at the age of 70 after 50 years in charge of the company.

Times were hard during the inter-war years when Dundee was badly hit by the recession, and the decline of Ballingall's continued after the Second World War. By the 1960s, fewer than 100 barrels a week were being produced at the Park Brewery, and in January 1964 the harsh commercial decision to stop all brewing was made.

No account of drinking in Dundee would be complete without a short expedition around a selection of some of the notable howfs that abound in the city today. A pleasant starting point for a few rounds is the Speedwell Tavern in the Perth Road. An original Edwardian public house, the Speedwell takes its name from Provost James Speed, who built it in 1903. To Dundonians, however, it is invariably known as Mennie's, after a long-serving and formidable landlady. Mrs Mennie, who was a relative of Provost Speed, served her last drink back in 1976.

Today's owner is Jonathan Stewart, who also owns the Campbelltown Bar in the Hawkhill and the Fisherman's Tavern in Broughty Ferry. 'The Fish' is a fine watering hole which in 1994 had the distinction of being voted the best pub in the United Kingdom by the 50,000-strong membership of the Campaign for Real Ale. It was established in 1825 for the fishermen of the Ferry, who used to gather outside the building to read the barometer which once hung from a nearby wall, and the smooth and creamy pints pulled at the Fish have won it many admirers over the years. Fine beer is also a feature of the third member of Stewart's triumvirate, the Campbelltown Bar, where drinkers unwittingly step over a remnant of the first Tay Railway Bridge, which was salvaged after the 1879 disaster, when they cross the threshold.

According to Mr Stewart, who has spent a quarter of a century in the trade and whose career has taken him from the heights of Shakespeare's in the Hilltown down the literary slope to McGonagall's in the Perth Road, the pub scene in Dundee has never been healthier. 'I know that Dundee pubs are the best run in Scotland and that, I think, is a result of our licensing board and the hardy and independent breed of publican that flourishes in the city,' he said. 'The licensing board, while being reasonable, are always firm, and when you compare Dundee pubs with those in other cities, we are simply streets ahead.' Behaviour has improved dramatically since drinking hours were extended past ten o'clock at night. According to Mr Stewart, 'We used to get people finishing their work and they were so worried that they would lose valuable drinking time that they would drink as fast as possible. Now they go home, have something to eat and then come out. This has made pubs a bit less profitable, because we are basically doing the same business in twice the hours, but the sociological benefits are such that it has been an amazing success.'

Dundee's drinkers are rediscovering their drinking heritage as the city's publicans hold out against the sterile uniformity of theme-pub domination. The young and beautiful of the city hang out in Laing's or congregate in the cluster of taverns in the West Port. In the Nethergate, the traditional Phoenix is a fine bar serving a superb selection of food and drink. A high standard of pub cuisine is also an outstanding feature of Deacon Brodie's, where there is a meeting of some of Dundee's finest legal minds at lunchtimes.

The lavish, stained-glass interior of the new and popular Trades Bar, part of the successful Morrison empire, recreates the splendour of the Victorian era in a modern setting, and establishments such as the nearby Pillars and Broughty Ferry's Royal Arch recall two of Dundee's lamented architectural treasures.

A trendy crowd now gathers in the Dundee Contemporary Arts centre, but beer connoisseurs know that Dundee drinking was elevated to an art form a long time ago in places like the Clep Bar in Clepington Road, which is famed for its delicious pints of heavy.

Today a few wildly ambitious drinkers still seem intent on recreating the heady days of the past by emulating the intake of their forefathers, but, overwhelmingly, drinking in Dundee has taken on a civilised hue that would come as a surprise to Neddy Scrymgeour.

Mary Slessor stained-glass windows (courtesy of Dundee Art Galleries and Museums)

11

Emerging from Obscurity
How Dundee Women Have Made Their Mark

Norman Watson

The perception that Dundee is a 'women's town' has lingered since it was transformed into a world centre for jute, employing an overwhelmingly female labour force. For 100 years women outnumbered men in the city's population, more women worked in Dundee than in any other city, and eight out of ten of them were the largely unwilling subjects of King Jute. Working women were the city's backbone. Yet Dundee's women were hidden from history, condemned to be the unseen wives or widows of prominent men or as the mischievous, anarchic figure of mill girls. They emerged only in recent years, not, as they richly deserved, to grace the pages of the city's history, but to become an almost mythical figure encompassing the character and idealism of women of the past, too often in a picture painted of a city struggling to shake off the jute legacy.

Now, however, that gender-jaundiced perception of Dundee is changing. Today, as never before, the city's women weave a welcome thread through Dundee's rich tapestry of community life, with an increasing bearing on the city in terms of access, presence and action. Today, they are seen 1,000-strong running in the 'Race for Life' at Camperdown Park, supporting each other and others by doing so; seen working together and sharing cultures in ethnic harmony in the Dundee Women's International Centre; seen in community choral and dance groups; seen as ever-increasing numbers of higher-education students, graduates and staff; and seen as personnel in the city's crusading health sector.

In 1999, the thoughts and aspirations of many women with political ambition turned to the new Scottish Parliament and its promise of gender equality in the new millennium. In embracing proportional representation for the first time, Dundee's women mirrored the uncertainty of women gaining the Parliamentary vote 80 years ago after the long struggle to take part in the political process. The credible but otherwise painfully serious *Dundee Advertiser* in November 1918 captured the novelty of the granting of the vote to women:

One woman revealed a remarkable conception of what the function of recording a vote meant. She was shown into her booth and told to approach the polling clerks. She stared at these gentlemen with a puzzled expression, and at last exclaimed, 'That's no' the candidate I want tae vote for. It's Reid I want; where is he?' Evidently she expected to find her favourite enthroned on a dais with a hand stretched out to receive her vote.

Passing years have diluted that excitement and perhaps many women today take the democratic right to vote for granted. Two female pressure groups, the Fawcett Society and the Women's Communication Centre, recently blamed growing female apathy on politicians failing to address the specific concerns of women. If Dundee women are like any others, the main political concerns today are childcare measures, domestic violence, part-time workers' rights, low and equal pay, support for carers, breast-cancer research and pensions. If such issues are taken seriously, say these groups, women, who already vote in larger numbers than men, could have a significant collective impact on future general elections.

Ironically, it was Dundee's women who threw body and soul into the campaign to win those votes. The first act of suffragette militancy in Scotland occurred in Dundee in 1907; the first demonstration of the suffragettes' tactic of disrupting meetings took place in the city, and although there was no figurehead in the votes-for-women movement in Scotland, its recognised leader was the Dundee artist Ethel Moorhead. Moreover, some of Britain's most militant suffragette deeds, many of the campaign's largest demonstrations, its political imprisonments and most violent confrontations took place in Dundee. If we project forward into the twenty-first century and picture women disrupting a royal visit to Tayside, setting fire to postboxes or burning down the Caird Hall, we can imagine the impact such militant tactics had 90 years ago. However, the contribution of the majority of Dundee suffrage supporters was to persuade people – men *and* women – of the constitutional justice of a woman's vote rather than to engage in militant activity. A contemporary extract from *The Dundee Advertiser* indicates that being a footsoldier in this women's movement was anything but a romantic commitment, issues being absorbed to the extent that the women involved were highly politicised. In it, the young Dundee teacher Helen Wilkie describes her visit to the Kincardineshire by-election in the spring of 1908:

As we came nearer the town we saw chalked on walls and gates 'Votes for Women' and 'No Votes for Women' and so on, but we saw no references to the Small Landholders' Bill, the Licensing Bill or Tariff Reform, which are, or will be, the burning questions of the Kincardine election. By and by we met Miss Munro busily chalking notices of that night's meeting on the pavement. We were pleased to hear that she had almost recovered from the ill-effects of Holloway Gaol. After tea we went for a walk around the square and through the main streets. We walked in the middle of the road, and carried sandwich boards as a final advertisement. The large sheets of cardboard were a most effective protection from the rain. I should have liked an umbrella, but I became resigned when someone told me that rain water was good for the complexion. We had two small bells, and their shrill clanging brought the people to their windows and doors, and later to the Town Hall. When we took our seats on the platform we could see the people standing in crowds out to the street door. It was the first women's suffrage meeting held in Stonehaven and the people listened with keen interest. We felt we had done a good night's work keeping the Liberal out.

It is as voters that the majority of Dundee women will continue to make political headway in the new century, and it was as novice voters in 1922 that newly enfranchised Dundee women may have voted as a cohesive block for the first and only time in British politics to rid the city of Winston Churchill in favour of Edwin Scrymgeour, the first and only Prohibition MP. Then, in 1929, the year in which all women over 21 were given the vote, Scrymgeour secured the biggest single vote in the city's history to be returned to Parliament. *The Courier* noted that his poll had been increased by 71 per cent and that the new electoral register had increased the number of female voters by 77 per cent. The paper felt that the 'significance of the two figures cannot be missed'. Two years later, with nearly 20,000 unemployed in Dundee and with Labour councillors elected in ten of the twelve municipal wards, it might have been considered the city's political destiny for a Labour candidate to be returned. Instead, the Conservative Florence Horsbrugh overturned a huge electoral deficit to record the most surprising victory in the city's political history. It may also have been the case that the expanded female electorate in Dundee in 1929 made a difference in terms of political outcome that year – Horsbrugh, after all, was the first woman to stand in Dundee.

Despite Dundee boasting significantly greater numbers of women Parliamentary voters than men since the war – for example, 50,935 men and 65,895 women in 1946, and 65,290 women against 50,990 men in 1948 – the prospect of further mass voting by women in favour of specific policies or candidates failed to materialise, as did a second woman MP. Indeed, between 1918, when women were first allowed to stand for Parliament, and the 1997 general election, women provided just 16 candidates in Dundee from a total of 187. Only Baroness Horsbrugh was successful. As the new millennium dawned,

Limbering up for the 'Race for Life', Camperdown Park, June 1998 (courtesy of D.C. Thomson and Co. Ltd)

however, there was a steady increase in women candidates as a percentage of the total standing in Dundee. In 1983, for example, 22 per cent of candidates were women, and although the figure dropped to 20 per cent in 1987, it rose to 25 per cent in 1992 and 31 per cent in May 1997, this last figure greater than that of Edinburgh, Glasgow and Aberdeen. Interestingly, research suggests that where women make up more than 30 per cent of a decision-making body, the nature of debate and policy-making changes.

Out of these early efforts to win voting rights and representation emerged the vanguard of the women who help to guide Dundee's domestic affairs today. One of note was Agnes Husband, a doughty campaigner for women's rights and a pioneering member of Dundee School Board and Dundee Parish Council, the forerunners of today's local-authority education and social-work departments. Husband became one of only a handful of women to be given the freedom of the city, and modern-day historians number her among those who have shaped Dundee. As for Dundee Town Council, or Corporation, or City Council, as it is called today, women have only recently taken their place at the heart of municipal affairs and addressed traditional gender imbalances in local-authority control. Since 1935, when the secretary of Dundee Trades and Labour Council, Mrs Lily Miller, at the sixth attempt became the first woman to stand successfully for election to the town council in Dundee, women candidates as a percentage of those standing have risen steadily to around 30 per cent. In 1995 a record number of ten women were elected to the council. But it remains to be seen whether any twenty-first-century candidate can ever match the achievements of Mrs Miller, the first woman to stand for election to the council, the first to be elected, the first bailie and the first woman to sit on a magistrate's bench in the city.

It is probably safe to say that Dundee's formidable force of working women never shared common interests with Lily Miller as political actors. The type and nature of the work carried out in the textiles industry made Dundee the most readily identifiable 'women's town' in Britain, not only in terms of women over men in the general population – 17,521 more females than males over 20 years of age in 1901, for example – but also because of other factors and patterns, such as their dominance in the workplace to the exclusion of adult men, the number of married women employed and the number of girl workers in its textiles industry. Dundee, said the British Association in 1912, 'was pre-eminently a city of women and of women workers'. For the 100 years between the mid-1800s and mid-1900s, Dundee was a manufacturing town largely limited to this single industry. It was 'Juteopolis' – the jute capital of the world – and 'without women's labours,' said Dundee Social Union's female investigators in 1905, 'the city would sink to the level of a small burgh; as a manufacturing centre it would possibly cease to exist'.

Thus the most striking feature about employment and life in Dundee over those years was the extent to which the city depended on women to operate this hugely dominant industry. By 1870 it boasted 70 mills and factories and a jute workforce of nearly 40,000, some 30,000 of them women and girls. This gave it a lopsided economic profile of women earners and unemployed men – the so-called kettleboilers. But it was also an industry where spontaneous strikes, walk-outs and lock-outs were commonplace. Between 1870 and 1880, 46 strikes occurred within the jute industry alone. Yet if Dr David Lennox could warn in his 1902 monograph that the 'true reason for the employment of women is an economic one; they lack the faculty of efficient organisation', it was not for the want of trying. The absence of a jute trade union prompted one 'Mill Lassie' to write to *The Advertiser* in 1874:

> I dinna ken what's the use o' us women that we dinna hae a Union, since a' the men, even the vera scaffies, hae ane. Gin we could only get some chap tae tak' it in hand [or] twa or three sensible women.

The Dundee women's champion was the Reverend Henry Williamson of the Unitarian Church, which now bears his name in the city. In the spring of 1885

Political first: Florence Horsbrugh triumphs in the male world of Conservative politics to become Britain's first ever woman Tory MP (courtesy of Dundee Central Library Photographic Collection)

he founded what is accepted as Scotland's first female trade union, the Dundee and District Mill and Factory Operatives' Union, because, as he put it, 'no other person offered to do it'. If this was a hint that jute women were apathetic towards political participation, Williamson soon discovered that his prime directive – appeasing employers and the avoidance of strikes at all costs – did not sit comfortably with the women's radical past. Thus his union grew slowly. By the turn of the century it had around 7,000 members, some 6,000 of them women, while the textiles workforce in Dundee in 1901 was given by the census as 38,936.

In spite of Williamson's best efforts, however, stoppages by non-unionised women continued. There were major disputes in 1895, when 18,000 walked out on strike and a further 10,000 were thrown idle over a demand for a 10 per cent rise; in 1898, when three works were closed; and in 1899, when 35,000 workers were locked out – numbers inconceivable today. It was directly as a response to Williamson's no-strike stance that Dundee's more militant Jute and Flax Workers' Union was formed, a union which grew in size and power up to 1918, when it had 20,000 members, mostly women, out of a total textiles labour force of 47,000. Both unions deserve their place in history for progressing women's equality in the workplace. Indeed, both had a majority of women on their executive committees.

As for the Dundee mill girl, she continues to be seen by tradition, folklore

Women getting their hands dirty at Camperdown Works during the war, while the men look on (courtesy of Marine Design Consultants Ltd)

and legend as a barefoot, shawl-clad and aproned lass, mischievous to the point of anarchy, capable of hard work and spontaneous rowdyism, plagued by the highs and lows of production. The product of a Dundee half-time school, she worked from 6 a.m. to 6 p.m. as a preparatory shifter or rover in a low mill, or a spinner, and her place was not to be confused with the better-paid, 'higher-class' factory weaver. She had her own shopfloor rules, and even, it is said, her own unintelligible shopfloor patois. The jute historian William Walker said of the mill girls, 'Unruly, raucous and madcap, [they] were the despair of reformers and an embarrassment to employers and workers alike,' while the *Dundee Yearbook* concluded in 1893, 'Below the surf of industrious, respectable factory workers ebb and surge the flotsam and jetsam of the stream – the mill workers.'

Such an attitude and such a way of life is now hard to imagine in the sophisticated City of Discovery. Today, women fill a diverse spectrum of prominent roles in industrial, commercial and business concerns and have a developed political consciousness. Record numbers of girls go on to higher education and the half-time school is confined to history books. Manufacturing has largely given way to service industries. Dundee's past is its past.

What did emerge from the jute era, however, was a comradeship born of loyal reliance. Evidence suggests that Dundee's women frequently turned away from traditional family-centred domesticity to seek an independent life. 'Some of the most attractive little homes in Dundee are those of women and girls living as companions. The friendship begins in their youth, often persists till old age

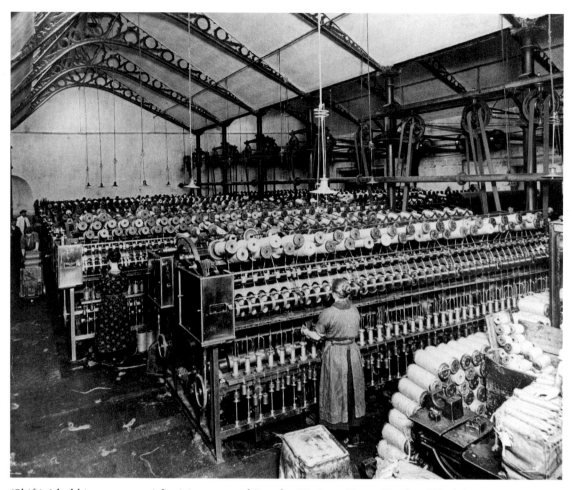

'Shiftin' bobbins coorse an' fine' (courtesy of Dundee Heritage Trust, Verdant Works)

and is only broken by death,' reported Dundee Social Union in the jute heyday. As such, the 'inevitable' job in the mills was seen by some women as a pathway to economic independence. Dr David Lennox reported in 1902 that there were 44,065 ordinary accounts in Dundee savings banks, equal to 30 per cent of the population, and a considerable saving power indicative of a community capable of financial prudence. He cited the average Dundee balance as over £12, while the UK average was under £5. The money did not belong to jute barons, however. In 1904, 33 per cent of new depositors were people engaged in spinning, weaving, dyeing and engineering. This, in effect, was the beginnings of the expansion of the city's hitherto insignificant middle classes. Dundee's greatest social-welfare pioneer, Mary Lily Walker, spoke of these women in 1912:

> She leaves her home, sometimes taking some of her brothers and sisters with her, sometimes setting up joint housekeeping with a companion of her own age and sex. The home she makes is bright with gay floorcloth and

polished brass. The windows are draped with muslin, the bed with chintz. These are not the girls who marry casual labourers or mill workers and work after marriage. They are interested in the questions of the day, they attend lectures and classes, take an active part in Church life, are members of various unions and societies and are ready to help others.

Support for others is a characteristic common among Dundee women and one that can be seen today in organisations such as the Women's Royal Voluntary Service and Women's Aid Dundee. Away from the arena of politics and the workplace, groups of Dundee women have down the years gathered together in welfare, charitable, church and voluntary organisations, often providing the first formal forums for women's issues and concerns. The Dundee Female Society of Lochee Road was to be found in 1871 'visiting and relieving aged females in distressing circumstances'. A Dundee branch of the Scottish Ladies' Association for Female Education in India also appeared that year, with a sizeable committee of 13 women. There was a Clothing Society and, as early as 1848, an institution called The Home, for 'the reformation of females'. By the turn of the century there was a Dundee Women's Temperance Union and three branches of the Dundee Young Women's Christian Association, which provided classes in 'reading, cooking, sewing, ambulance work and accommodation for occasional boarders'.

While the textiles unions took up the attention of working women in the early years of the twentieth century, the pioneer of community concern in the city was Dundee Social Union, whose ground-breaking report by women inspectors in 1905 – which involved evaluating working-class life in 5,888 houses in the city – was used for a Royal Commission on housing and was discussed in the House of Commons. In 1924 the Union noted proudly, 'The crippled children, the nursing mother and the welfare of infants were three all-important branches of work begun through the Union,' and although by then they had been taken over by the town council, they 'had the credit of initiation'. Elsewhere, the organisation of women which faced up to a rapidly transforming city with a female population newly enfranchised was the Dundee Women Citizens' Association.

When women of today look around the city – how it operates, its traffic system, its policing, its local-authority departments, the distribution and management of housing, even its by-laws – they might be forgiven for assuming that they are seeing the legacy of patriarchal control. Yet the Women Citizens' Association, with 1,000 members in the Dundee branch alone, became such a significant forum for action on matters such as housing, education, child law and social improvement that it was a model of feminine solidarity, influence and collective action, so much so that in the 1920s the town council recognised it as

If it wasn't for the work o' the weavers . . . (courtesy of Dundee Heritage Trust, Verdant Works)

the 'body representative of the women of Dundee'. Its members' determination to bring about change in the city has struggled to surface in histories of the period and are recorded here to provide an indication of the breadth of the women's movement as its network expanded.

The DWCA was founded in 1918 with a remit to progress women's influence and power. One of its early objectives was realised in 1920 when it persuaded the all-male town council in Dundee to co-opt two of its women members on to the council's housing and education committees. It would be a further 15 years before a woman was elected by right to the council. The branch later persuaded the council to build single-person houses for Dundee mill girls when the Housing Act (Scotland) of 1919 stated an ideal minimum of two-bedroom homes. It was instrumental in securing the first women police officers in the city, drunk-free Dundee trams and even 'morally acceptable' films in the city's cinemas!

Thus there is a legacy of hard-working, responsible women's groups who have been distinct and determined forces for good in the city, a tradition carried on today by the likes of Dundee Soroptomist International and, indeed, the

Dundee branch of the Women Citizens' Association, extant after 80 years. Dundee Soroptomists, formed in 1932, is an organisation which has continued the tradition of co-ordinating clusters of women and networking women's groups. The Soroptomists, from the Latin for 'best sister', were founded to cement women's growing role in society, and Dundee branch members have proudly continued the march of women into all corners of society. Its first president, Dr Edith Philip Smith, was a pioneering university lecturer in botany. The first treasurer, Miss Christian Bissett, became the first woman (as Mrs Christian Tudhope) to hold the position of Depute Town Clerk in Dundee. Margaret Fairlie, chair of obstetrics and gynaecology at Dundee University and Scotland's first woman professor, was a member in the 1940s. Catherine Scrimgeour, branch secretary from 1946 to 1953, was the first local woman to head a legal practice in Dundee. Eva Laburn, the first woman to train as a chartered accountant in the city, was club president from 1961 to 1963.

These are crashes through the gender glass ceiling, but advances a-plenty await in the twenty-first century. The climb by Women Citizens' and Soroptomist members to the top of their professions are important but largely symbolic milestones. Persuading the local authority to allow women on to the education committee was significant for Dundee Social Union, but in 1999 there were no female rectors or heads in Dundee's 11 secondary schools. Putting policewomen on Dundee's streets in the 1930s was a notable achievement for the DWCA, but in 1999 Scotland could boast only one woman assistant chief constable. Entry to the Depute Town Clerk's office by a Soroptomist in Dundee was commendable, but in 1998 there was not one woman chief executive of a Scottish local authority according to the annual *Gender Audit* by the women's organisation Engender, which also pointed out that 'women made up between 50 and 70 per cent of the workforce of most local authorities'. It has been a long road to equality for women in the workplace. In a leader-page comment on 'equal pay for equal work' as long ago as 1922, *The Dundee Advertiser* argued the following.

> The time was when many cognate problems could be dismissed by the lordly masculine declaration that 'women's sphere is in the home'. That is no longer possible.

Some 80 years on, equal pay for equal work remains a distant hope for many of the city's women.

And what of Dundee's working women after the decline of jute? While no full analysis of the impact of new employers and industries in Dundee is known, incoming industries clearly formed a watershed in the development of the city by creating a considerable electronics and light-engineering sector. The post-

Second World War period witnessed a movement of 20,000 jobs out of the jute heartlands to peripheral industrial estates and into companies such as Timex, the National Cash Register company, Ferranti, Veeder-Root, Holo-Krome and Burndept (later Vidor). By 1952, town planners could write, 'So successful has been the selection and development of these new industries that, in complete contrast to the inter-war period, there have actually been signs of a shortage of labour.' (City and Royal Burgh Advisory Plan Report, 1952)

A second key point to record is that jute workers, particularly female operatives, showed themselves to be adeptly skilled to meet the challenges of the electronics age. One of the factors which influenced L.S. Meyer's choice of Dundee for their new clock-making venture in 1946 was the belief that suitable labour would be available, and results justified this confidence. 'The operators have proved themselves to be dextrous, efficient and adaptable, adjusting themselves from their former types of work to up-to-date clock manufacture and assembly.' When the NCR president Stanley Allyn visited Scotland in August 1950, he said of the Dundee workforce, 'Production is good. Efficiency and morale excellent. Why? Because Scots people are industrious and conscientious.' Ferranti, writing of the Dundee factory in December 1958, said, 'Since the firm came to Dundee four years ago they have been more than satisfied with the quality of the labour available in the city.' In August 1968, Mr R. Boyd, Veeder-Root's director of manufacturing, claimed his company was 'more than satisfied' with the type of employee it had found in the city. 'They had an inherent ability to learn the new techniques,' he said.

That the jobs were earned and not given to the women as a matter of course is also significant. The intricate nature of watch assembly, for example, required patience and a keen eye. In May 1947 Mr John Strachey of the Timex parent company told the *Glasgow Herald* that 'the girls' employed in his Scottish Timex factory were considered at least equal in skill and aptitude to the third generation of American workers – 'operatives, that is, whose parents and grandparents had been employed in the firm's American factories'. The Scottish writer Jack House visited NCR in 1949 and observed its production line. He reported his findings in the firm's *Factory Post* magazine.

> A girl sat putting the twenty-one finicky wee bits together . . . I was amazed at the intricacy of the work. Apparently Dundee people are very good at this sort of thing, perhaps because jute work on which most of the inhabitants were employed at one time can be a finicky thing.

At Burndept in 1952, the manufacture of dry batteries employed several hundred people, mainly women. 'In the early days of production, women were found to be more adaptable than men in this particular type of work,' they said.

Ferranti claimed in 1958 that its workforce of 'women and girls have proved themselves most adaptable and capable'. Tributes to the women's skills were also made by the American directors of Timex in 1949 and 1952, by which time there were 400 women employed by the company in the city: 'The girls with nimble fingers on assembly are really the people who count. In over ten different stages, sitting under powerful lamps with tweezers and magnifying glasses, they pick up minute parts, place them in the correct positions, and inside an hour a watch all but case is ticking in a testing room.' And according to the *Daily Express* in April 1979, the employees at Levi's – 80 per cent of them women – were voted the company's best workers 'in the world'.

Marathon woman: the indefatigable Jenny Wood Allen (courtesy of D.C. Thomson and Co. Ltd)

What Dundee had rather unconsciously witnessed was the successful mass movement of women into these vibrant new industries. Of Burndept's workforce of 550 in 1947, 450 were women. Half of NCR's start-up workforce in 1946–47 and two-thirds of Ferranti's 350 employees in the mid-1950s were female. Between 1943 and 1951, three out of four employed at Hamilton Carhartt Ltd were women. By the early 1950s, over 600 of Veeder-Root's workforce of 1,000 were women. And by the early 1970s, Timex alone employed 3,000 women in Dundee, when there were only 2,500 female operatives remaining in the jute industry. Effectively, light engineering and electronics had replaced textiles as the principal employer in a transformation which, as the twenty-first century unfolds, may eventually be viewed as the significant connecting link between two extraordinary eras in Dundee's industrial story.

That the new industries fell into decline is also part of Dundee's story. The sit-in by Timex workers in 1983 which prefaced the closure of the company's Milton of Craigie factory to make way for a supermarket was followed in 1993 by a strike involving the company's by-now only 350-strong largely female workforce at the Camperdown factory. As television pictures of the women with their Intifada caravan on the Harrison Road picket line were flashed around the world, *The Times* rounded on the striking women, infamously calling them 'The Witches of Dundee'. But the shop-steward conveners involved in the 1993 stoppage were men, the leading union officials were men, the local MPs were men, the largest marches were led by men and the public speakers at protest meetings were mostly men. In tribute to those indomitable Timex women who stood on the picket line week after week and who contributed towards a memorable, trouble-free and happy Women's Day on 11 June 1993, redressing the balance after weeks of ugly scenes around the factory gates, it is worth raising the possibility that had those so-called witches of Dundee been given greater access to negotiations, Timex might well have been content to continue its long association with the city into the next century.

Individually, women's contribution to Dundee's history, culture and identity is increasingly apparent. There has been a resurgence of interest in the exceptional missionary Mary Slessor and the skilled social reformer and women's-rights pioneer Fanny Wright. Jute heiress Mary Baxter would be astonished at the development of the university she fought to create in 1883 and at the numbers and contribution of its female students and graduates, whose presence she insisted upon as a condition of her endowment. There, in 1995, Scotland's only chair in gender relations was established, followed by the appointment of a research-based Professor of Gender Studies.

Mary Lily Walker's selfless contribution to the development of social work in turn-of-the-century Dundee is seen today in the work of Grey Lodge, the home she bequeathed to allow the continuation of her pioneering ideas. The political orator turned mill poet Mary Brooksbank is currently the subject of academic study. Liz McColgan and the remarkable Jenny Wood Allen have blessed the world of athletics for two decades, becoming household names across the UK and beyond. And who can forget the 1,000-plus women in both 1997 and 1998 who took part in the Imperial Cancer Research Fund's 'Race for Life' running event in Camperdown Park to raise funds for research into cancers which affect women? Many of them had been treated for cancer themselves or had friends and family affected by the disease. Side by side with them in the belief that cancer will be beaten eventually walks the indefatigable Jacqui Wood, whose efforts have encouraged the raising of millions of pounds for local medical causes.

In general health matters, scores of senior citizens have benefited from the physical revolution sparked by Dorothy Dobson's exercise classes at the University of Dundee, which have led to over 50 classes using her name and techniques nationwide. Margaret Grant founded the Brittle Bone Society in

Dundee 28 years ago and has drawn the country's attention to the plight of sufferers of osteogenesis imperfecta. The society is a major source of support for the 3,500 people in the UK who suffer from the condition. Meanwhile, a host of women scientists and healthcare personnel, such as Professor Elaine Rankin of the ICRF chair of cancer medicine at Dundee University, are striving for new cures and better treatments for a variety of diseases at Ninewells Hospital and Medical School and at the Wellcome life-sciences centre in the Hawkhill, while other women throughout the city are involved in counselling at times of crisis, specialist help and enabling support. Dundee, indeed, is in good hands.

Magdalen Green Band Stand, treasured by locals who fought for its preservation

12

It's a Singing City

*A Look into the Future of Dundee's
Alive and Kicking Music Scene*

Helen Brown

Music is, by its very nature, an inclusive art. Everyone, regardless of taste, listens to music, enjoys music and whistles, hums or sings along to music as an integral part of everyday life, and nowhere is that more true than in Dundee. Scratch a Dundonian and you'll find a singer.

Dundee's grass-roots music, of whatever style, has always got people involved. Dundonians are rarely content to sit back and be passively entertained, and for people supposedly dour, thrawn and introspective, below the chipped veneer of many an imperturbable Dundonian surface lies the heart and soul of a natural-born show-off. Over decades, even centuries, perhaps, those attempting to put bums on seats have bemoaned the fact that it's hard to get an audience for any kind of show in this city, but organise something where people can come and take part and you'll be virtually guaranteed queues around the block.

Traditional singer Sheena Welling-ton's memories of growing up in Dundee are of a musical feast. Sheena, now traditional arts development officer for Fife, remembers Blind Mattie – 'She wasn't a big woman but you could hear her from one end of the Overgate to the other!' – and singing at parties in Dundee as a way of life. 'Just look at the way karaoke took off in Dundee and you'll see how people still love to sing and dance,' she says. 'There was a great tradition of dance bands and

Blind Mattie – 'She wasn't a big woman but you could hear her from one end of the Overgate to the other!' (courtesy of D.C. Thomson and Co. Ltd)

215

dance halls in the city. In the communities, groups like Discover Dundee Voices, based at the Brooksbank Centre, sing all kinds of music, from pop to Vera Lynn.

'Dundee has a great song tradition, more so than many other cities. I think it's because it's small enough to have a real sense of community and belonging and yet big enough to welcome the influence of "incomers". I was always told that 'A Guid New Year' was written in Dundee! Nigel Gatherer's *Songs and Ballads of Old Dundee* is well known, and individual singers like Annie Watkins had an amazing collection of songs. You only have to look at the response to singing events or workshops here to see that it's still the same today. There's a hunger here for music and song. It's a singing city!'

It's a singing city all right, but it's also much more than that. Dundee's music is that of a place that is, and always has been, a city of many voices. According to John Purser in his definitive book *Scotland's Music*, Dundee, along with Aberdeen, Edinburgh and Glasgow, had a 'Sang Schule' in the early 1500s. Dundee was also the home of the Wedderburn brothers, whose *Good and Godlie*

From top to bottom: RSNO conductors Neeme Jarvi, Sir Alexander Gibson and Bryden Thomson, who are all noted for their recordings at the Caird Hall (courtesy of the Royal Scottish National Orchestra)

Ballads is one of the earliest collections of hymns, psalms and songs set to popular tunes of the time. The Wighton Collection of music, currently housed in Dundee Central Library, is a fine collection of early Scottish music dating from the sixteenth century onwards and there are plans to develop around it a heritage centre for the study, performance and appreciation of Scottish music. A lot of recent work on the collection has been done by Dundee-based musicologist Brian Clark, who has an international reputation in his field.

Dundee has maintained a tradition of producing singers and songwriters with a distinctive tone from Mary Brooksbank right through to Michael Marra. It has one of the most active amateur circuits in the country with literally thousands of people involved in everything from revues to grand opera, choral singing to bands and full orchestras, and it has a track record of community involvement in music mixed with drama that is second to none.

With the city's strong working-class traditions, it's a haven for blues, jazz and soul in pubs and clubs. There are several fully equipped recording studios, including the Seagate and Stage 2000, that cater for many diverse performers and styles. Radio Tay is committed to supporting a wide range of musical organisations and events in Dundee and beyond. The city is also home to the Caird Hall, without doubt one of the greatest concert halls in Western Europe. It has a guitar festival, inspired by Dundee-born and Dundee-based guitarist Allan Neave, that is now regarded as the leading event of its type in Britain, and it was from here that the very first classical performance to be broadcast live across the world via the Internet took place.

Dundee has a lot to offer and a lot to be proud of, but the difficulty at this stage seems to be that although there are many significant musical things happening in Dundee, for reasons partly social, partly industrial and partly economic there doesn't yet exist a lively musical cultural network that will draw locals into regular attendance at all kind of events and attract outsiders to come and see Dundee in a different musical light. But the building blocks are there, ready to be stacked. The great thing about Dundee's millennium music is that across the community of musicmakers, both amateur and professional, there seems to be a great desire to get involved. The trick, in the new millennium, will be to join all Dundee's disparate musical dots, tap into the undoubted interest and goodwill of potential participants and audiences alike and create a diverse and delicious musical menu that will appeal to all tastes and is accessible across the board.

So how does a city find its voice, its own distinctive sounds? It looks both within and without. Dundee has always been a city with strong musical roots where committed individuals have, for many years, worked hard to establish musical events and to create an audience for their work. Now links are being forged and initiatives are already in place to harness the energy coming both

217

Dundee People's Orchestra performing The Salmon's Tail *at the Rep, 1992 (courtesy of Steve Smart)*

from the grass-roots and from a range of organisations keen to support and be a part of music in the city. There's Music Plus, formerly the Dundee Music Partnership, a three-year project supported by the National Lottery's 'New Directions' programme and managed by Dundee City Council's arts and heritage section. It brings together the Royal Scottish National Orchestra, the Dundee Guitar Festival, the Dundee Music Consultation Forum, the Dundee Jazz Festival and the Traditional Music and Song Association. The city now also has its own music development officer, Rachel Gardiner, based at Dundee Contemporary Arts, one of the first in Scotland. Her remit is to liaise with musicians, artists and members of the community to encourage music in all its forms and to aid the creation, development and presentation of quality live music in Dundee.

'It's important to build up a picture of what's happening in the city, who is involved, where people can go either to be entertained, to look for music tutoring, to learn, even to book a band for a certain occasion,' she says. 'From the other perspective, it's also important for musicians to be put in touch with groups and individuals who can help them, with new developments, with others who are working in the city and contributing to the range of events and projects.

'Making and maintaining regular contact is a vital step and we're keen to do that as a kind of first base. Although the council has a website, there's definitely a call for a comprehensive listings guide, for example, both for locals and for visitors, so that people know what's going on and get into the habit of taking a look at it.'

Workshops and education projects take musicians out into the community to build a rapport and a relationship over the musical spectrum. As well as using the Rep and the Gardyne Theatre as venues for its Opera-Go-Round and Essentials tours, Scottish Opera For All has in the past also undertaken educational workshops with local schoolchildren. The RSNO has a strong commitment to its performances at the Caird Hall, one of its favourite venues. It is so much the favoured choice of Neeme Jarvi, now its conductor laureate, under whose baton the orchestra has recorded there, that he came back to Dundee in 1997 to conduct 'Carmina Burana'.

Simon Crookall, chief executive of the RSNO, explained, 'We're working over the next three years with half a dozen or so community groups on a range of activities and skills related both to our programmes and to their needs so they can get experience of different aspects of the orchestra.

'Our first afternoon Kids' Prom was in Dundee in May 1999 and there's also a three-year project for schools, two primaries and two secondaries, where the kids will have the opportunity to build up a relationship with individual players. They'll be looking at works from our programme, then composing their own pieces based on what they learn and performing them before the RSNO concert, which will feature the originals.

'We've worked with living composers like James MacMillan and Michael Torke and we're planning to do that in Dundee, getting a composer to write what we're calling a "windows" piece with gaps where the kids' work will fit in. That way, they play it not before the main orchestra performance but as an integral part of it. Here in Dundee, because of the relationships building up between different disciplines, we're hoping to link up with dance and the visual arts too. There are no little boxes!'

Rock schools are also aimed at young people in many different areas of the city and traditional music workshops and weekends in areas like the Hilltown, for example, cover both Scottish traditions and those of the Asian community. In Dundee, the Bengali Singers are well known. Sheena Wellington recalls hearing them sing Burns songs translated into Bengali, the perfect example of crossover culture and appropriate in Scotland, where it is reckoned there are more native speakers of languages like Urdu than there are speakers of Gaelic. Regular events rooted in different communities will be designed to establish music there and eventually it is hoped to have a traditional music weekend event for the whole of the city, as well as stronger performing and educational links with Celtic Connections, the Glasgow-based showcase for traditional music.

Whether classical or traditional, these ideas are not just meant to put bums on seats. 'They're intended to create a musical frame of mind,' says music development officer Rachel Gardiner. 'These project initiatives will build audiences for a range of music and, vitally, will also build confidence amongst those who want to work and perform here. The aim is to give Dundee the most varied package of quality music and get the city known as a music venue so that it becomes a natural touring stop again. It has a reputation as being a difficult place to get audiences, but everyone's working on that!'

The problem of getting those audiences is a thorny one, as is the issue of venues. Dundee isn't short of them, but what most musicians seem to be looking for – amateurs, professionals, classical players and rock guitarists alike – is not just a good hall but a real musical focal point for Dundee. The failure of the campaign to regenerate the King's Theatre was seen by many as a real blow, but there are still the Caird and Marryat Halls, the latter currently used by the BT Scottish Ensemble, the Bonar Hall, the Gardyne Theatre at the Northern College at Broughty Ferry, Dundee Rep, the Bell Street Music Centre, the Whitehall Theatre, several university halls including the Chaplaincy Centre and a series of acoustically beautiful churches dotted around the city. All have their own qualities and many are excellent in their style. But if one theme recurs when speaking to all kinds of musicians about their vision of Dundee's musical future, it is the plea for a multi-purpose music centre and mid-sized – around 500 seats – performance space with facilities both for visiting artists to perform and for the locals who live and work here to centre their musical life.

The founder of the Dundee Guitar Festival, internationally renowned guitarist Allan Neave, is one who sees this as a real way forward. 'I think we need a music centre in every sense, not only with performance, technical and rehearsal facilities for musicians but also with the ability to build up a culture of events so that people expect to have a range of things available. That way they will get used to going along and listening to musical styles they haven't tried before as well as those they know they like. I think it could be a real nerve centre for local musicians, whether they're classical or rock-trained, to play, develop their abilities, rehearse, record and so on, and it would provide a top-class venue for big names to come here to play.'

Planned developments at the Caird Hall, including the installation of new sound and lighting systems, the purchase of a moveable proscenium arch and the use of special curtaining to reduce the seating capacity, may expand its use beyond the traditional orchestral or large-scale choral concerts and programmes of distinguished organ recitals on an instrument admired worldwide. Even those whose natural home it is, such as Dundee Symphony Orchestra and the RSNO, would support the idea of a new venue as part of the wider picture.

Donald Gordon, treasurer of the 106-year-old Dundee Orchestral Society whose playing arm is Dundee Symphony Orchestra, explained that with a larger audience and a greater number of players enabling it to tackle major works like Bruckner's Fourth Symphony, DSO is now back at the Caird Hall for the foreseeable future for the first time in many years. 'Increasing our own activities, plus the finance and support of local trusts, has made a big difference to us and it's wonderful to be back at the Caird Hall with future plans for major events. But I think that a medium-sized venue would be wonderful for Dundee and Dundee audiences, and I think most musicians I know would support it.'

Susan Allen, president of the Dundee Chamber Music Club and secretary of the Music in Dundee Initiative (MIDI), was given the brief by MIDI to get people together to create an impetus for a millennium venue of around 500 seats. Meetings have already taken place with a consulting architect and a quantity surveyor and questionnaires have been circulated to a wide variety of promoters throughout Scotland to assess the interest in a venue constructed specifically for musical performance in Dundee. A wide spectrum of musical interests backed this move; the initial group comprised Susan Allen, Frank McLevy of the Musicians' Union, director of Dundee Guitar Festival Allan Neave, president of MIDI and founder of Dundee People's Orchestra Kevin Murray, composer Gordon MacPherson and university music adviser Graeme Stevenson, with interest also expressed by Kit Clark of Swiss Family Orbison, jazz musician Tony Sellars, Heather Duncan of the BT Scottish Ensemble and music development officer Rachel Gardiner.

The Chamber Music Club has recently celebrated its 70th anniversary and is enjoying great success and, significantly, increased audiences for high-calibre chamber concerts. With a generous bequest as the basis, Susan and interested parties outside as well as within the club are looking to form the nucleus of a group to support a National Lottery bid to finance the purchase of a top-class Steinway piano for the city. This, it is hoped, will form part of the facilities of the new performance venue.

Kevin Murray added, 'We also have the MIDI website, established three years ago as the Virtual Music Centre, providing contact worldwide for all kinds of musicians. It has led to invitations to Dundee performers to appear as far afield as Russia and the Caribbean, where I was touring recently. It's still not easy to live and work here at the moment, but to me one of the great things about Dundee musicians is their ability to keep alive a determination to function even in difficult conditions. Apart from that, I think the city has more talented musicians per square foot than other places can claim!'

Gordon MacPherson, like Allan Neave, is another native son who has chosen to make his home here in Dundee. As well as building distinguished international careers, the two have often collaborated. One of their recent joint efforts was working with Dundee-born poet Don Paterson to create the music for the opening of Dundee Contemporary Arts, work composed and recorded not only for a CD but also to be listened to through headsets in different parts of the building.

Gordon creates music for musicians all over the world as well as maintaining

*Exploring musical collaborations: Dundee composer
Gordon MacPherson with guitarist Allan Neave aboard
the* Discovery *(courtesy of D.C. Thomson and Co. Ltd)*

a strong commitment to teaching at the Royal Scottish Academy of Music and Drama in Glasgow. His Kamperduin overture, commissioned by Dundee City Council to commemorate the victory of Admiral Duncan at the Battle of Camperdown in 1797, was premiered here in Dundee by the RSNO, but he also composes for companies from London to Vienna, ranging from amplified ensembles like Icebreaker to the National Youth Orchestra of Scotland.

'Classically there isn't a great tradition here and I don't necessarily think that everything can grow out of community involvement, although Dundee has a great background in that and a lot of it is very exciting,' he says. 'What I like about what's happening now in visual arts here is the fact that it's looking outwards as well as inwards. People may say, in terms of what DCA is showing, what has Andy Warhol got to do with Dundee, but I don't think links have to be that direct for people to relate to them. The more people get used to having things around, the more they try new things, branch out a bit, take a new view. It's the same with music. I think the more people can hear of different styles, the more they'll see that a lot of them do mean something to them, even though the subject matter may not be directly about their lives.

'What I'd like to see is support for musical activity right across the board, from education through to performance, everything. It's important to encourage excellence in any area. I would say I'm all for élites and all for making them bigger!

'What would also be a really interesting development would be a festival with a real focus, not just a selection of events grouped together at the same time. It seems to me that something like that could grow out of what's happening here, particularly the guitar festival, which covers so many different styles from rock and jazz to classical and has such a strong local involvement in terms of workshops and participation. It also has one of the few composers' courses around.'

Since its beginnings as a small-scale weekend event designed for local kids and musicians, the Dundee Guitar Festival has grown in stature to become an international event. According to Allan Neave, it has over the years earned the trust of its audience, who support it enthusiastically, and of participants the world over. Early enquiries about the 1999 festival came from Japan, America and Iceland, among many other countries. The festival was very much Allan's own brainchild and a manifestation of what he felt could be done in his native city. Dundee now has a worldwide reputation in guitar music and in a multiplicity of disciplines including classical, jazz, flamenco and Celtic music. Plans for the new millennium include building on 1999's collaboration with the RSNO and a determination to bring the very best performers to the city.

'A festival would have to be something that grew out of the scene here rather than being grafted on, because I don't think people would go for that,' says Allan Neave. 'I didn't like the idea of bringing bits of the Edinburgh Festival to Dundee, for example, because I thought that was rather patronising.

'I am proud of the guitar festival and I know that the climate in the city with regard to supporting these things has changed a lot since we started out. Again, it's a case of working our way towards becoming part of a link-up of groups and events so that there's something going on all the time. Then we can say to people, "Come to Dundee because it's got this event to offer, that festival to experience, this series of concerts, that tradition of live entertainment."

'It's taken us a long time to get where we are and a lot of hard work, but I'm

The world-renowned Tayside Police Pipe Band outside Scone Palace (courtesy of Tayside Police)

a great believer in thinking positively about what can be done and I'm hopeful about the future. A lot of determined and tenacious individuals have done a lot over the years to get things going and I think we'd all like to see a climate here that makes things easier for musicians, writers and performers who want to live and work in Dundee.'

Dundee Rep is another epicentre of arts in the city. It is home not only to drama but also to the Dundee Jazz Festival and the Scottish Dance Theatre, which has itself commissioned music for new dance work not only from Scottish composers with an international reputation like Craig Armstrong but also from local Dundee bands like Quarter. The Rep also has a policy of creating work with local relevance that is far from parochial. It taps into wider concerns but keeps its place in the locality, and again music is at the heart of many of these plays.

'The songs and poetry of Mary Brooksbank allied to the music of Michael Marra formed the backbone of Billy Kay's *They Fairly Mak Ye Work*, and Marra also contributed the songs for musician-turned-sculptor-turned-writer Chris Rattray's celebration of the heyday of jute *The Mill Lavvies*. Both the Dundee-based women's drumming group Ells Belles and Dundee Rep's Women's Singing Group grew out of community initiatives and around 40 singers of all ages and backgrounds have involved themselves in a range of activities, from an oral history and songwriting project based on the theme of women and work in Dundee to the recording of a CD, *Recognise That Feeling*, and a large-scale community musical planned for late 1999.

On the Line was another theatrical and musical landmark for Dundee, tackling one of the most significant events in the recent history of the city and winning major plaudits, including the Theatre Managers' Association Best Overall Production award, into the bargain. The music was an integral part of Alan Spence's play right from the start, bringing back Deacon Blue frontman and songwriter Ricky Ross to his birthplace to tackle a very different kind of musical project that harnessed local energy and talent in a unique way. Ross said at the time, 'I didn't want it to become a musical. It's a play with music. People anywhere can understand what it's about – you don't have to be from Dundee for it to mean something to you.'

It was obviously an experience to treasure as there's now another collaboration to celebrate, reuniting Ross and Dundee Rep and using the verbal verve of Liz Lochhead. There is also perhaps a way forward here in encouraging live music in the city. The Rep, after all, has a pit and it would be particularly appropriate if local musicians could perhaps be hired to provide live music to accompany the acting.

To that end, training and encouraging performers of the future is a vital part of any music policy. With traditional job security a thing of the past, those with a talent and a bit of grit may as well go for it, as they're as likely to be able to make a living out of singing and dancing, playing an instrument solo or in sessions, sound engineering, DJ-ing, working with music technology, recording or composing as they are working in an office or a bank. And if the Dundee music scene develops the way many think it should, they may well be able to do it on their own doorstep. And for would-be performers, there is now even a one-year full-time national certificate course in Performing Arts: Music at Dundee College.

According to Charlie Maynes, co-ordinator of expressive arts for Dundee schools, as far back as 1893 archive reports record that 'Dundee Corporation continues to employ seven lady piano teachers in the Harris Academy and Logie Secondary areas'. There are currently 25 staff in Dundee teaching instruments from piano to bagpipes, and group-teaching techniques have resulted in a significant increase in the number of pupils who play. Dundee can even boast its own schools' music centre in Bell Street, dedicated to rehearsals, workshops and staff training, with particularly fine acoustics. Morgan Academy has a modern music technology suite used by staff and pupils, with twilight training courses regularly held by principal teacher Paul Clancy, and across primary and secondary levels there are no fewer than a dozen different ensembles, from training, intermediate and senior string orchestras to a big band, junior and senior choirs and a symphony orchestra.

Dundee has produced many top-class professional musicians, including classical accordionist James Crabbe, Pamella Dow, principal percussionist with the RSNO long before Evelyn Glennie achieved solo fame, young clarsach player Catriona McKay, pianist and professor of music Norman Beedie, lutenist Rob McKillop and composer and author of *The Songs of Scotland* – and numerous cook books! – Wilma Paterson. Ailsa Cochrane, Mark Wilde and Colette Ruddy are only three of a feast of young singers on the brink of major careers, while the 'Voices of Discovery' competition encouraged national participants. Famous rock names range from the Average White Band to Deacon Blue via Danny Wilson, and there has been a fair number of original, quirky, not to say downright eccentric voices. The Dundonian trait of bone-dry, mordant humour has often caught many a listener by surprise, as has a predilection for the deeply surreal, seemingly at odds with a dour character and a forbidding exterior. Dundonians know exactly what St Andrew, late of the Woollen Mill and the now legendary *The Word on the Pavey*, is all about, and native son Michael Marra has the ability to marry sharp sarcasm with real pathos and tenderness. Anyone who has heard Marra's masterly debunking of Flora Macdonald's royal friend in 'Mincin' wi' Charlie' will never be able to look the lace-jabot-and-shortbread school of Scottish culture in the face again.

Perhaps the reason that community-based arts initiatives have always done

Thomson-Leng Musical Society's production of The King and I *at the Whitehall Theatre (courtesy of D.C. Thomson and Co. Ltd)*

Ann Wallace as Joice Heath, the oldest woman in the world, in Downfield Musical Society's production of Barnum *at the Whitehall Theatre (courtesy of D.C. Thomson and Co. Ltd)*

The Dundee Operatic Society's cast of Oklahoma! *at the Whitehall Theatre (courtesy of D.C. Thomson and Co. Ltd)*

Sounds Spectacular *at the Whitehall Theatre (courtesy of D.C. Thomson and Co. Ltd)*

well in Dundee is because it is a city of participators. The sheer number of people involved in making music, from the amateur musical societies to the flourishing Strathspey and Reel Society, the world-renowned Tayside Police Pipe Band, the City of Discovery Brass Band and early music groups like the Craigowl Consort and the newly established Cantiones Sacrae, is huge, especially in relation to the overall population. New combinations are being forged all the time, such as the large choir of local singers established to perform in a special Caird Hall millennium concert in June 2000, accompanied by the well-established Tayside Symphony Orchestra, which draws players from all over the area.

Dundee Choral Union is the archetypal mix of local participants and top-class professional soloists and accompanists. With their millennium performance of Verdi's monumental *Requiem* in view, they have assembled not only the massed ranks of the Scottish Opera Orchestra to accompany them but also an impressive quartet of top-notch soloists: Dame Sarah Walker, Arthur Davies, Evgeny Nesterenko and soprano Lynne Dawson, who sang an excerpt from the *Requiem* at the funeral of Diana, Princess of Wales. Future projects for 2000 and 2001 include works by Elgar, Berlioz, Lloyd Webber and Bernstein.

Many church choirs – including that of St Paul's Episcopal Church, who have recorded a CD – continue the tradition of encouraging young singers, and adults have several choirs to choose from, including the Cecilian choir, the Dundee Gaelic choir and many other active local groups.

Amateur music-making is often sneered at, but in Dundee it's important to underline the root of the word in the sheer love of performing. Tayport Amateur Musical Society, which performs regularly in Dundee, recently celebrated its 50th anniversary. Thomson-Leng was the first Scottish society to take part in the Waterford Festival in Ireland and the inaugural Newport Festival in Wales, while Downfield have competed with great success at Waterford and had the major honour of representing Scotland in the National Opera and Dramatic Association's centenary celebration at the Royal Albert Hall in May 1999. Generations of Dundee children have been brought up with the Scout Gang Show and with Margaret Mather's Junior Showtime, and there is now the Whitehall Youth Theatre Guild, affiliated to the National Youth Music Theatre, and groups like the Really Young Theatre, Monifieth.

Tayside Opera sponsors an award for promising opera singers at the Royal Scottish Academy of Music and Drama in Glasgow in memory of its founder, the late Bill Dewar, and has inspired the creation of Tronder Opera in Trondheim, Norway. This was the result of a collaboration with international tenor and music professor Harald Bjorkoy, who has sung with the company in Dundee. In the year 2000, the two companies hope to mount a joint production to be staged both in Dundee and at the Trondheim Festival.

Dundee Operatic is the city's original amateur group, founded in 1923 but with roots going back to the 1870s, and Broughty Ferry is the second oldest, with a strong Gilbert and Sullivan tradition and a recent popular association with pianist John Scrimger and international singers Donald Maxwell, Linda Ormiston – whose mother Muriel Brown was a former Broughty producer – and James Nicoll. Many other companies from around the wider Tayside, Fife and Angus areas perform at the Gardyne Theatre and at the Whitehall, one of the few theatres in Britain owned and run by a trust. The brainchild of the late Bill Crowe, it was created by the local amateurs and plays host to both amateur and

Dress rehearsal of Dundee University Operatic Society's production of The Boyfriend *at Bonar Hall (courtesy of D.C. Thomson and Co. Ltd)*

professional performers. There is also the phenomenon of *Sounds Spectacular*, drawn from a range of local talent, which packed the Whitehall Theatre for 13 years.

The university, although it has never had a music faculty, has a regular concert programme and a wide range of activities participated in by students, from the University Operatic Society to two choirs, an orchestra, a big band and its offshoot, a quintet. 1999 saw the opening of music rooms and the appointment of Graeme Stevenson as music organiser, succeeding Dr John Brush. The regular and varied lunchtime concert programme at the Chaplaincy Centre attracts a 'town and gown' audience, and there are also evening concerts there and in the Bonar Hall with top-class artistes including Dundee-born pianist Murray McLachlan, oboeist Nicholas Daniel and organist John Kitchen. Graeme hopes to expand the already growing membership of the choir and orchestra and to encourage borrowing of the small collection of musical instruments. He is also keen to link up with music-making at Aberdeen University.

Linking up, collaborating and working together seems to be the keynote for the future. At the end of the twentieth century, Dundee has a lot to say, not only to its own citizens but to the wider world. As the new millennium arrives, what the City of Discovery is learning to listen to and love is the sound of its own individual, distinctive and infinitely varying voices.

229

St Salvador's, a glorious interior (courtesy of Alan Richardson)

13

The Sixth Incarnation of Dundee
Designs on Dundee's Past, Present and Future

A Personal View by Charles McKean

Winston Churchill's observation 'We make our buildings, and they make us' applies with equal force to how we interact with our cities. Cities throughout history have been characterised by symbols or imagery designed to reflect their identity and personality – like the 'Athens of the North' label for neo-classical Edinburgh. Danger lies if the image is partial, or if it dominates perceptions of the city, for perceptions and reputations of cities have a critical impact on their fortunes. For a hundred years, Glasgow boasted of its reputation as 'the Workshop of the World'. Once heavy industry finally left the city in the 1970s, however, the question of whether it had any future at all was often the subject of discussion in the Sunday colour supplements. The revived Glasgow has been achieved, at least in part, by the rediscovery of the Merchant City, displaying that Glasgow did have a life before it became the Workshop of the World. And it was in the Merchant City of the tobacco lords and the cotton kings that central Glasgow began its revival.

In comparison with the Athens of the North, the Granite City and the Workshop of the World, Dundee's imagery was pretty demotic, characterised by the three 'J's – jute, jam and journalism. Yet even while these three industries were at their peak, the city was furiously attempting to refashion itself and cast off its history, partly through its fledgling university with its team of young, radical thinkers – including that great urban analyst Patrick Geddes – and partly through schemes of great civic ambition to transform Dundee into the most modern city in the country. These visions of the wholesale replacing of old Dundee with variations of a twentieth-century 'beautiful city', partially executed in the 1930s and in the 1960s, failed to replace jute, jam and journalism with anything more attractive, however.

Jute and jam are long gone, although journalism in Dundee continues to thrive. Even if the three 'J's used to be an appropriate way to depict the city, they are no longer. The difficulty is that, unlike Glasgow – which retained the Merchant City of the tobacco and cotton periods – Dundee appears to have nothing to fall back on. It has few striking physical features save the broad sweep of the Tay estuary, and no great castle, cathedral or comparably grand civic monument. Furthermore, a principal legacy of the 'jute, jam and journalism' period has been the belief – held by Dundonians and visitors alike – that there was nothing else to the city. That is patently not the case. What is required is a new appreciation of Dundee, which can only come about through a study of how it grew. We have to know more about its history, for whatever may be the opinion of Scots, English and even Dundonians themselves, Europeans have little difficulty in sensing the continued presence of the second city of Renaissance Scotland and appreciating the (albeit fragmentary) quality of what they find in it. As Dundee enters its sixth incarnation, that of a university city, it will become crucial that it capitalises upon its undoubted strengths, for a university city dependent upon incoming students and academics has to compete with more obviously attractive or historic institutions. If it is to sustain itself in the future, Dundee, like Glasgow, has to discover a multi-layered past which is richer than a single-industry proletarian workplace.

THE MYTH

The most composite summary of the myth is that of Sinclair Gauldie: 'The eighteenth-century burgh never experienced that expansion of a civilised middle class which ensured the success of Edinburgh's New Town . . . Subsequent generations [did not] possess the resources and fierce determination . . . A modest burgh with a fairly typical eighteenth-century social stratification . . . became within a matter of decades an industrial city with an overwhelmingly proletarian population.' The town's other histories of linen, tanning and shoe-making, shipbuilding and whaling have been submerged beneath jute, as indeed was its vibrant British (and yet distinctively Scottish) civic culture – and that had developed during the eighteenth century. The image of jute Dundee – gaunt mills, a forest of tall smokestacks, canyons of unrelieved and often grim workers' tenements, and poor poets in drinking dens – came to dominate people's perceptions of the city and to represent its entire culture.

Extraordinary theories were developed to explain why Dundee did not expand with the graciousness of other Scots cities. Its rock was too hard, or it had no middle class, or what little middle class it had had left the town for Broughty Ferry by 1800, or its entrepreneurs lacked imagination, sophistication or culture, or it was too poor, or the town had inherited nothing of value from any earlier period. None of these assertions is true. For example, the percentage of Dundee's population in 1841 that were of the professional classes was significantly higher than Glasgow's; and far from being the insanitary working-class Babylon whose middle classes had fled to the Ferry *c.* 1800, the town remained socially integrated decades after old Glasgow and old Aberdeen. Indeed, by 1871, the year of the City Improvement Act, Dundee retained possibly the most extensive medieval city centre then surviving in Scotland. Much of it, however, was overcrowded and in poor condition, and some of its streets were unconscionably narrow.

The myth about Dundee grew, partly as a consequence of the physical difference between the town and other substantial communities of the period, namely the absence of a new town. While other towns and cities were building their new towns (Edinburgh from 1767, and again from 1802; Paisley from 1782; Perth from at least 1801, if not earlier; Aberdeen from 1800; Ayr from 1803; Greenock from 1780 and 1809; and Glasgow from 1786, and again from 1791 onwards), Dundee missed out on that essential phase of urban development and never recovered the lost ground. It is evident from the reactions of people who complained that Dundee's streets lacked 'even the trivial grace of a straight line' that they were almost certainly comparing the city to the new towns of the other Scottish cities. They had to rationalise the aberration, and the easiest way was to presume that as early as 1800 Dundonian middle classes, fleeing the cholera and the other epidemics of an insanitary town centre, were emigrating to Broughty Ferry at a time when the altogether more sophisticated burghers of Perth, Aberdeen, Edinburgh and Glasgow were emigrating to the formidable neo-classical blocks of gracious terraced houses.

Yet the houses to which the Dundonian bourgeois would flee would not be built for another 50 years. The plan of the late 1820s for a spanking neo-classical suburb in Broughty Ferry went unbuilt and the Ferry remained an agglomeration of cottages by the beach well into the 1840s. The reality was that Dundee was unusually healthy in comparison with its peer cities and remained unusually socially integrated long after the classes in the cities with new towns had begun to segregate. It did not appear to put the same priority upon class distinctions as its rivals. Fourteen merchants, three booksellers, three agents, eleven grocers and four surgeons, *inter alia*, lived alongside four vintners, a slater, a saddler and a reedmaker in 1822 Murraygate. When the city architect, James Black, was asked in 1835 to comment on whether more public wells should be provided in the poorer parts of the town rather than areas inhabited by the richer classes, he replied, 'They are so much mixed that you cannot distinguish them.'

So Dundee pursued a development pattern unique in Scotland. The relevance to today is that as Dundee enters its sixth incarnation, the image of a grim, class-segregated, post-industrial town lacking a function – albeit partially and temporarily true – will be of little help to its future. It is far too narrow a vision of Dundee, as the surviving buildings can tell you.

THE DUNDEE REINCARNATIONS
History matters. An understanding of Dundee and an appreciation of its quality are only possible by understanding how it came about, observing, in passing, the extent of the undamaged historic town centre Dundee retained in 1871. The simplest method is to divide up its story into periods of differing imagery and symbolism and consider how the legacy of each stage is still visible within the city today.

1 St Mary's

Towns have always been careful about the buildings or symbols by which they are represented. Early maps show Dundee – perhaps the second city of Scotland in 1590 (only Dundee and Edinburgh sent representatives on James VI's wedding trip to Denmark) – dominated by the steeple of St Mary's. Rudely

Gardyne's Lane, from Lamb's Old Dundee *(courtesy of Charles McKean)*

interrupted by the sack of General Monck in 1651, Dundee had rebuilt or refitted itself by 1686 (dated by buildings on Fish Street), becoming possibly the most modern town in Scotland. Glasgow had rebuilt its street fronts in 1652 but, judging from Lamb's *Old Dundee*, Dundee's rebuilding appears to have extended into the minor streets and the closes. The population might not have shrunk, but it had certainly retreated from the east to the west; fewer people lived in the Cowgate or eastern Seagate, surrounded by abandoned buildings and crumbling walls. Uphill to the west it was a different story, and the quality of the rebuilt town may be inferred from David Hunter's 1697 'great lodging with portico, gallery, well, garden and houses' on the north side of the Overgate. The many drawings in Lamb's *Old Dundee* show smart dwellings with large windows rather advanced for the late-seventeenth century, newly in from Holland. The city was a place of growing

Head of Commercial Street, from Lamb's Old Dundee *(courtesy of Charles McKean)*

confidence and prosperity, with a Physick Garden and a Cabinet of Curiosities (a museum). In 1700, its council won the right from the Scots Parliament to levy taxes for the building and repair of the harbour. What few illustrations exist of the town's hospital, on the site of the new arts centre, show it to be a large, fashionable U-plan civic building with octagonal stairs and a cupola of the late-seventeenth century.

The period of St Mary's left the legacy not just of St Mary's tower but of the underlying street pattern of Dundee itself and, mouldering behind Georgian and Victorian rebuildings, substantive relics of the original Baltic trading port.

2   The Town House

In 1735, the new Town House, representative of the thriving mercantile Dundee of the eighteenth century, replaced St Mary's as the symbolic focus of the burgh. William Adam, then Scotland's finest architect, was employed to design quite the most imposing Town House in Scotland, if not beyond – which, if nothing else, signified ambition. It took over three years to build.

By the 1740s, Dundee had become the leading Scottish centre for coarse linens manufactured from low-grade Baltic flax. It invested in three new 'very handsome' shoreside packhouses and warehouses in 1758, and the following year the harbour was described as 'one of the best ports for trade in all Scotland'. In 1768, the town invited Britain's most celebrated engineer, John

Smeaton, to advise it on how to control silting in the harbour caused by the fast-flowing Tay, and four years later Dundee had 32 ships engaged in foreign trade, 78 in coastal trade and four whalers. The town's population more than doubled between 1775 and 1800, and its shipping tonnage increased by more than 15 times between 1745 and 1791.

In 1772, the Trades funded a new chapel (later St Andrew's Church) in the countryside to the east, designed by the town's wright or architect Samuel Bell so that its spire faced axially down Murraygate. The burgh's principal attraction had become its 'large and well-built Market Place', the spacious 360-foot-long by 100-foot-broad High Street (the same width as Edinburgh's). In addition to the Town House half-way along the south side, Bell added the new Trades House to close its east end and the English Chapel to close off the west end in 1783. The High Street – the town's 'dealing floor' – thus retained the necessary protection against wind to keep it comfortable for outdoor trading. In 1793, the pride in the town, and its ambition, was proved by the publication of the *Old Statistical Account* by Robert Small as a separate *History of Dundee*, with specially commissioned illustrations and an updated and illustrated plan of the town. In 1794, subscribers to the new Infirmary appointed Robert Adam's chief assistant John Paterson to design it (Adam had just died), and a similarly ambitious attitude to patronage was exemplified in the appointment of Scotland's best architect, William Stark, to design the lunatic asylum in 1812.

The ambition had its downside. Dundonians have never seemed to value their past. The pseudonymous Philetas, writing in 1799, paints a picture of Dundee in 1746 as a small, crumbling town of no consequence, whose buildings were disfigured by timber projections – 'The buildings were generally of wood. There were not then above half a dozen stone houses in the High Street or market place.' In fact, the houses were very rarely timber houses, but stone buildings with timber projections, which gave a dry arcaded passage beneath in wet weather, almost certainly the timber balconies and galleries customary on street-fronting buildings of the Renaissance. The 1799 perspective was that wood was old-fashioned and had to be stripped from the façades to make the town look more modern. It was not to be the last time that the town would be preoccupied by modernity.

Although most of Dundee's eighteenth-century monuments have been demolished, the legacy of the period lies in Castle and Crichton Streets, South Tay Street, the scant remains of Irvine Square, St Andrew's Church, Milne's Buildings and some plain and worthy houses facing Nethergate. However, a more significant legacy of the period was the marginalisation of the town council. Under Provost Alexander Riddoch, the burgh had refused to share the improvement mania under which all other Scottish towns of note were embellishing themselves with new towns. Seeking to contain the town's expenditure within its revenue, it had invested in neither harbour nor development plans and was characterised by parsimony, short-sightedness and allegations of corruption. The energetic individuals and new manufacturers who had funded the town's new institutions were determined to break loose, however, and in 1815 succeeded in the establishment of independent Harbour Trustees. Thus the town entered its next phase.

3 The Harbour

Whilst Dundee lacked the broad, neo-classical streets and axial vistas which now adorned all other Scottish cities of note, it had more practical attractions. For example, the extensive pier, spacious and convenient docks and commodious and well-arranged warehouses had been admired by Alexander Campbell in 1802. Dundee had 34 ships in the foreign trade, 78 coasters, four Greenland; shipbuilding carried on with great spirit; there were 2,000 looms, threads, osnaburghs, tanned leather, shoes, glass, snuff, ropes and cordage. The thriving burgh was now to be represented by the sea, for it was the harbour developments and the Harbour Board – a body of entrepreneurs and manufacturers generally different from those represented by the Merchants' Coffee House – that began to drive the city and led to its replanning with new roads.

The success of the first dock, rapidly joined by a second and then in the 1830s by a third and fourth, indicated that Dundee was coping with demand. In 1838, visitors failed to notice the substantial new civic monuments which the town had built, and the new Union and Reform Streets. It was the harbour. 'The town and harbour of Dundee . . . present attractions of the deepest interest to all who delight to contemplate scenes of national prosperity . . . in which manufacturers and commerce have attained unprecedented status and extent.' It was the harbour that led to the creation of the unusually wide and gently sloping Union Street in 1825, then South Union Street, the Shore, Dock Street, Commercial Street, Exchange Street and,

A Renaissance archway (courtesy of Charles McKean)

237

Union Street and St Mary's (courtesy of Charles McKean)

Architectural detail from the Albert Institute which now houses the McManus Galleries

eventually, Trades Lane. The enormous quantities of goods coming through the harbour had to percolate through the town somehow.

According to Professor John Wilson, the celebrated columnist who wrote as 'Christopher North', in 1845, 'There is little regularity of plan. The High Street wears much of that opulent and commercially great and dignified appearance which characterises Trongate or Argyle Street of Glasgow but there is little regularity of plan. Excepting the numerous new but in general short streets . . . not even the trivial grace of straightness of street line is displayed. Most of the old streets are of irregular and varying width; and many of the alleys are inconveniently and orientally narrow.' He failed to observe the town's fine civic monuments probably because the town lacked the new streets, squares and axial vistas generally required to give such buildings the prominence and nobility they required. The 1823 Theatre Royal, probably by David Neave, slid into Castle Street and the 1828 Thistle Hall (Assembly Rooms or Masonic Club) into Union Street.

The principal early/mid-nineteenth-century institutions – the High School, the Sheriff Court, the Exchange, the Albert Institute, the Watt Institution and many of the new churches – lay to the north of old Dundee in the newly opened Meadowlands. The town's new civic buildings were of a quality to rival those in other major cities, and yet the town itself did not, and still does not, appear

to do so. Reform Street itself – intended to be the axis between the Town House and the High School – was squint, as was Lindsay Street (former School Wynd) up to the Sheriff Court. There were several proposals – by James Brewster in 1832, George Mathewson in 1834 and Charles Edward in 1846 – to bring regularity to the Meadows, but none succeeded. It took 24 years for Reform Street to be completed (91 years after the beginning of the New Town of

Caird Hall, City Square; Central Reading Rooms; St Roque's Branch Library; Coldside Branch Library (courtesy of Charles McKean)

Edinburgh), after all the railways had arrived and industry had penetrated deeply to the last backyard of old Dundee.

The grand urban planning had begun too late, and the market for such developments had moved on. Significantly, those behind the new civic monuments – the Watt Institution, the Albert Institute, the Royal Exchange, the Theatre, Baxter Park – were still not the council but the town's entrepreneurs,

241

many of whom still took no part in council affairs. The council remained largely marginalised, tainted with the inherited reputation of ineffectiveness and lack of vision. This reputation was largely justifiable, for the town's continuing failure to think strategically meant that it had failed to take advantage of the newly opened lands north of the medieval centre and provide a new road from the west. That failure meant that, until 1871, all the east–west traffic from Edinburgh and Perth to Aberdeen had to squeeze through the Narrows of the Murraygate, condemning it to inevitable demolition. Only with the Improvement Act in 1871 did the town council regain power.

4   The City Beautiful

At no point did Dundee actually choose to be represented by jute, jam and journalism. Indeed, as juteopolis developed the character of grimy smokestacks, canyons of grey, threadbare, working-class tenements and an overcrowded, unkempt and inconvenient city centre, the city began a century not just of redevelopment but of the pursuit of what eventually became characterised as the 'city beautiful'. The period of St Nicholas – the harbour and the development of trade – had provided much commercial opportunity but not a new identity, as the miserable saga of the 1851 Royal Arch had proved. The arch had been intended to be a symbol of Dundee's thriving commerce, but its retrospective neo-Norman style had proved totally inappropriate for innovating manufacturers and international traders. Furthermore, the merchants who had funded the 1853 Royal Exchange as a symbol of pre-jute Dundee were faced with an aborted project once its fantastic crown spire had had to be lopped off as it was too heavy for the foundations. It would be a magnificent millennium project to resurrect that crown spire in lightweight glass-reinforced cement or plastic.

The 1871 City Improvement Act was the first step in the century-long reformatting of the city, culminating in the obliteration of the last significant area of ancient Dundee in the Overgate in the 1960s. Few valued the old centre (an attitude that was to last throughout the century) and the council was driven, both by the need to rationalise historic inconveniences like the Narrows of the Murraygate and the Seagate and by civic ambition, towards the insertion of a street resembling a Parisian boulevard into the medieval labyrinth surrounding Fish Street, approximately along the line of Whitehall Close. Each wave of demolition was made possible by the perception that Dundee's inherited character had nothing of value; indeed, the 1952 Development Plan identified only 16 buildings or streets of any importance in central Dundee, including seven churches, the McManus, High School, Customs House, Sheriff Court, Technical College and the east side of South Tay Street. Not only were Reform Street, Whitehall Street and Commercial

The Geddes Quadrangle on the University of Dundee's campus (courtesy of Charles McKean)

Street deemed of little value, but the medieval relics they concealed had not even been spotted.

The first to go was the district at the east end of the High Street at the head of the Murraygate and Seagate, extending Commercial Street in a north–south swathe of Parisian-like shops and offices joining the Docks to the Meadows. Then followed Whitehall Street, less for city improvement than for traffic improvement. Some 20 years later, the idea was continued by James Thomson, who proposed to redesign the city in a manner worthy of its status and grandeur. His proposals included a majestic domed civic centre in Earl Grey Dock, streets being widened and focused axially on statues, a formalised South Union Street and an enormous esplanade sweeping out to the west. The area behind the Town House was to become a two-storeyed market, like Edinburgh's Waverley market, with a formal garden on top. He planned to clear the Luckenbooths at the east end of the Overgate. Thomson also designed the first garden city houses in Britain in Logie and Mid Craigie and was responsible for an extraordinarily fine series of libraries. Although he believed that his 'city beautiful' schemes of 1912 would be best executed over a long period, the time was not ripe. Although the foundations of the Caird Hall were laid in 1914, it was not until 1932 that the Vaults – the area behind the Town House – were demolished, along with the Town House itself, and levelled up to that of the High Street to form City Square and Thomson's proposed Caird Hall.

In 1952, W. Dodson Champman and Partners were asked to prepare an advisory plan for the city's development. Advised by Hugh Martin, they proposed an updated version of 'city beautiful' plans for the recasting of Dundee. The most significant change in the 40 years since Thomson's plans was the increased priority given to road transport; the plan envisaged the current ring road and vast roundabouts. It also proposed the substantial demolition of Dundee's buildings and their replacement by avenues of trees between three-storeyed blocks of shops and offices, interspersed with large quantities of isolated Y-plan blocks of flats. This plan largely governed how Dundee developed during the post-war decades.

5   City of Discovery

To retrieve the RRS *Discovery* and install it on the riverfront as a museum and the principal marketing attraction for Dundee was the main identity change of the late-twentieth century. There were many advantages to this new symbol of the city. It would remind Dundonians of its forgotten ship-building and whaling past, and surprise non-Dundonians by presenting something altogether different from jute, jam and journalism. Visitor attractions are vital for a city, but they are no substitutes for the broader urban experience. The Docks have been selected as the next focus for urban regeneration, although it is less a case of regenerating than one of creating new activities. Like the *Discovery*, the Victoria Dock suffers from being on the wrong side of the tracks and detached from the town centre, lying some way to the east. There could be a risk of extending Dundee's economy too far east or west, or, alternatively, of attracting people only to the docks so that they never visit the town centre, as has happened in Swansea.

These developments are well within Dundee's tradition of seeking symbolism wherever it can be found: now a ship, then a mill, again a ship, then a dock. Each, like the Royal Arch saga back in 1851, is interesting but insufficient in itself. By comparison with other cities, Dundee is ill provided with public monuments as visitor attractions. It demolished its historic Town House in 1932 and its replacement is no substitute. St Mary's, the city's most ancient church, is mostly an 1841 rebuild by William Burn in rather cosy Gothic style with little of ancient mystery. When open, its steeple is magnificent. Although St Paul's, on the Castle Hill, has a fine tall space within, it is not always open. The McManus Galleries, although very near the centre, feel miles away – and will continue to do so until the closes running up to the Meadows from the High Street are reinvigorated. Equally, the Abertay campus, greatly enhanced by its new library, still has to embrace its part of the urban fabric, as has the university. Buildings of considerable age and quality remain neglected even in Bell Street, and the new student residences provide no adequate substitute for the previous buildings on the site. A radical plan for developing Bell Street on the model of Strathclyde University's occupation of Rottenrow could provide the north city centre with the catalyst that it needs.

West of the urban chasm that is the Marketgate (which the 1952 plan showed as being closely hemmed in by substantial buildings rather than the windswept tundra that it is today) lies the university campus, now enhanced by the city's two outstanding twentieth-century arts buildings – Dundee Contemporary Arts in the Nethergate and the Dundee Rep in Tay Square – and a growing number of restaurants. The Nethergate remains Dundee's principal historic route. From the Queen's Hotel you can see its majesty as it curves round into the distance into the High Street without noticing how it has been cut. That cut – the Marketgate – is both psychological and economic, for it inhibits members of that enormous financial generator that is the university from making casual visits into the centre for impulse-buy visits or interchange with townsfolk. So long as it remains as it is, the Marketgate reinforces the perception of a city with a hole in the middle, split from east to west.

Detail from the tower of Morgan Academy

THE SIXTH INCARNATION: UNIVERSITY CITY

The council's focus since the war has been on supporting existing industry and attracting new businesses. Until recently, it hadn't grasped the extent to which further and higher education had been expanding, now employing 5.2 per cent of the city's population – double that of Glasgow and Edinburgh. Dundee University itself has become the city's fourth largest employer, ahead of both D.C. Thomson and NCR. Between the universities of Dundee and Abertay and Dundee and Northern Colleges, there are over 22,000 full- and part-time students in a total population of around 150,000 people – a student:citizen ratio not dissimilar to that in Germany's oldest university city Heidelberg, which has 24,000 students in a total population of around 139,000. In a world of competing academic cities, Dundee is making its mark with students and academics who choose to come to study at local institutions, attracted by the qualities of the host city as well as the academic reputation of its universities.

OPPORTUNITIES FOR THE FUTURE

Despite everything, Dundee's historic plan survives largely intact and many of its layers of history also survive hidden in the 30-odd closes and wynds that partially survived the waves of rebuilding. Behind later façades in the High Street, Nethergate and Seagate, there lie fragments of much earlier buildings and courtyards. The Sea Captain's House off Candlemaker Lane has been most gloriously restored, and old Dundee's greater treasure, the predominantly fifteenth- to seventeenth-century courtyard house of Gardyne's Lodging, with its splendid fourth-floor early-eighteenth-century panelled room still looking out over the High Street below, awaits its turn. The layering becomes physical rather than metaphorical when you walk down a turnpike stair to find that beneath the 1828 Merchants' Coffee House (now the Bouquet Garnie restaurant) there survives a much earlier warehouse courtyard surrounded by vaulted cellars at sea level.

The surviving closes offer three opportunities for twenty-first-century Dundee. They retain the clues to the previous incarnations of the city, and can deepen the experience of resident and visitor alike. The time has come to open the closes and the blocked-windowed buildings facing into them and to explore their history. Secondly, they could provide – as some do already – splendid short cuts from one part of the city to another, sheltered from wind and passing through places of varying but always interesting character. Finally, building relics of great value – archways, blocked windows, ancient inscriptions, façades, rings, staircases, gardens, trees and even vaults – reside within. They range from the minor tactile curiosity to something worthy of major urban rescue. However great or small, it is these backland buildings – currently almost universally neglected – that tie together the different incarnations of Dundee.

The conservation and restoration of the Sea Captain's House by the Tayside Building Preservation Trust symbolises the potential of the ancient centre of Dundee as a whole. The appearance of the house and its panelling are of the 1820s, yet the house itself largely dates from the 1780s and contains five-foot-thick walls of the 1500s (as does the mid-Victorian Calendar to which it is attached behind).

Equally, there are many opportunities for high-quality contemporary architecture to be juxtaposed with the old, such as the Dundee Contemporary Arts building. Where in the High Street once sat the three pedimented monuments of eighteenth-century Dundee, the Trades Hall, the Town House and the English Chapel, is now characterised by emptiness. Architectural competitions for new structures on those old sites would bring people and activities back to the centre, recreate the wind-protected spaces and finally achieve the necessary critical mass.

The sixth incarnation of Dundee as a university city must win genuine popular support and offer some palpable attractions to the citizens as well as to the academics if it is to avoid resentment amongst those who might feel excluded. The first step must be to reawaken a confidence in Dundee citizens about the quality of their city – and that requires a more open perspective of the city's various incarnations than that provided by jute, jam and journalism.

Desperation: Desperate Dan meets desperate Tam Shields (courtesy of Tom Shields)

14

Meh Dundee Roots

A Postscript

Tom Shields

I am eminently unqualified to write about Dundee. My father was born in Lochee, but then so was Daley Thompson's mother and Daley is famous. My grandparents, John and Maggie Shields, lived and worked in Dundee for a few years before the First World War. My father, Charles, was born there on 9 May 1909 but the family moved back to Glasgow when he was four years old. That's where the family connection with Dundee begins and ends.

Dundee remained for me a dot on the map and a name in the Scottish football league until, as a raw recruit to the D.C. Thomson school of journalism in 1969, I was required occasionally to visit the city. It was a place I associated primarily with paternalism and parochialism. A bit like Glasgow, really, but smaller. And quite decent pubs with cheap beer and a bit of crack, although I didn't follow much of the local patois.

I knew that my father had been born in the city by the Tay but I was not inspired to go in search of my Dundee roots, however slender and shallow they were. Then I met Harry McLevy, a Dundee man who was transplanted to Glasgow in the mid-1980s through his work as an official of the engineering union. I remembered the name McLevy from the *Dundee Standard*, the left-wing newspaper that existed all too briefly as an alternative to the established press. 'McLevy' was the title of the feisty and argumentative column that Harry contributed to the *Standard*.

A not-too-unwilling exile to the West End of Glasgow, Harry McLevy would proselytise constantly on behalf of his home city. He was a great story-teller. He told of the canteen at the Caledon shipyard, where the soup of the day would be Bilermaker's broth – 'thick as a plank', and of his horror on seeing the handiwork of his youthful supporters when he stood for yard convener: a vast slogan painted on the side of a ship reading 'For a bevvy, vote McLevy'.

Harry was most passionate on the subject of the traditional strength and worth of the women of Dundee who worked in the mills by day and also raised a family. He would quote Mary Brooksbank on how they fair made them work for their ten and nine. But more often he would quote the examples of his own politically active mother and his other Dundee women kinfolk. I mentioned that my own granny had lived in Lochee and worked in the local mill. Harry told me about Tipperary, as that redoubt of the Irish immigrant was known, and about the Camperdown mill. We made many plans for forays to Dundee, where he would be my native guide to Lochee and to the Hilltown, the Hawkhill and other locales, the names of which tripped off his tongue, usually accompanied by an anecdote or ten.

It kindled in me an interest in Dundee, and with Harry's editorial assistance I used the occasion of the city's 'oxtercentenary' in 1991 to launch in the Glasgow *Herald*'s 'Diary' a search for 800 Fascinating Facts about Dundee. It was too ambitious a project and we ended up with 100 little anecdotes or stories, some of which were nearly factual.

It was also an opportunity to give Dundee a profile in a mainly West of Scotland newspaper, even if some of the stories appeared to be poking fun at the place. Like the tale of a crime which led to door-to-door inquiries in the Hawkhill area. One of the interviewees was an employee of Dundee District Council's cleansing department whose beat took in the locus of the crime. He was approached by one of Tayside's finest, who had surmised that the street sweeper might have seen something of value to their investigation. 'What is your name?' he asked. The cleansing operative told him. 'Address?' This information was duly given. 'Occupation?' the policeman asked. The road sweeper looked at his dustcart, looked at his cleansing-department uniform and said to the policeman, 'Actually, I'm a brain surgeon at the Dundee Royal Infirmary.' The police were not amused and took the unfortunate scaffie down to the nick, where he was kept in custody for an hour for obstructing police inquiries. He was released with a warning 'not to be stupid in future'. Unrepentant, he replied, 'Well, you started it!'

Another legend concerned Jim McLean, former manager, chairman and God of Dundee United. In a way he epitomises the city. Mr McLean has a reputation for having an uncompromising nature, and this was enhanced by a tale about his reaction to a letter from a young fan. The young Arab (as United fans are called) put pen to paper, as is every paying punter's right, to inform Mr McLean that he thought some of his team selections were wrong. The letter duly went into Mr McLean's in-tray. After Ayatollah McLean had dealt with the day's business (tormenting apprentices, rebuilding the stadium, checking the Tannadice bank balance), he set off home, stopping on his way at the address from which the letter had come. He knocked on the door and asked the lady of the house if the boy was in. The boy duly appeared, to be told by Mr McLean, 'Look, I pick the team.'

Dundee's 800th birthday party in 1991 was great fun. I got to meet

Desperate Dan and to sample the room-service speciality of the Angus Hotel. The night porter's 'piece on chips' (for one) consisted of a silver salver containing eight slices of buttered bread, enough chips for four and a gravy boat of tomato sauce. After a hectic night on the town it was a heavenly delicacy.

But I never got to do the Dundee trip in the company of Harry McLevy. Just as he neared retirement from his job with the engineering union and debated whether to stay in the West End of Glasgow or move back to Dundee, or somehow become a citizen of both places, he died suddenly at the age of 58. The day I went to Dundee with Harry was for his memorial service and to see him off at the Camperdown cemetery. It was a secular burial service but there

Harry McLevy (courtesy of Alan Wyllie)

was a minister there, a former shipyard chaplain, to conduct matters at the graveside. As Harry's coffin was lowered into the ground, the minister read the bit by Karl Marx about 'workers of the world unite, you have nothing to lose but your chains'. He then asked all those present not to report him to the Church of Scotland, as he would probably get his jotters.

Since then I have tried a few times to retrace the Dundee connection of my father and my grandparents. I had a day out with my three sisters, and the highlight was a visit to the Verdant Works, the jute mill which has been made into a museum. Except it is not a museum. It is a living testament to how the folk of Dundee survived in the mills. The detail of how the mills worked is educational; to see the harsh reality of the conditions endured by the mill women is quite astonishing; to have an insight into how life was lived in the teeming tenements of Dundee is deeply moving, simultaneously inducing tears and laughter.

I went in pursuit of the place where my father was born in Dundee. It has to be said that Lochee failed to meet the aspirations of this pilgrim. Worse than those teeming tenements of yesteryear are the bleak shopping precincts of the 1970s on main street Lochee. A saving grace for Lochee, however, is the conversion of the various buildings of the vast Camperdown mill into a shopping centre and housing. In the unlikely setting of the Tesco supermarket cafeteria, I found on the walls some fantastic old photographs of the mill and the people who had worked there when it was an industrial powerhouse. It was even better that the old lady whom I asked to talk me through the photographs had worked in the mill and now lived in a sheltered-housing flat in the converted finishing shed.

I have not yet got to the bottom of the Shields' Lochee connection. I phoned a Catholic church in the area hoping to be allowed to check out some parish records. The priest suggested I contact the Mormons, who, he said, 'were better at that sort of thing'. I phoned the Mormons but they weren't in. Probably out knocking on doors. I took the easy way out and went to renew my acquaintance with Dundee's fine pubs. The Phoenix does an absolutely wonderful steak sandwich the likes of which we Glaswegians can only dream of. On another visit supposedly dedicated to the genealogical trail, I spent the time enjoying the delights of Dundee Contemporary Arts, the city's shining new palace of visual culture.

I may have to come back to Dundee quite a few times before I finally get the research completed. I enjoy Dundee, even though I am still nowhere near fluent in its language. I have been trying to learn from a CD, *The Word on the Pavey*, by a chap called St Andrew. It is an eclectic collection of songs in various musical styles. The unifying theme is the lyrics, which are pure Dundee:

> *Crivvens, help ma boab, and jings,*
> *This world is full o' a number o' things.*
> *Sahlt and pepper, sugar and muwk,*
> *Eamonn Bannon and Acker Bulk . . .*
> *Chippers, larries, bogies, trams,*
> *The Sporting Post on the bus to Glamis.*

Despite the linguistic differences, there is more that unites Glasgow and Dundee than separates the two cities. The people of both have been ill served by their industrial and commercial masters. The planners and developers have laid waste to great swathes of both cities. But both have managed to save significant chunks of their Victorian architectural heritage and turn them into places for people to live.

Maybe it's the strong beer in Mennie's bar of an evening, but I feel that Dundee and Glasgow are soulmates in a way. Dundee photographer Joseph McKenzie recorded the faces of the people of the Gorbals in Glasgow in a way that no Glaswegian with a camera ever managed. McKenzie's photos of the Hawkhill and other Dundee scenes strike an immediate chord of recognition with Glasgow folk. Dundonian Michael Marra wrote the best song ever about

Glasgow. He sang of Mother Glasgow watching all her weans. He sang of Father Glasgow walking all his charges into hell. It is an affectionate, realistic view of the city far superior to the strident, simplistic and otiose tones of 'I Belong to Glasgow'.

There are writers in this book better qualified than I am to set out the joys and glories of Dundee's literature, music, architecture and people. For me, it is still a city of discovery. I know little of my grandparents' time in Dundee. My grandfather was killed at the Somme in 1916, and my granny worked as a hawker in Glasgow and her hard work was punctuated by spells of hard drinking. I never heard her speak of the days before her man was killed. I do know that as a teenage girl before her wedding she walked all the way from Glasgow to Dundee in search of work. I told Harry McLevy about her journey, and he told me his granny had once walked all the way from Dundee to Glasgow to find work. This crossing of paths seems to me a suitable metaphor for the tale of both cities.

Bibliography

Alexander, John, *Dundee Pubs Past and Present*

Atkinson, Kate, *Emotionally Weird*, Transworld (1999)

Barnard, *The Noted Breweries of Great Britain and Ireland*

Barron, Captain William, *Old Whaling Days*, Conway Maritime Press (1970)

Billcliffe, Patrick Roger, *James McIntosh Patrick*, Fine Art Society for Dundee District Council (1987)

Buchan, James, *The Expendable Mary Slessor*, The Saint Andrew Press (1980)

Burnside, John, *Swimming in the Flood*, Jonathan Cape (1995)

Burnside, John, *A Normal Skin*, Jonathan Cape (1997)

Burnside, John, *The Mercy Boys*, Jonathan Cape (1999)

Butchart, G.F., *Temperance and Counter Attractive Establishment in Victorian Dundee* (1988)

Chalmers, Patrick, *The Adhesive Stamp*, Effingham Wilson (1881)

Cooke, A.J., ed., *Baxters of Dundee*, University of Dundee Department of Extra-Mural Education (1980)

Crumley, Jim, *The Road and the Miles: A Homage to Dundee*, Mainstream Publishing (1996)

Douglas, Sheila, ed., *Fair Upon Tay*, Tayside Regional Council (1993)

Dunn, Douglas, *Elegies*, London Faber (1985)

Dunn, Douglas, *Northlight*, London Faber (1988)

Forrest, Louise M., *Publications of Clan Lindsay Society*

Gatherer, Nigel, *The Songs and Ballads of Dundee*, John Donald (1986)

Gauldie, Enid, ed., *The Dundee Textile Industry 1790–1885*, T. and A. Constable (1969)

Gibson, Henry J.C., *Dundee Royal Infirmary 1778–1948*, William Kidd (1948)

Henderson, David S., *Fishing for the Whale*, Dundee Museum and Art Gallery Publication

Herbert, W.N., *Dundee Doldrums*, Galliard (1991)

Herbert, W.N., *Cabaret MacGonagall*, Bloodaxe Books (1996)

Bibliography

Herd, Tracey, *No Hiding Places*, Bloodaxe Books (1996)

Howe, W. Stewart, *The Dundee Textiles Industry 1960–1977*, Aberdeen University Press (1982)

Jeffrey, Andrew, *This Dangerous Menace: Dundee and the River Tay at War*, Mainstream Publishing (1991)

Jones, S.J., ed., *Dundee and District*, British Association for the Advancement of Science (1968)

Kay, Billy, ed., *The Dundee Book*, Mainstream Publishing (1995)

Kidd, William and Sons, ed., *Dundee Past and Present*, William Kidd

Kidd, William and Sons, ed., *The Chartist Agitation in Dundee*, William Kidd

Knox, William, ed., *Scottish Labour Leaders 1918–1939 Biographical Dictionary*

Lamb Collection, The Wellgate Library

Leneman, Leah, *Martyrs in our Midst*, Abertay Historical Society (1993)

Lenman, Bruce, Lythe, Charlotte and Gauldie, Enid, *Dundee and its Textile Industry 1850–1914*, Abertay Historical Society (1969)

Lockhart, R.H. Bruce, *My Scottish Youth*

Lubbock, Basil, *The Arctic Whalers*, Brown, Son and Ferguson (1937)

McCraw, Ian, *The Fairs of Dundee*, Abertay Historical Society (1994)

McGonagall, William Topaz, *Poetic Gems*, London Duckworth (1989)

MacIntyre, Lorn and Adamson, Peter, *Dundee: City of Discovery*, Alvie (1988)

McKean, Charles and Walker, David, *Dundee: An Illustrated Introduction*, Royal Incorporation of Architects in Scotland/Scottish Academic Press (1984)

McKean, Charles and Walker, David, *Dundee: An Illustrated Architectural Guide*, Royal Incorporation of Architects in Scotland (1993)

Mackie, R.L., ed., *Dundee and District*, British Association for the Advancement of Science (1939)

McMaster, Charles, *Edwin Scrymgeour and the Scottish Prohibition Party*, Scottish Brewing Archive

McMaster, Charles and Dean, Kenneth A., *Ballingall's Brewery*, Scottish Brewing Archive

Marshall, Peter, *The Railways of Dundee*, Oakwood Press (1996)

Marshall, Sheila, *James Scrymgeour and the Dundee Band of Hope*, lecture, August 1997

Martin, George M., *Dundee Worthies*, David Winter (1934)

Maxwell, Alexander, *The History of Old Dundee*, William Kidd (1884)

Millar, A.H., *The Dundee Advertiser: A Centenary Memoir*, John Leng (1901)

Miller, A.H., *Glimpses of Old and New Dundee*, Malcolm MacLeod (1925)

Miller, A.H., *James Bowman Lindsay and Other Pioneers of Invention*, Malcolm MacLeod (1925)

Morrison, J., *The First Hundred: Dundee's Art College 1892–1992* (1992)

Murray, Janice, ed., *Glorious Victory: Admiral Duncan and the Battle of Camperdown*, Dundee City Council (1997)

NCR (Scotland) Ltd., *Cash Advance: The Story of NCR in Scotland 1946–1996*

Ogilvy, Graham, *The River Tay and Its People*, Mainstream Publishing (1993)

Paterson, Don, *Nil Nil*, Faber and Faber (1993)

Paterson, Don, *God's Gift to Women*, Faber and Faber (1998)

Paterson, Don, *The Eyes: A Version of Antonio Machadio*, Faber and Faber (1999)

Paterson, Tony, *Churchill: A Seat for Life*, David Winter and Son (1980)

Phillips, David, *No Poets' Corner in the Abbey*, David Winter (1971)

Price, Norrie, *Up Wi' the Bonnets*, Norrie Price (1994)

Robertson, Alec, *History of Dundee Theatre*, Precision Press (1949)

Savours, Ann, *The Voyages of Discovery*, Virgin (1992)

Scott, Andrew Murray, *Discovering Dundee*, Mercat Press (1989)

Shields, Tom, *More Tom Shields' Diary Too*, Mainstream Publishing (1993)

Smith, Annette M., *The Nine Trades of Dundee*, Abertay Historical Society (1995)

Smith, Robert, *The Whale Hunters*, John Donald (1993)

Smith, W.J. and Metcalfe, J.E., *James Chalmers: Inventor of the Adhesive Postage Stamp*, David Winter (1970)

Southgate, Donald, *University Education in Dundee*, Edinburgh University Press (1982)

Southgate, Donald, *Edwin Scrymgeour (1866–1947) Prohibitionist and Politician*

Stephen, Alexander, *A Shipbuilding History*, Edward J. Burrow (1932)

Stewart, Bob, *Breaking the Fetters*, Lawrence and Wishart (1967)

Swinfen, David, *The Fall of the Tay Bridge*, Mercat Press (1994)

Thomas, John, *The Tay Bridge Disaster*, David and Charles (1972)

Thomson, J. Hannay and Ritchie, George G., *Dundee Harbour Trust Centenary 1830–1930* (1930)

Walker, William M., *Juteopolis: Dundee and its Textile Workers 1885–1923*, Scottish Academic Press (1979)

Watson, Mike, *Rags to Riches*, David Winter and Son (1992)

Watson, Mike, *The Tannadice Encyclopedia*, Mainstream Publishing (1997)

Watson, Norman, *Daughters of Dundee*, Linda McGill (1997)

Watson, Norman, *Dundee's Suffragettes* (1990)

Whatley, C.A., Swinfen, D. and Smith, A., *The Life and Times of Dundee*, John Donald (1993)

Whatley, C.A., ed., *The Remaking of Juteopolis: Dundee c. 1891–1991*, Abertay Historical Society (1992)

Wilkie, Jim, *Across the Great Divide*, Mainstream Publishing (1984)